## DATE DUE

| | | |
|---|---|---|
| OCT 13 1995 | | |
| OCT 27 1995 | | |
| | | |
| | | |
| | | |
| | DISCARDED | |
| | | |
| | | |
| | | |
| | | |
| | | |
| | | |
| | | |
| | Printed in USA | |

# BE MYSELF

# BE MYSELF

*Memoirs of a Bridgebuilder*

## WARREN W. WIERSBE

**VICTOR BOOKS**

A DIVISION OF SCRIPTURE PRESS PUBLICATIONS INC.
USA CANADA ENGLAND

Copyediting: Barbara Williams
Cover Design: Scott Rattray
Cover Photo: Bill Bilsley

**Library of Congress Cataloging-in-Publication Data**

Wiersbe, Warren W.
   Be myself / Warren W. Wiersbe.
      p.    cm.
   Includes bibliographical references.
   1. Wiersbe, Warren W.    2. Clergy—United States—Biography.
  I. Title.
   BR1725.W449A3    1994
286'.1'092—dc20
[B]                                94-8115
                                        CIP

1  2  3  4  5  6  7  8  9  10  Printing/Year  98  97  96  95  94

# CONTENTS

# With Appreciation

I owe a lot of people my sincere appreciation for helping me with this book; so, my grateful thanks to:

● **my wife Betty,** who saved every piece of memorabilia for over forty years, filed it away carefully, and produced each item at the proper time, thereby saving me many hours of searching and muttering to myself. She also read the entire manuscript, corrected my calendar errors, and helped me say things better. Without her help, it would have been impossible to write this book with any degree of historical accuracy; and without her daily encouragement, my writing it would have been an intolerable burden. "Many daughters have done well, but you excel them all" (Prov. 31:29, NKJV).

● **Ed, Tat, and Doris,** who remember things better than I do, for reading the manuscript and making corrections and suggestions.

● **Mark Sweeney,** vice president of Scripture Press and director of Victor Books, for encouraging me to write these memoirs and daring to let me be myself.

● **Carol Thiessen,** who supplied me with the "Eutychus" information and the copy I needed from *Christianity Today.*

● *Christianity Today,* for giving me permission to quote copyrighted material.

● **Mrs. Margaret Carlson,** who was kind enough to copy out her diary entry and send it to me.

● **Herb Epp,** who was kind enough to read the chapters on my

"Back to the Bible" years and share his wisdom with me.

● **Curt and Claudine Lehman,** our pastor and his wife, for being such good friends and counselors all these years we've been in Lincoln. Curt doesn't know it, but when we'd lunch together, I'd often discuss some of the things in this book. I profited greatly from his responses.

# PART ONE
# The Early Years

# CHAPTER ONE

$$\boxed{1}$$

B efore we go any farther, I need to answer a question: Why am I writing these memoirs anyway? After all, my hometown has turned out people a lot more famous than I'll ever be, like movie actor Jack Hubbard; opera star Vivian Della Chiesa, who for a short time lived up the street from us; ABC anchorman Frank Reynolds; Dr. James P. Comer, associate dean of Yale Medical School; Dottie Vance, record promoter for Dinah Shore, Perry Como, and a host of other musical greats; NBA All-Star Vince Boryla; radio "Quiz Kid" Richard Williams, who became a U.S. consul in China; movie and TV actress Marian Collier (we knew her as Marian Chulay); and John Templeton, the world's foremost painter of the Indiana dunes.

My fellow Scandinavian Dag Hammarskjöld wrote in his book *Markings*, "The longest journey is the journey inwards," and as I write these pages, I'm discovering that he's right. American humorist Josh Billings said just about the same thing, only a lot less philosophically: "Autobiographies are the most difficult things to write correctly, for there is nothing that a man knows less about than himself." Maybe that's why people write them: they're trying to find themselves.

Russell Baker, whose autobiography, *Growing Up,* is a favorite of mine, said just the opposite: "The biographer's problem is that he never knows enough. The autobiographer's problem is that he knows too much."* But it makes no difference how much you think you know about yourself; *if you can't make sense out of it, you really don't know how to tell your story.* As a Christian believer, I'm convinced that life is made up of appointments, not accidents, and that there's a pattern to each life if only we can find it. Somewhere, there's a metaphor that pulls the whole thing together, and when you find that metaphor, you say, "Yeah, that's right! That's what it's all about!"

The metaphor that helps me make sense out of my own life is that of a *bridge-builder.* As I look back, I can see that I've always been building bridges. Some of the bridges I've built are the kind that *everybody* has to build for themselves if their lives are going to be meaningful; a few of my bridges were special assignments from the Lord. If I hadn't believed that, I could never have made it.

Everybody has a story to tell. I'm not writing my story because I'm famous or a candidate for some great prize, or even because people are clamoring to know about me. I'm writing it to fulfill another assignment in bridge-building, this time between me and you. I hope it does both us of some good.

## 2

*I was born at an early age in a log cabin I helped my father build. I was born at home, because I wanted to be near my mother; and when she saw me, they had to take her to the hospital. I'm not saying I was an ugly kid, but when my mother kissed me good night, she put a bag over my head.*

*I was a sickly kid and had to take a lot of cod-liver oil. In*

---

*William Zinsser, ed., *Inventing the Truth* (New York: Book-of-the-Month Club, 1987), 49.

# Chapter One

*fact, I took so much cod-liver oil, they had to fish me out of the bathtub with a net. I was a bottle baby, and when I turned three, they let me out of the bottle.*

*Those were depression days and we were a poor family. We were so poor, the wolf was always at the door. One day my father invited the wolf in and it starved to death.*

None of the above is true, except for three facts: I *was* born at home; I *did* grow up during the Depression; and I *was* a sickly kid who had to take a lot of cod-liver oil. The speech quoted above was part of the opening "patter" for the magic show I presented scores of times during my teen years when I was active as an amateur magician. I wasn't a very good magician, but I soon discovered I could make people laugh with one-liners I found in joke books. I had listened to Jack Benny's radio program so much that my sense of timing was excellent, and my sense of humor gave me the ability to *ad lib* a bit. So, in my magic shows, I'd do fifteen minutes of jokes interspersed with fifteen minutes of magic tricks, and for this I was paid twenty dollars, which was a lot of money in those days. During my teen years, I probably had more undesignated funds in my pocket than my father had in his, and he had to work a lot harder. He delivered milk for the Borden Dairy.

The date of my arrival in East Chicago, Indiana, was May 16, 1929, five months before the crash that kicked off the Depression. The reason I was born at home was simple: I came on the scene before my mother could get to the hospital. In fact, I showed up before Dr. Cox did.

That crisis birth experience probably explains why all my life I've arrived early, much to the consternation of family and friends who stroll through life at a more leisurely pace than I do. When I walked to Sunday School as a child, I invariably arrived before the church doors were unlocked, and I'd have to go to the pastor's house to get the key. Our family attended the Indiana Harbor Mission Covenant Church.

In spite of it being in May, the day of my birth was very chilly; my Uncle David Forsberg, my mother's brother, had to come and haul in coal so we'd have heat in the house.

With a depression around the corner, the neighbors probably felt like expressing sympathy when they heard that Fred and Gladys Wiersbe had their fourth child—and a sickly one at that. I joined two brothers, Edward and Clarence, and a sister Doris, all of whom were probably wondering how six people would manage to live happily in a five-room flat with one bathroom and two bedrooms. I'm sure my older brother Ed wasn't too excited about my arrival, because he had celebrated his birthday the day before, and a baby brother wasn't exactly his idea of a birthday present. Like any normal six-year-old, he would rather have had a dog.

"East Chicago" is the official name of the city, but a canal from Lake Michigan divides it into two parts, and the other part, the part where we lived, was called "Indiana Harbor." "East Chicago" and "Indiana Harbor" were known as "the Twin Cities," but they were definitely not identical twins. People on the East Chicago side of town would usually say "the Harbor" with just a touch of disdain in their voice, making the statement almost equivalent to "the other side of the tracks." But our house was located in a comfortable neighborhood close to Washington Park with its zoo and swimming pool, and to St. Catherine's Hospital, where I would make many a pastoral visit in later years, and to Washington School, which I attended for thirteen years.

The people on our street didn't whine because the General American Tank Car Corporation was just two blocks away. Sure, we were occasionally awakened at night by the squeaky new tank cars being pulled out of the sheds by switch engines, but we just turned over and went back to sleep. The citizens of Indiana Harbor didn't complain about the grimy steel mills or the smelly oil refineries and chemical plants. Back in those days, we didn't worry about pollution and didn't know anything about ecology; people were just happy to have jobs.

Our family saw no reason to be embarrassed about living on "the Harbor side of town." After all, in our extended neighborhood we had the Horn family, wealthy pillars of the community who owned the big lumberyard; A.C. Senour, superintendent of schools, the man with the awesome authority to close all the schools when there was a snowstorm; Paul Marcovich, owner of the drug store at the corner of Euclid Avenue and Columbus Drive, where I spent many a nickel; several doctors and lawyers; and even Warren "Sonny" Sheetz, northern Indiana's gambling czar who ran "the Big House" in a questionable neighborhood on Michigan Avenue, near Lake Michigan. He lived in the 41st block of Ivy Street, just north of us, and if he happened to be in front of his house when I was on my way to school, he would say hello to me in a friendly way. Once I was even *in* his house and did some card tricks for him.

I don't know where she lived, but Ana Cumpagnas, John Dillinger's "Lady in Red," was from Indiana Harbor; so you can see that we didn't lack for celebrities.

# 3

Our family occupied the first floor of a brick two-flat building my father had a contractor build for us before I was born. The house was in the center of the block, and during the summer the neighborhood kids usually gathered there to talk, "fool around," and plan strategy for the day. ("Planning strategy" meant figuring out a way to get rid of us younger kids so that the older ones could have more fun.) It wasn't unusual for us to have eight or ten kids milling around the backyard or sitting on the back porch, calling my parents "Ma" and "Pa" just the way the Wiersbe kids did.

We had a neat bunch of kids on our block and we got along fairly well with each other and had a good time, in spite of all the problems the Depression brought us. If we were deprived, we didn't know it, and it didn't seem to leave any permanent scars. As the baby of the family, I wore hand-me-downs, and Doris wore clothes that some of the older girls in the neighborhood had outgrown. We didn't have everything we wanted but we did have everything we needed.

Nicknames abounded in our neighborhood. If I listed all of them, you'd think I was doing a rerun of Abbott and Costello's "Who's on First?" The two Yeager boys, who lived across the street from us, were nicknamed "Bud," which is sensible, and "Li'l Apple," which is insane. (It had something to do with "The Big Apple" dance that was popular about that time.) Barbara Jones was "Bobby," and Ramona Mapes was both "Mona" and "Tony." Harold Manley was called "Hootch," Arthur Markovich was "Moe," and Warren Stanley was "Forse" (or "Fours"), a nickname that stuck to me for several years because my name was also Warren. (However, some family etymologists think that my three nicknames—"Forse," "Forsby" and "Orbie" originated from my mother's maiden name, Forsberg. Fortunately, none of these nicknames lasted, although even today one of my siblings might call me "Orb.")

In one of his essays, William Hazlitt wrote, "A nickname is the heaviest stone that the devil can throw at a man"; but all of us on the 42nd block of Ivy Street managed to survive the assault. I guess we didn't take these names too seriously.

My parents were both born in Chicago, my father in 1895 and my mother in 1900. The Wiersbe family originally came from Germany, and my Grandfather Wiersbe, whom I never knew, was a successful butcher in Chicago and owned several shops. At a young age my father left home to go to work, first on the railroad and then with the East Chicago Dairy, where he met my mother, who was a bookkeeper in the office. We never knew too many of our Wiersbe relatives. It was as though Pa shut a door on his past when he got married, and we never tried to force it open.

My mother's full name was Gladys Anna Octavia Forsberg. Her parents, Otto and Elizabeth, were part of the Swedish migration that brought hundreds of immigrants to the greater Chicago area to work in the factories, especially the Standard Forgings Company in Indiana Harbor, which became known as "the Swedish Penitentiary." In 1900, Chicago had more Swedes than any other city except Stockholm. Forsbergs and Carlsons and Johnsons and Ericksons and Niquists and Nelsons and Rodells and Aldrins all flocked to northern Indiana to earn their daily bread. Our grandfather Otto Forsberg worked at the Standard Forgings Company, affectionately called "the Forge," and so did Uncle Roy and our great-uncle Hjalmar Carlson (turn the *hj* into a *y* and you've got it) and a host of other shirttail relatives who wouldn't have thought of working anywhere else. For a Swede to leave the Forge would be like a Calvinist losing his salvation; it just didn't happen.

**My parents, Fred and Gladys Wiersbe, 1938.**

Even though my father was German, our family followed the Swedish traditions, which meant we woke up almost every Saturday morning to the delicious aroma of Swedish bread and coffee cake baking in the oven. We had Swedish meatballs for supper at least once a week (we ate "supper," not "dinner"), and Ma baked plenty of Swedish pastries at Christmas. My mother enjoyed eating some of the more cultic Swedish foods like headcheese and lutefisk; but when it came to those dishes, we kids remained true blue Americans.

In case you aren't among the initiated, lutefisk is a white fish that's soaked in lye for some days, washed thoroughly, and then served with a special sauce that could hold bricks together. Some Scandinavian wit called lutefisk "the piece of cod that passes all understanding."

Of course, following the Swedish way of life meant that we four children attended Sunday School at the Mission Covenant Church at 139th and Grand Boulevard. The church had been founded in 1906 by a small group of dedicated people, among them my great-grandfather John Carlson. These were people who remembered the friendly "mission halls" back in Sweden and wanted to maintain those familiar religious traditions in the new land. Of course, as successive generations came along, some of those traditions gave way to innovations, but the fellowship was still quite Scandinavian when we started attending, except that the services were now all in English. My great-uncle Simon Carlson pastored the church at one time and then served as interim-pastor after his retirement.

I'm grateful that I grew up learning Scandinavian hymnody, singing songs like "Day by Day" and "Security" and "If I Gained the World." We sang "How Great Thou Art" long before it became popular in the Stuart K. Hine translation. (The translation in *The Covenant Hymnal* was done by E. Gustav Johnson. With a name like that, he surely knew something about the Swedish language.) There was a great deal of musical talent in our little church, although some people who didn't have any talent sang special numbers. But we didn't care. They were singing the Lord's song in a strange land and looking forward to that Better Land where everybody would sing in Swedish and everybody would eat lutefisk and not complain about it.

The Indiana Harbor Mission Covenant Church wasn't the easiest congregation to pastor and our little fellowship had its ups and downs over the years. Perhaps too many people in the church were related to each other and the only way for an outsider to be accepted was to marry into a founding family. Ed and Tat and Doris and I were among the elect because our mother was a Forsberg and her grandfather helped to found the church. Carl Wall, Sr., the Sunday School superintendent, was married to our great-aunt Lydia; and many of the church officers were either blood relatives or relatives by marriage. You didn't dare gossip about people because they might be closet members of your family.

My earliest memories of the church go back to the time when Bill Taylor was the pastor. (Later he became Dr. William Taylor, missionary statesman and General Director of the Central American Mission, now CAM International.) Bill came to us fresh from the Moody Bible Institute. He loved people, worked hard, preached the Word, and must have prayed a lot, because under his leadership the church exploded. If you wanted to be sure of a seat in the morning service, you carried your chair from the Sunday School room into the auditorium. Bill and his wife, Stella, started a Friday, after-school Bible club for the children, and that's where I learned the books of the Bible. When Bill and Stella left to serve as missionaries in Costa Rica, we felt like our world had come to an end.

Wayne Child, another Moody graduate, took over the flock, and the work continued to prosper. His gentle disposition and the fact that he married Edna Larson helped him get along with the Swedish patriarchs of the congregation. Edna's mother Judith Larson was the daughter of our great-uncle Hjalmar Carlson, a pillar of the church; and Edna's two brothers, Roy and Eddie, and her sister Agnes were devoted church workers and fine musicians. A star football player at Washington High School, Eddie was my Sunday School teacher for a time, and he went on to become an effective Mission Covenant pastor and denominational leader. Agnes married Carl Davis and they served the Lord effectively in The Evangelical Alliance Mission (TEAM) in Pakistan. Our congregation wasn't especially large but it sure sent a lot of people into Christian service.

But the ministry didn't always go smoothly and I'm sure a few of our pastors went away with broken hearts. One of my relatives is supposed to have told a pastor, "Vell, things have been dis vay for over thirty years and ve're not about to shange them now!" The word "change" just wasn't in the church constitution. Occasionally, if the morning service went too long, one of the elder statesmen (who shall be nameless to protect the author) got up on the pew and wound the clock that hung on the north wall. One Sunday, between Sunday School and morning worship, Hjalmar Carlson encountered some exuberant children running in the church, and shouted: "Stop your running! Vat do you tink this is, a Vild Vest Show?"

Each Lord's Day, the Sunday School assembly opened with the singing of "More about Jesus"; and to this day, whenever I sing that song, I experience dejà vu. I see a thin blond boy, Bible in hand, lesson all prepared, sitting meekly in a pew, contemplating the fact that he still had a few more hours of freedom before he'd have to go back to school on Monday morning. He'd run home after church, lie on the floor and read the *Chicago Tribune* Sunday comics, then eat Sunday dinner (usually pot roast), read a book, and climax the afternoon by listening to "The Shadow" on the radio. It was a good life, if only he didn't have to go to school.

I owe a lot to the people at the Mission Covenant Church who sowed the seed of God's Word in my heart. Most of the people in the church would have pointed me out as a "good Christian boy," but I had never really been born again. I was faithful in my attendance and was even confirmed in 1944, but I had never made that life-changing decision to trust Jesus Christ as Lord and Savior.

Everett Ostrom was the pastor when I was confirmed. There were only three of us in the class, but he was faithful to teach us and pray for us. I didn't know until years later that every Saturday after Confirmation Class, Pastor Ostrom would fall on his face on the study floor and weep over me and pray for me. He knew I was pretending to be a Christian and he yearned to see me make a true decision for Christ.

A year later, the Lord answered his prayers.

# CHAPTER TWO

From kindergarten through high school graduation, I attended the same public school, Washington Elementary and High School on Columbus Drive, just two blocks from home. I could leisurely walk to school each morning, come home for lunch at noon, and take my time going back. Some of the students had to ride bikes to school, walk long distances, or take the bus; I had it made.

When Doris entered school, she started in the first grade because there was no kindergarten in the school system then. The city couldn't afford it. But by 1934 when I turned five, the economy had improved, kindergarten was back in business, and I lost an extra year's vacation at home.

I remember how my left arm swelled up and ached from the vaccination Dr. Yoder gave me in preparation for kindergarten. Dr. Yoder was a family friend because he often made calls at our house to treat my sister. Doris had an asthmatic condition that created bronchial congestion and made it hard for her to breathe. My mother would call Dr. Yoder and he'd come over with his bag of herbs, ask for a drinking glass, and concoct what we kids called "the brown medicine." Doris would courageously drink the potion and before long all that phlegm would come up and she'd be able to breathe easily again.

# Be Myself

My first two weeks in kindergarten were a disaster because I didn't like the teacher. I was assigned to the morning session, from 8:30 to 11:45, and almost every day during recess, I would run home. Ma usually let me stay home, but the next day I would have to go back and apologize for my transgression. Pa was delivering milk to the school and usually got an earful from the teacher. I'm sure I was punished for my disobedience, but I didn't care. I just didn't like the teacher and I wasn't going to stay in school.

But it turned out that she was only a substitute. When the "real" teacher, Alice Furmark, arrived home from a summer trip to Europe (she'd been delayed in Hitler's Germany), I immediately fell in love with her, much to everybody's relief. Doris was happy because now she wouldn't be embarrassed by having to go to the kindergarten room to retrieve whatever I'd left behind when I made my escape, and Pa could deliver milk to the kindergarten room without fear of intimidation. Happy days were here again.

But those happy days didn't last too long. I soon discovered the deep dark secret that terrorized almost every student at Washington Elementary School, and her name was Evelyn McFeely. She was over six feet tall, built like a football player, and was the principal of the school. A strict disciplinarian, she carried a piece of rubber hose as the badge of her office, and she wasn't afraid to use it. We pupils would rather face a loaded gun than confront the piece of rubber hose in Evelyn McFeely's hand.

But she had another weapon almost as deadly as her rubber hose, and that was her tongue. When Miss McFeely scolded you, she usually did it before your classmates, and the experience was a combination of going through the third-degree at police headquarters, having surgery, and falling into molten iron at Inland Steel. It wasn't a scolding, it was a scalding and a scourging, and you carried the pain and scars for a long time. Even worse, your fellow pupils would never let you forget it.

I don't understand why the school board permitted Evelyn McFeely to frighten, humiliate, and crush the sensitive kids committed to her care. Any school principal today doing some of the things that she did to us would probably be fired. She was smart enough not to attack the sons and daughters of influential people in our school district, but she sure made up for it in the way she treated us commoners. For seven painful years, Washington Elementary School was a chamber of horrors to me, and there was nothing I could do but endure it.

But that wasn't all. Like every school, Washington had its share of bullies, and one of them zeroed in on me. He was good-looking, popular, and a good athlete, but a poor student, and he took great delight in persecuting me during recess. Once he threatened to beat me up if I didn't pay him off. I suppose I could have gotten Ed or Tat to take care of him, but I was too proud to tell anybody about the problem. During my grade-school years, life was difficult. If I was inside the school building, the dark shadow of the principal was haunting me; if I was outside, my persecutor was hunting for me. The only thing that saved me from total ego collapse was the fact that I was a good student and got good grades, so the teachers liked me. Another plus was the fact that I could run very fast.

One more thing added to my scholastic misery: I was definitely not an athlete in a school where athletic ability was the measure of the child. For six years, I was the last boy chosen for every team in gym class; nobody expected anything great to happen when I was up to bat or at the free-throw line. My two brothers were excellent athletes in every sport, but the genes that blessed them abandoned me and left me probably the greatest nonathlete in the history of Washington School.

Most of the people in northern Indiana considered sports more important than academics. The annual basketball tournament was known as "Hoosier Hysteria," and our "Washington Senators" ruthlessly fought the crosstown "Roosevelt Rough Riders" for the coveted "Brown Derby" football trophy. During my junior high and senior high school years, I enjoyed attending the games and screaming my encouragement to the players, but I didn't always understand the rules and I couldn't have participated on the field or floor for five minutes. I went to the games because my friends were there and it was cozy to be a part of "the gang."

# Be Myself

Because I could run fast and maneuver quickly, soccer was the one game I could play skillfully, but back in those days, few people considered soccer a sport worthy of interscholastic competition. The only boys who played soccer were the ones who couldn't play any other game, which made me eminently qualified. The trouble was, we had to play on a blocked-off street because the athletic field was in the hands of the real athletes. If you ran into another player or missed the ball, you might find yourself skidding down the pavement on your face or your knees. One day I kicked at the ball and missed it and ended up resurfacing Hemlock Street with the skin of my face. The school nurse, Miss Oscarina Lundquist, a Swede, had to paint my face with Mercurochrome. I looked like a circus clown; when my mother saw me after school that day, she almost fainted.

To compensate for my athletic incompetence, I concentrated on my studies and got excellent grades; then my academic record began to haunt me almost as much as my fear of Evelyn McFeely. I *had* to succeed. I *had* to get the best grades in the class. I *had* to have perfect scores on every test. I would toss and turn in my sleep, dreaming about the agony of getting an S on my report card when I should have been awarded an E. (Our system was E for excellent, S for satisfactory, U for unsatisfactory, and F for failure. I usually had all E's.)

So, this thin little boy had to deal with the combined pressures of fear of the principal, fear of the class bully, failure in sports, and fear of failure in academics. The only way he could do it was to retreat into his own world of champions, people like The Lone Ranger, The Shadow, Jack Armstrong, Tom Mix, and a host of other radio and movie heroes. I felt like I was living on an abandoned island, with no way to reach out and touch the real world.

Then I met Miss Bennett and she helped me build my first bridge.

# Chapter Two

Mary Bennett was everything Evelyn McFeely was not. She was short, gentle, soft-spoken, pleasant, and had the ability to make learning an enjoyable experience. The atmosphere in her second-grade classroom was nonthreatening because she kept reminding us that we weren't competing with each other but with ourselves. The greatest thing she did for us was to introduce us to the world of books; one beautiful spring day, she marched the entire class up Grand Boulevard to the public library where we all received our first library cards.

My parents weren't avid book readers. They preferred reading our local newspapers, *The Hammond Times* and the Sunday *Chicago Tribune* ("The World's Greatest Newspaper" — it said so, right on the front page), and subscribed to assorted magazines like *The Saturday Evening Post, Collier's,* and *Liberty.* Ed and Tat read *Open Road for Boys* and Doris read Grace Livingston Hill novels borrowed from friends at school or church. The first clothbound book I ever owned was called *Farm Babies,* a Christmas present from my parents. It was about calves and colts and chicks and goslings and other assorted rural progeny, and it seemed an odd gift for a boy who lived in the city and cared nothing about farms. In later years, I used the book for a lap board when I would sit in the living room listening to the radio and molding things out of clay. The clay wrecked the covers of the book.

The East Chicago public library on Grand Boulevard, just beyond Broadway, eventually became my home away from home where I could escape principals and bullies and terrible feelings of inadequacy as the baby of the family. My precious library card was a passport to people and places I never dreamed existed. *Books became my bridge into worlds that couldn't threaten me.* During the school year, I spent a good part of almost every Saturday at the library; during summer vacation, it wasn't unusual for me to be at the library two or three times a week. It was a seven-block walk from home to the library and I usually whistled all the way. Today in East Chicago, a beautiful new city library is located just two blocks from my boyhood home, but I wouldn't have exchanged those long walks for anything. They gave me opportunity to think and dream, and the walking was good exercise for a boy who avoided sports.

The head librarian in the children's division was Bessie Glawe (rhymes with Maui). She and her assistants got to know me quite well, since I was their best customer and they knew I was serious about reading. Miss Glawe often suggested books to me when she detected that my interests were changing. One summer I focused on science and read about chemical elements, minerals, stars, and insects. Then I got interested in history and biography and read many of the biographical series written especially for children.

But the greatest literary event of all occurred the day Miss Glawe introduced me to Sherlock Holmes. "I think you'll enjoy this," she said as she handed me *The Boy's Sherlock Holmes;* she was right. Since that day, Holmes and Watson, Inspector Lestrade, and the foggy streets of Victorian London have become as real to me as the clothing I wear; I've read each of the Holmes stories and novels dozens of times. Watching the new Granada Television Sherlock Holmes series, featuring Jeremy Brett, is a delight to me.

During my childhood, I used to sit by the radio on Sunday evenings absolutely transfixed as Basil Rathbone and Nigel Bruce dramatized "The Adventures of Sherlock Holmes," and I was grateful to the anonymous people who manufactured Grove's "Bromo-Quinine" tablets for footing the bill. I never did find out what "Bromo-Quinine" tablets were good for, but if the network had ever threatened to cancel my favorite radio program, I would have swallowed a ton of those tablets to keep Sherlock Holmes on the air. Years later, while ministering at "The Cove" in Asheville, North Carolina, my wife and I stayed at The Grove Park Inn, built by Mr. Grove of "Bromo-Quinine" fame, and as I walked the halls, I silently gave thanks for his contribution to a young boy's life.

# Chapter Two

Let me jump ahead several years to the time I was a seminary student in Chicago and was engaged to marry a girl who lived in Clinton, Wisconsin, just over the Illinois–Wisconsin line. I was taking the train from Chicago to Wisconsin to visit her and on impulse had purchased in the railroad station a one-volume edition of all the Sherlock Holmes stories and novels. I hadn't read a Holmes story in years, so I became a child again and lost myself in Conan Doyle's tales as the train carried me from Chicago to Wisconsin. It was one of the most delightful journeys I ever made; as I rode along I thought of Bessie Glawe and "Bromo-Quinine" tablets and Sunday evenings with Basil Rathbone.

That introduction to Sherlock Holmes was the beginning of a lifelong interest in good detective fiction. Soon I had read all the mystery and detective books in the children's division of the library (there weren't many), so Miss Glawe graciously gave me a pass to go upstairs to the adult division where the shelves were crammed with books by Agatha Christie, Mary Roberts Reinhart, Ellery Queen, S.S. Van Dine, and all the other greats whose imaginary detectives could solve every crime that baffled the police.

"This is *only* for the detective fiction section," Miss Glawe reminded me as she gave me the pass. I suppose she was afraid I'd wander off to some shelf that contained books that a young boy was not yet supposed to read. But there was no danger. There were no such books in our library, and I was so fascinated by the vast treasury of detective novels that nothing else attracted me. Furthermore, the librarian at the desk in the adult division would have thrown me bodily out of the building if I'd tried to violate the privileges stated on my pass.

Her name was Birdie Peters, and she sat at the main checkout desk like a female Buddha, but not the "laughing" variety. To her, the public library was a sacred temple, the books were icons, and the patrons were worshipers; woe to that person, young or old, who spoke above a holy whisper, who dropped a book, who scraped a chair, who chewed gum, or who laughed out loud. She had marvelously sensitive ears for an older woman; if she heard any noise other than the turning of pages, she would leave her throne and make a solemn march around the reading room, looking neither to the right hand nor to the left, knowing that her austere presence was enough to paralyze anyone bent on mischief. The first time I saw a picture of the aged Queen Victoria, I was reminded of Birdie Peters; in later years, I came to appreciate Miss Peters more, and she and I almost became friends. At least she smiled at me occasionally when she checked out my books.

In his charming essay "The Lost Childhood," novelist Graham Greene says, "Perhaps it is only in childhood that books have any deep influence on our lives." Whether that statement applies to everybody is debatable, but this much is true: fortunate are those people whose love for books and reading started early in life and was cultivated by people who could encourage them in the right direction.

At Christmas, Grandpa Forsberg usually gave each of his grandchildren a dollar, which in those days was really worth something. We could purchase an ice cream cone for only five cents, an ice cream sundae or soda for a dime, and a clothbound Triangle Books edition of a novel for only forty-nine cents. Quality paperback books were sold in every drug store for only a quarter. During my early teen years, I built up quite a library of detective novels which one day, while in a generous mood, I donated to the USO so the servicemen could get their minds off foreign wars by concentrating on domestic murders.

My Christmas dollar was always spent on books, except for the year my mother decided she wanted to buy two new matching floor lamps for the living room. The lamps were on sale at some local furniture store, and reluctantly we four children surrendered Grandpa Forsberg's gifts so there could be light

My sister, Doris, my mother, and me, 1938.

My father and me.

◀ Warren Abraham and I eating spaghetti on the back porch of my house.

29

# Be Myself

and beauty in our home, not to mention peace. The lamps were duly purchased and plugged in, but Ed and Tat and Doris and I still missed our fortunes, and frequently in the months that followed, one of us would say, "I want my dollar back!" In fact, years later, in any family gathering, all somebody had to say was "I want my dollar back!" and we'd all break up laughing, with Ma usually laughing the hardest.

My parents often shopped at Sears Roebuck in nearby Gary, Indiana, and the store had a small book section. It was there I bought my first copy of *Roget's Thesaurus* for ninety-nine cents, and I thought I'd acquired the Hope Diamond. Here was a book of *words,* thousands of them, all neatly captured and categorized and now at my command. I didn't have the foggiest notion what Roget's verbal categories meant and couldn't have told you the difference between "abstract relations" and any other relations or what distinguished "special forms" from "superficial forms." But Roget's system fascinated me and I have been a thesaurus collector ever since. At last count, I had six different versions of Roget in my library, along with more than fifty different dictionaries of one kind or another. Yes, I confess it: I'm a word addict.

I wish I could say that everybody in my family approved of my interest in books and libraries, but they didn't. I don't know how many times I was asked, "Is that all you have to do is stick your nose in a book? Why don't you go out and get some fresh air?" (I realize now that in those days there wasn't a great deal of fresh air to be found in northern Indiana, especially when the steel mills were pouring, but back then, we didn't know that.) During the summer, Ed and Tat were usually active in a sandlot baseball league; and in the fall, they played football in Washington Park. (One day Ed ran smack into a bleacher and broke a front tooth.) Doris would roller skate with her friends and ride her bike, when I wasn't using it. When winter came, all of them enjoyed ice skating and the boys played ice hockey. But all year round, my main form of exercise was walking to the library and back, carrying books and turning pages.

But it wasn't just books and reading that gripped me. *Anything* that was related to the study of words was nourishment to the inner boy. I guess that's why I got interested in crossword puzzles and codes. As a child, I used to labor for days over crossword puzzles, erasing my dumb mistakes and scanning whole sections of the dictionary in an attempt to find the right word. The code messages in my big brother's *Shadow* magazines took weeks to solve. Today, I usually solve a crossword puzzle and a cryptogram every day because I find the exercise keeps my mind alert and helps me be creative.

I was an inveterate reader of the advertisements in the magazines that came to our home and often sent away for free catalogs, most of them from booksellers. It was fun to receive mail and then at my leisure pore over the catalogs and try to figure out why anybody would publish books on those subjects. Especially on Friday afternoons, when the dismissal bell rang, I'd run home as fast as I could for two reasons: there might be some mail for me from my postcards of the previous weekend; and Friday was Pa's day off, and when he and Ma went shopping, they sometimes brought home special treats, like chocolate eclairs. After a dangerous week at school, the combination of a new book catalog and a chocolate eclair was hard to beat.

Not only are you born into a family, but you're born into a neighborhood, and that neighborhood will influence your life. Chesterton wrote, "We make our friends; we make our enemies; but God makes our next-door neighbor." (It's nice to have somebody to blame.) Chesterton also said, "The Bible tells us to love our neighbors, and also to love our enemies; probably because they are generally the same people." Our family had its share of that kind of experience, thanks to the antics of the four creative Wiersbe children in the neighborhood.

# Be Myself

To the north, our immediate neighbors were the Burgesses and to the south, a family I'll call the Allans. Glen Burgess was my age and was built a lot like me, thin and blond and a fast runner. I often played with Glen and his younger brother Gene, but frequently we would disagree about something and end up not talking to each other for weeks. Then something would happen to bring us together again and we'd pick up where we left off. Childhood friendships are either pragmatic and superficial, always changing, or else profoundly intense, creating heartache when they're broken. I can't remember any friends I was so attached to in my childhood that when they walked out of my life, I felt hurt. At that stage in life, I was closer to Sherlock Holmes and Dr. Watson than I was to some of the boys I went swimming with at the Washington Park pool.

The Allans were a quiet family who had two daughters about the ages of Ed and Tat. The younger daughter, whom I'll call Julia, had a physical problem that caused her to faint without warning, no matter where she was or what she was doing. Whenever she fainted, her mother would become frantic and shout, "Julia! Julia! Now snap out of it!" My father had a theory that Julia was fabricating the whole thing just to get attention, and one evening he had an opportunity to test his theory. He was sprinkling the lawn in the backyard and Julia was talking to him over the fence. She had one of her "spells" and fell to the ground, so Pa turned the hose on her. Instantly she jumped to her feet and ran into the house, at least temporarily delivered from her affliction. If *I* had done that to Julia, Pa would have whipped me with his belt, but for some reason, he didn't feel too guilty.

The Allans often went on picnics to Whiting Park or even as far as the Indiana Dunes, and sometimes they asked me to go along. I think they felt sorry for their skinny little neighbor boy who seemed "abandoned" by his siblings. Maybe they wanted me to be a companion to Julia and help take her mind off her problems. At a moment's notice, Ma would make me a peanut butter sandwich and put it in a paper bag with some potato chips and cookies—Mrs. Allan always provided the drink, usually root beer or lemonade—and off I'd go in their car.

## Chapter Two

This experience as a picnic draftee may explain my lifelong aversion to outdoor eating in general. I can't understand why a family will work hard and save money to be able to have a house with a kitchen and a dining room and then go out to a dirty table in a messy park and eat cold food with the flies, ants, and mosquitoes. The girl I married was raised in a family that thrived on picnics, so over the years I've had to alter my views somewhat, but I'm still prejudiced.

In my pre-kindergarten years, my best friend on the block was Warren Abraham. He was an only child and lived with his parents in the apartment house two doors to the north. Florence Abraham was Swedish and her widowed mother, Mrs. Hedwall, lived across the street and her brother lived up the block. During the spring and summer, Warren Abraham and I would go with our mothers to Washington Park where we boys would enjoy the playground and the ladies would sit on a bench and chat about whatever mothers chat about. During those depression days, my mother worked hard caring for our family, and I'm sure she enjoyed those brief times out of the kitchen and the basement laundry.

During one of those expeditions to the park, two lions were delivered to our little zoo, and we boys were quite excited as we heard them roar. Later, somebody told us that Frank Buck, of "Bring 'em Back Alive" fame, had caught them, but that was probably a rumor. However, hearing that story, plus seeing Clyde Beatty "tame" lions at the Chicago World's Fair in 1934, motivated me a few years later to read all the Frank Buck books I could find at the library, as well as the books by Martin and Osa Johnson.

Clyde Beatty starred in one of the movie serials we watched on Saturdays at the Indiana Theater on Michigan Avenue, and sometimes Glen and Gene Burgess and I would go to the park and play African safari. The way we argued, it's a wonder any of us came back alive.

The Indiana Theater was the prime movie house on the Harbor side of town and the mecca for hundreds of children every Saturday afternoon. There was another movie theater on Main Street called The Garden, but no respectable person from our part of town would attend there, because that's where the "riff-raff" went. One of our high school teachers missed a movie at The Indiana and went to see it weeks later at The Garden; when her fellow teachers heard about it, they reprimanded her. The Garden wasn't the place for a refined and educated lady.

At The Indiana every Saturday, for a thin dime, we children could enjoy a full-length feature, coming attractions, at least three cartoons, and an episode in an exciting serial. An extra nickel would provide enough candy to satisfy you the whole afternoon, except when there was a double feature. Every Saturday morning, somebody deposited on our front porch a nicely printed "show bill" that told us what was playing that week. There were no movie ratings in those days. Just about every film was suitable for family consumption and our parents never questioned us about what we saw.

"What we saw" were primarily comedies from Abbott and Costello, Jane Withers, Mickey Rooney, and the Three Stooges; westerns from Gene Autry, Tom Mix, Hopalong Cassidy, Ken Maynard, and Buck Jones; and dramas suited to a juvenile audience, often featuring Shirley Temple, Deanna Durbin, or Freddy Bartholomew. There was usually one gushy romantic scene in the more serious films, and that was our signal to either go to the restroom or replenish our supply of candy.

On one occasion, I went to see a Paul Muni film that was not only over my head (I didn't even understand the title) but was so boring I wanted to get my dime back. I finally walked out in the middle of the movie and went home. I met Julia Allan and told her that I had walked out on a Paul Muni film. She was so upset she had one of her spells. Apparently one didn't walk out on a great actor like Paul Muni, but I did.

## Chapter Two

I had adult friends in our neighborhood as well as juvenile friends, and number one on the list was LaVerne Mapes, Ramona's father. Maybe he saw in me the son he never had (if so, his expectations weren't very high), or maybe he just found in me a willing partner with lots of free time to fit into his plans. But it wasn't unusual for him to come to my bedroom window at 8 o'clock on a summer morning, tap on the screen, and invite me to join him after breakfast for a drive to Chicago or a game of Chinese checkers on his front porch.

Mr. Mapes was a self-employed accountant who had offices both in his home and in the back room of Fritz Veit's barber shop on Michigan Avenue. Ed and Tat and I used to go to Fritz for our haircuts, and sometimes we'd see Mr. Mapes in his back-room office, figuring somebody's taxes or playing cards with some of his cronies. In that office, he did general accounting work for clients; and on Inland Steel paydays, he'd park his car near the Inland gate and cash checks for the workers, charging them a small fee for his services.

But I think his first love was his postage stamps. I used to go with him to a Roman Catholic missionary organization in Chicago where he purchased gunnysacks full of domestic and foreign stamps that the priests saved for him. The best part of the trip was stopping at a drive-in on the way home and getting an ice cream cone or a "blizzard," which was a cold drink made of crushed ice and flavoring. That was my payment for giving up a part of my vacation to keep Mr. Mapes company.

Once home, he would soak the stamps in water, carefully remove them from the envelopes, sort them out, and bundle them into packages of 100 each. At one time he had boxes and sacks in his basement containing 3 million stamps, all in those little bundles. Whenever he found a stamp that he needed, he added it to his own collection, which was large and valuable. The rest he sold to other collectors. In an article about stamp collecting, the *Chicago Daily News* called my neighbor "a renowned Midwestern collector"; so the neighborhood had another famous man beside "Sonny" Sheetz, and I was his friend.

But LaVerne Mapes was never so busy that he couldn't take time for a game of checkers, Chinese checkers, or gin rummy, which he taught me to play much against my mother's wishes. Although I often played juvenile card games like "Fish" or "War" with Glen and Gene Burgess, we never had a deck of cards in our house until I started to do magic, and Ma opposed my using cards even then. Mr. Mapes and I would sit on his front porch on a summer's day and play as many as twenty or thirty games of Chinese checkers, and occasionally he'd let me win.

Another adult friend was Bob Weirich who was our block captain during World War II. A "block captain" was a person in charge of informing the residents of the block what they were supposed to do in case of an air raid or an invasion, neither of which anybody in East Chicago expected to see. Mr. Weirich used to enlist me to go from house to house distributing pamphlets containing valuable information about invasions and incendiary bombs, and since he paid me fifty cents to do it, I was only too happy to perform this public service on behalf of the war effort.

My father and Mr. Mapes were too old to be drafted, although at one critical period during the war, they both had to register just in case they were needed. Mr. Mapes' only comment was, "Yes sir, yes sir, things are pretty bad if they need fossils like me to help win this war!" He was a rabid Republican and had an intense dislike for Democrats in general and President Franklin Delano Roosevelt in particular. He would read the morning *Chicago Tribune* first thing each day and, after doing the crossword puzzle, spend the rest of the day fuming about the news and the way the Democrats were wrecking the country.

My father was an air raid warden and I think Mr. Mapes was his assistant, or it may have been the other way around. The government sponsored training sessions at the high school auditorium, and some evenings, I went along with my father and my neighbor, hoping the Civil Defense people would show a movie and that either Pa or Mr. Mapes would treat me to an ice cream cone on the way home. I suppose if a Japanese bomber had strayed through our coastal defenses and made it to the Chicago area, or if a German submarine had wandered into Calumet Harbor, Pa and Mr. Mapes would have heroically risen to the occasion. I know the war was serious, but I must admit that, even now, as I picture those two middle-aged men leading us in defending our block from invaders, I burst into almost uncontrollable laughter.

# CHAPTER THREE

F rom my limited point of view as the baby of the family, I
watched our family face three crises during my childhood years.

The first was a strike at the Borden Dairy, organized by a
group of workers who wanted all the drivers to join the Teamsters Union ("The International Brotherhood of Teamsters,
Chauffeurs, Warehousemen, and Helpers of America") so they
could pressure management into raising wages and providing
better benefits, both of which were noble goals. My mother had
to watch the budget very carefully until the strike was over, and
it wasn't easy. When we kids heard the "Good Humor Man"
ring his bell each evening, we wanted to ask for money for ice
cream, but we knew it would be selfish. Our only income during those days was the rent from the upstairs flat.

The second crisis occurred very early New Year's morning,
1941, when a drunken driver hit Pa's car while he was on his
way to work. (On holidays, he had to go out very early to
deliver the milk.) He was laid up for several weeks and one
doctor told him he'd probably lose his left leg. He survived and
returned to work, but those were austere weeks for all of us. As
I look back, I wonder how many personal sacrifices my parents
made so that we four kids could have the things we needed.

You don't really understand some of these things until you have children of your own, and then you wish you could set the clock back and have another chance to show your parents that you understand and care.

Pa was driving a new Dodge when the accident occurred. Twenty-five years later, I was driving a new Pontiac, and a drunk driver going eighty or ninety miles an hour hit me and almost killed me. Sometimes history does repeat itself.

The third crisis hit more than one family in our neighborhood when on December 8, 1941, the United States entered World War II and the eligible young men started being called up for service in the armed forces. Ed was two years older than Tat and had been deferred because he was involved in specialized war work as a machinist at the Edward Valve and Manufacturing Company, a division of the Rockwell Manufacturing Company. But after Tat graduated from high school, the war effort caught up with both of them. They were drafted in 1943 and enlisted in the United States Marines. They went through basic training together at Camp Pendleton in California and stayed together in the Sixth Marine Division during their entire three-year stint.

Except when we were angry, we Wiersbes didn't let anybody know that we had emotions. Whether it was our German stoicism or our Swedish pride that motivated us, we always did our suffering in private. I wasn't home the day Ed and Tat left for the Marines, but I was on hand when the postman arrived with a package containing their civilian clothes. Ma took the package down to the basement. "I'll have to put the clothes in the washing," she said, but I knew that she went down there to cry.

The only time I ever saw my mother cry publicly was one Thanksgiving Day when my father wanted to invite his stepfather to dinner and Ma was against it. We called our German step-grandfather "Glasses Grandpa" because, unlike our Swedish Grandpa Forsberg, he wore glasses. With his little bald head and little round glasses, he looked a lot like the scientist Dr. Huer in the "Flash Gordon" comic strip. He lived in a shabby part of town and spent most of his time reading old magazines, smoking, drinking, and gambling. One reason Ma didn't want me doing card tricks is because she was afraid I'd end up a gambler like Glasses Grandpa.

I can still see Ma standing in the kitchen, sobbing into a dish towel and saying, "He'll wreck our marriage yet!" Glasses Grandpa came to share our Thanksgiving dinner, but the marriage wasn't wrecked. My father had a struggle that day, wanting to please his family and yet wanting to help his stepfather. There was nobody else to care for the old man and I guess Pa felt sorry for him.

Before leaving home, Ed and Tat worked out a code system to keep us informed of their whereabouts on Planet Earth. For example, if Tat wrote, "I'm glad to hear that Roy and Bee [our aunt and uncle] sold their house," that meant their unit was in the Philippines. "Tell Louise [our cousin] to stick with her voice lessons" meant they were heading for the South Pacific. Some of their letters were heavily censored, but I don't think any of the coded statements were ever deleted. As long as their letters got through, we pretty much knew where they were.

Ed and Tat were among the second wave to land on Okinawa on April 1, 1945. Later they were transferred to China. It was a happy day for all of us when they arrived back on Ivy Street in 1946 and took up civilian life again. The only member of the Ivy Street gang who didn't come back from the war was Harold "Hootch" Manley who was lost in action while serving in the Air Force. Whenever I walked past the Manley house, I couldn't help seeing the gold star in the window. It was the only gold star on the block.

When school started in September 1941, I left Washington Elementary School and entered Washington High School. It was one of the happiest days of my life. Israel must have felt that same kind of liberating joy when they were delivered from Egypt. No more Evelyn McFeely and no more campus bullies!

During my last week in grade school, Marie Jablonski, one of my favorite teachers, called me aside and gave me what turned out to be an invaluable piece of advice.

"Warren," she said, "you're moving into junior high school and then high school; I want you to promise me you'll always do two things: do a lot of reading—all kinds of reading, and do a lot of writing. You've got a gift for writing, and I want you to use it."

Then she showed me a file of my work that she'd been keeping: two-page essays on subjects she'd assigned from time to time, short stories and poems on holiday themes, and even book reviews. She saw something in those juvenile productions that I didn't see, but I took her advice to heart and have been grateful ever since.

One day, our Uncle Dave brought an ancient Underwood upright typewriter to our house and asked if we wanted it. If the Smithsonian staff had seen it first, they would have acquired it for their collection, but I beat them to it. I should have enrolled in a typing class at school, but I decided to teach myself to type, and before long, I was pounding away rather successfully using my thumbs and two fingers on each hand. By the time I was qualified to take Typing 101, I had so many incurable bad typing habits that I would have been thrown out of class the first week. Bad habits notwithstanding, in the years that followed, I did all of my high school, college, and seminary writing using the Wiersbe four-finger method, and went on to write over a hundred books, not to speak of scores of press releases, magazine articles, and radio scripts.

When school let out each day at 3:30 P.M., I often stopped at the high school library to see what might be available for me to read. Ruth Lucas, the head librarian, had taken a liking to my sister Doris and had asked her to serve on the student library staff, so this gave me an "in" with the powers that be, and I took advantage of it. Like Miss Glawe in my childhood years, Miss Lucas steered me toward the best books and even took time to teach me how to use the reference section. Maybe Miss Jablonski had whispered something in her ear.

Without destroying my interest in detective fiction, Miss Lucas taught me to appreciate the classics. Miss DePew and Miss Oilar were supposed to do that in their respective American and English literature classes, and to some extent they succeeded, but stories and poems you read as assignments just aren't the same as stories and poems you read for fun. Miss Lucas must have been an omnivorous reader, because she could discuss intelligently almost any book or writer you might mention. I hate to confess it, but I learned more about good literature after school than I did in class. The appetite for good books that Miss Lucas helped cultivate has brought me a great deal of pleasure, and the things I've read have greatly enriched my life and my ministry.

Before I leave my early high school years, I have to mention two more teachers: Miss Gaber and Miss Hustad. Miss Gaber was in charge of school productions and ran the stage crew on which both of my brothers served. Each year there would be a junior class play, a senior class play, several major concerts, and the annual "Washington Hi-Lights" revue; Miss Gaber produced them all. I've forgotten the name of the class she taught, but I was in it for one semester, and during those weeks, she taught me to love poetry. She used to play recordings of great poets reading their works, and I'd sit there fascinated that words could be put together with such power. Vachel Lindsay's reading of "The Congo" captivated me and I found a copy of it in the library and memorized the first part. I can still recite it.

Mildred Hustad was Norwegian with the blonde hair and blue eyes to prove it, and she sang like a nightingale. She could whistle too and would sometimes end our weekly music class by playing some popular song and whistling as she played. She was so good and so good-looking, we wondered why she wasn't in the movies. Just as Miss Gaber taught me to love good poetry, Miss Hustad taught me to appreciate classical music. My family wasn't into the classics; we leaned more toward the country-western music we heard over the WLS "Barn Dance" or the hymns we heard over WMBI.

This was a whole new world for me, and I couldn't get enough of it. I fell in love with *The Nutcracker Suite* and *Peter and the Wolf* and Edward MacDowell's *Woodland Sketches*. I discovered "The Northwestern 400 Hour" on WGN, hosted from 7 to 8 each weekday morning by Norman Ross; and during summer vacation, I'd often get up early and listen to a whole hour of beautiful music. (During our years at Moody Church, I used to listen to Norman Ross, Jr., host a late-afternoon classical music program over one of the local FM stations.) I still love classical music and poetry and wish I had more time for enjoying and understanding both.

I recall a funny thing about my early music career. When I was in elementary school, once a week our class would be dismissed to the music room for an hour with Miss Boyce. She was built like a Wagnerian prima donna and had a voice to match. One year we were rehearsing Christmas music for a concert and I was having a hard time with words of familiar carols that were new to me. Instead of singing "With angelic hosts proclaim," I was singing "With and jelly hosts proclaim." Nobody corrected me, so I kept it up; but I was perplexed. I knew what "jelly" was, but what was "with," and why were we "proclaiming" both of them? What did they have to do with Christmas?

During my high school years, I continued to get good grades except in physical education class, where I usually got a reluctant "Satisfactory" from a coach who happened to be in a generous mood. I wasn't interested in sports and I had no athletic ability, and these two factors combined to make me a coach's nightmare. I couldn't have played basketball any worse if I had been on crutches, and football and baseball absolutely bewildered me.

Although I liked Coach Clark (his nickname was "Pottsy"—you can figure out why), I hated swimming class with a passion. It was usually the first class in the morning; and in spite of taking a shower, I smelled like chlorine all day. And I usually caught at least one good cold each winter because we had to run between buildings with wet hair and sometimes with wet clothes. The class was lethal.

**Pastor Everett Ostrom and the 1944 confirmation class: Doris Carlson, Gloria Davis, myself, and Lillian Stevens.**

Noting that I could run fast, Coach Walker entered me in the all-city "Field Day" one spring. I was assigned to bring glory to Washington High School by running speedily down the track, leaping gracefully over a number of low hurdles and arriving victoriously at the finish line ahead of everybody else. The running part presented no difficulty, but the low hurdles were a serious problem: they weren't low enough. I knocked over six hurdles, chipped a metatarsal bone in my left foot and never did make it triumphantly to the finish line. Shortly after that, Coach Walker vanished from our little campus and was reported to be in the army. I always wondered if he was drafted or just enlisted to get away from me.

## Chapter Three

During the war years, somebody in Washington, D.C., decided that the American schoolboy was weak and flabby and needed toning up. One Monday when we returned to school from our weekend off, we discovered that an obstacle course had been installed on the school athletic field, and Coach Adolph Schweingruber (believe me, that was his name) told us the facts of athletic life in wartime. His speech went something like this:

"Boys, there's a war on, and all of us have to *do* our best and *be* our best. The government has set some standards for us and we're here to help you reach them. *[Most of the coaches standing there were definitely overweight and not in good shape.]* The first thing we'll do in gym class each day is run two laps around the track and make two successful passages through the obstacle course. This we will do rain or shine, cold or heat, and there will be no exceptions."

Achtung! Schnell! Schnell! Sieg Heil!

From the warmth and comfort of his upstairs office, and with a cup of steaming coffee in his hand, Coach Schweingruber would watch us struggle through this so-called bodybuilding ordeal day after day. He watched us because he wanted to make sure nobody asked anybody for help in scaling the wall or conquering the barricades, because to ask for help was to violate the first commandment of successful athletic endeavors: "Thou shalt do it thyself!" To me, the whole thing was ridiculous, and all it ever did for my body was bruise it, puncture it with little wooden slivers, and make it difficult for me to get over the cold I caught in swimming class.

But the sadistic sports program wasn't the only academic burden I had to bear in high school. There was also the shop program. Since Washington High School was located in a highly industrialized community, the local educators agreed that the male students must be exposed to as many facets of vocational life as possible, such as machine shop, print shop, wood shop, electric shop, and auto shop. (The girls had to take cooking, sewing, and home economics. From the odors that frequently filled the school halls, I think most of the girls flunked cooking.)

At the time in life when I should have been learning how to

drive a car, there was a war on and gas was rationed; so I steered clear of auto shop. Anyway, my mother didn't want me fooling around with gasoline; she was afraid I'd blow up the school and never graduate. As for machine shop, the only thing mechanical I knew how to run was my antique typewriter. This left me facing a semester each of wood shop, electric shop, and print shop.

Mr. Parker presided over the benches, stools, and vises in the wood shop, and since both of my older brothers had been his students, he expected me to excel in manual arts as they did. It didn't take him long to discover that he was wrong and that his latest Wiersbe student was a manual mutant. The other fellows in the class made bookends, foot stools, and cute little end tables, and proudly took them home to their parents, but all I had to show for a semester's work was a pile of shavings and some sawdust. But because Mr. Parker liked Ed and Tat, he gave me a passing grade.

I wasn't worried about passing electric shop because the teacher, Mr. Rencenberger, lived in the upstairs apartment my folks rented out. If he didn't give me a passing grade, I'd have my father evict him and his family! Mr. Rencenberger did his best to teach us about direct currents, alternating currents, voltage meters, relays, and how to build a small motor, but none of it stayed with me. I did learn that you should never use 220 voltage to run the little motors we made because they're supposed to run on battery voltage. I don't know who increased the voltage at my partner's bench that morning, but the pieces of Byron's motor flew all over the shop. Byron sat on his little metal stool and cried like a baby.

It was when I walked into Mr. Altenderfer's print shop that I knew I had found my natural habitat, and I've had printer's ink in my veins ever since. I was really in my element in the print shop, for here we not only *read* words but we *felt* them. We set type, assembled the lines in paragraphs, and then locked the paragraphs into forms that we put on the presses. We actually *printed* things, things that people would read, like football schedules, prom folders, concert programs, and above all else, the school newspaper, *The Anvil*.

## Chapter Three

In spite of his rough exterior, Mr. Altenderfer was a kind and patient man who taught me a lot about words, page layouts, different grades of paper and ink, punctuation, and proofreading. John Kail, my best friend from kindergarten to high school graduation (and a fellow amateur magician) was also in the class, and we had a good time working together on the school newspaper. I recall the day John picked up the form for pages one and four of *The Anvil* without first checking to see whether the form was locked. It wasn't. All the type spilled out, and John and I stayed after school, putting the paper back together.

I first broke into print in the pages of *The Anvil*. I didn't write anything sensational, but it was at least a beginning for somebody who would spend much of his life writing, editing, proofreading, and publishing.

When I was a junior, I collaborated on a humor column with my friend Phil Pecar, who was a sophomore and had a marvelous sense of humor. The column lasted two issues.

Reading this column now, I can see in it the embryo of the kind of humor that showed up years later in the crazy skits I wrote for Youth for Christ and also the columns I wrote for *Christianity Today* as "Eutychus X."

Miss Lucy Swindell, the school's journalism instructor, served as chief faculty sponsor for *The Anvil;* she allowed nothing to be printed that even hinted that something suspicious was going on. I remember how incensed she was when I wrote the following poem and submitted it:

Of all the *isms* on this earth,
To me, the most infernal,
The one that has the smallest worth
Is the one that starts with *journal.*

Miss Swindell didn't think it was funny.

While I'm on the subject of poetry, I must say something about Miss McCullough and her biology class. (Only she never said "*bi*ology"; it was always "bology.") She had gray hair that she tinged with a blue dye, and it always ended up looking purple. For some reason she had the idea that people couldn't live normal lives unless they could recite the various phyla that categorize the world of living things. During one particularly boring class, I wrote:

I see you moving, small amoeba,
Strutting like the Queen of Sheba.
And as you ooze in regal splendor,
You look to me like a peanut vendor.

Like Miss Swindell, Miss McCullough didn't have much of a sense of humor.

*The Anvil* majored on *important* things like listing the students who had perfect attendance, reporting athletic events, announcing school concerts and plays, promoting "good citizenship," and avoiding printing anything that the school board might consider subversive. During my senior year, I wrote the paper's "gossip column"; Miss Swindell read my copy carefully lest I sneak in something that only the student body would understand. Don't think I didn't try, but I never succeeded.

Not only was I trying to influence our campus through the pages of *The Anvil*, but from seventh grade to graduation, I was a member of the student council and served on numerous student government committees. I was also a student "defense attorney" and helped the campus "judge" run the campus court. The faculty thought we were learning "participatory government" and good citizenship, but all we were doing was having a good time. In fact, with the help of two of my friends, I even led a successful coup d'état right under the noses of the faculty and administration.

Bob Krajewski and Fred Corban and I were "the three musketeers" in Miss Swindell's journalism class. Bob and Fred were both a year ahead of me and Bob was one of our leading basketball stars. Later he became a teacher and then superintendent of schools for East Chicago. Fred was the philosophical type and had a subtle sense of humor.

I'd been reading in the school library about the "city manager" form of government that was growing in popularity in America about that time, and I suggested to Bob and Fred that we foment a revolution on campus.

"Let's replace the school's mayor–council system with a student manager system," I suggested, "and let's work it so Bob becomes the first student manager."

They bought the idea and we all went to work gathering information but keeping very quiet about our objectives. We knew that the plan wouldn't get faculty approval unless we made the whole enterprise look like "an experiment in democracy." How proud the faculty would be that the students thought enough of their school that *on their own* they wanted to improve its student government! It was breathtaking!

When we had the information ready, we shared it first with Mr. Palmer, faculty adviser to the student council. Since he taught history and government, he was thrilled with the idea and gave us permission to approach Mr. Robinson, principal of the school. Mr. Robinson read our plan, listened to our arguments, and told us we had his approval to share the idea with the whole student body.

"Council–Manager New Plan for Good Government!" announced a headline on the front page of *The Anvil* for April 11, 1945. The article said: "For sometime a number of students *[there were five of us in the cabal]* have been dissatisfied with the Mayor–Council form of government, and they have taken the responsibility of studying other forms in an attempt to get a change. The answer is in The Council or City Manager plan." The rest of the article explained the plan and why it simply had to be approved.

We presented the plan at a school assembly and wisely made Bob our spokesman. He was one of the most popular students on campus and this was actually the beginning of his campaign.

I don't recall that the opposition was ever given an opportunity to present their side of the issue; and when the vote was taken, the new system was enthusiastically voted in. Bob Krajewski became Washington High School's first Student Manager.

When he graduated the next year, Bob's picture was on the front page of *The Anvil* for April 3, followed by a laudatory article that concluded with, "And if that isn't enough, Bob was selected as Washington's first Student Manager, and it's not hard to see what great strides the Council has made this year with his leadership." Bob and Fred and I had many a good laugh over a successful coup d'état that hoodwinked the faculty, the administration, the student body—and even the school board.

Two very special events occurred during my sophomore year in high school: I published my first book, and I trusted Christ as my Savior and finally became a genuine Christian.

The book, *Action with Cards,* was published in October 1944, and contained a dozen original card tricks I had devised in my spare time. In spite of my mother's occasional protests, I did not dispose of my decks of cards but instead had practiced hard and become quite proficient at performing sleight-of-hand. I could stack a deck, deal cards from the bottom of the deck, do false shuffles that didn't disturb the order of the cards one bit, palm cards, and even make people choose cards that they didn't know I was forcing on them. Being the imaginative type, I found myself thinking up new ways to use old techniques, and the result was *Action with Cards.*

On Saturdays, I would sometimes take the South Shore electric train to the Chicago Loop and visit Ireland's Magic Shop on Dearborn Street, across the street from the old Carter's Restaurant. I'd study the new tricks that had come out, get advice about magic from Mrs. Ireland, make a few purchases to enhance my repertoire, then have a hamburger and malt at "Wimpy's" and take the train home. Occasionally Laurie Ireland or Ed Marlo would be at the shop, men whose skill at card dexterity was legendary in the profession; and I would watch them perform. Ed was especially encouraging and even took me to "The Magician's Round Table" at a nearby restaurant where he introduced me to some of the great magicians who happened to be in town. So, when I wrote the book, using my trusty Underwood, I decided to submit it to Ireland's; they bought it for thirty-five dollars. Nobody in my family knew about this transaction until it was finished, and I think they decided it was the best trick I had ever pulled off.

The book did well enough for Ireland's to accept *Mental Cases with Cards* two years later, and then *Tantalizing Thimbles,* a book on thimble magic, which was published in 1948. A gifted artist, my buddy Bob Krajewski did the explanatory illustrations for the thimble book. Once again, Bob and I were collaborating to fool somebody!

Granted, *Action with Cards* was just an eighteen-page pamphlet, but it was my first book and was published when I was only fifteen years old. I've averaged publishing two books a year ever since—but not on magic! How a Bible took the place of a pack of cards in my hands is a testimony to the miracle of the grace of God.

# CHAPTER FOUR

## 1

During the years I was growing up, spiritual ministry to young people in America was not the big thing it is today. Teenagers were just being discovered. Percy Crawford had been broadcasting the Gospel to youth since 1931; in 1937, Young Life was founded by Jim Rayburn and H.J. Taylor. Jack Wyrtzen had started his "Word of Life" ministry in 1940, and Crawford and Wyrtzen, both gifted evangelists, conducted large evangelistic rallies from city to city and won thousands to Jesus Christ. Both started camps and conference centers that ministered to young people and adults, and Young Life established several ranches. Our family often listened to Percy Crawford's "Young People's Church of the Air" radio program on Sunday afternoons.

When Youth for Christ exploded across America in the mid-'40s, we could tell that something new was happening, but we weren't quite sure what it was. Spontaneously, large YFC rallies were springing up in major cities like Detroit, Los Angeles, Minneapolis, and Chicago, and young people were being converted to Christ by the thousands. Local YFC committees were renting the largest auditoriums and stadiums and filling them to overflowing, and in many cities, denominational prejudices were disappearing as pastors from various churches worked and prayed *together,* some of them ministering together for the first time, in an all-out crusade to reach youth for Christ.

YFC President Bob Cook used to remind us, "If you can explain what's going on, God didn't do it." The constant prayer of YFC workers was, "Lord, keep YFC on a miracle basis." God answered that prayer. Hindsight doesn't always have 20/20 vision, but as I look back, I have the feeling that those early years of YFC in America were the closest thing to real revival that I've ever witnessed.

Torrey Johnson, founding pastor of the Mid-West Bible Church in Chicago, and his associate Bob Cook, were the catalysts God used to pull the whole thing together and give YFC the organizational and spiritual direction it needed. Burdened especially to reach the young servicemen walking the streets of Chicago, Torrey and Bob and their committee stepped out on faith and rented prestigious Orchestra Hall on Michigan Avenue, and on Saturday evening, May 24, 1944, "Chicagoland Youth for Christ" was born.

Torrey emceed the meeting; Bob led the singing; and Billy Graham, a young preacher from nearby Western Springs, was the speaker. Doug Fisher played the organ and Rose Arzoomanian was the soloist. The hall was packed, and when Billy Graham gave the invitation, scores responded. Chicagoland YFC stayed in Orchestra Hall all that summer, then moved to the Chicago Stadium and to Moody Church. They even held a special Memorial Day rally in Soldier Field and 75,000 people showed up. Chicago sat up and took notice.

By the end of 1944, dozens of youth leaders from the United States and Canada had met together twice, first at Winona Lake, Indiana, and then in Detroit, and the result was the organizing of Youth for Christ International, with Torrey Johnson as its first president. Its slogan was "Geared to the Times, Anchored to the Rock."

All of this may read like ancient history to you, but to us who lived in the greater Chicago area, Chicagoland Youth for Christ was a phenomenon. Our family often tuned in the broadcasts of the Saturday night rallies and caught some of the excitement of what was happening. Little did I know then the impact that

Torrey Johnson, Bob Cook, and Billy Graham would have on my own life in the years to come.

The Quaker leader Rufus Jones wrote in 1932: "Whenever the Church has taken a position of creative leadership and has summoned its youth to some great spiritual adventure significant enough to draw forth the potential capacities of its youthful members, they have always responded with zeal and alacrity, as they would do once more if the call reached them with kindling power...."*

In one simple sentence: young people will take notice when they see somebody burning out for what he believes. I like that phrase "kindling power." I'm reminded that Mel Larson's biography of Torrey Johnson is entitled *Young Man on Fire,* and that one of Torrey's most powerful messages was based on John 5:35, "He was a burning and a shining light."

## 2

Frustrated in their attempts to evangelize teenagers, many pastors and church leaders were asking, "Why can't what happened in Chicago happen in our own city?" Two Christian couples in East Chicago not only *asked* that question but went to the Youth for Christ office in downtown Chicago to get the answer. They were Jim and Henrietta Albaugh and Ed and Levida Bihl. (Carl "Kelly" Bihl, one of their sons, later became a YFC evangelist and also served as president of YFCI.) My mother and Mrs. Bihl were related through the Carlsons, but the Bihls had left the Mission Covenant Church and were worshiping at Central Baptist Church in Gary, Indiana.

The Bihl home at 3724 Hemlock Street was totally dedicated

---

*Harry Emerson Fosdick, *Rufus Jones Speaks to Our Time* (New York: Macmillan, 1951), 183. The quotation is from Jones' book *A Preface to Christian Faith in a New Age* (New York: Macmillan, 1932).

to the Lord and constantly open to the Lord's people. No stranger or pilgrim who came through Indiana Harbor was ever turned away from their door, and there were times when visiting evangelists and even entire missionary families lived with the Bihls for weeks at a time. East Chicago Youth for Christ began at a prayer meeting in their living room where a group of like-minded Christians asked God, "What do You want us to do?"

In the spring of 1945, this unofficial committee rented the Washington High School auditorium for three Saturday evenings and arranged for speakers from the Chicago YFC office. With their limited budget, the committee printed thousands of blotters that displayed a picture of an airplane and read:

---

Young People—ATTENTION!
YOUTH FOR CHRIST . . . Strictly on the beam!
May 12   May 26   June 9
Washington High School Auditorium
Hemlock near 141st Street
Indiana Harbor, Indiana
Starts 8 P.M.

---

Why they chose to use blotters for promoting a youth rally is a mystery to me, because not many kids I knew used fountain pens. Nevertheless, all of us in the Mission Covenant Church youth group passed the blotters out at school (you could do such things then), and other church youth groups did the same. When the doors opened at Washington Auditorium the evening of May 12, there was a fine crowd, and I was one of the ushers at those doors, passing out songbooks. They asked me to usher because I was one of the best Christian boys they knew.

Years later, Torrey Johnson told me that *he* was supposed to speak at the rally that night but sent Billy Graham instead. Torrey often did that for his younger colleagues in YFC so they could get a hearing and become better known. At that time, very few people knew who Billy Graham was, although some of us had heard him on the Sunday evening radio program "Songs in the Night" that was broadcast from The Village Church in Western Springs, Illinois. (Torrey had started the program at his Mid-West Bible Church, but when YFC duties began to multiply, he turned it over to Billy.) Torrey Johnson had convinced Billy to resign from the pastorate and serve as YFCI's first full-time evangelist. Billy was just one of scores of future Christian leaders that Johnson laid hands on and enlisted for the Savior.

Let me jump ahead a couple of years to an evening when I met Torrey Johnson at a YFC banquet and he asked me, "Young man, what do you plan to do with your life?" I told him I wanted to go to school and get some Bible training and then preach the Gospel. He then gave me a great piece of advice that I've tried to follow: "Young man, find the one thing you do that God blesses, *and stick with it!*"

Back to the YFC rally. That evening I was busy ushering and helping behind the scenes, so I can't recall what was on the program, but I can tell you that when Billy Graham began to preach, I was captivated. I stood against the back wall of the auditorium, unable to move and unable to take my eyes off the preacher. I heard every word he spoke and every Bible verse he quoted, and everything he said went right to my heart. Sure, I had heard it all before, but for the first time it came together and made sense. I saw that in spite of my character, my confirmation, my church attendance, and my host of religious relatives, I was a lost sinner who needed to trust Jesus Christ.

I didn't wait for the public invitation to be given. Right where I stood, I asked Jesus Christ to come into my heart and save me, *and He did!* I didn't raise my hand for prayer, I didn't fill out a card, I didn't even go forward when the crowd sang "Just as I Am," but I did trust Christ and become a child of God.

Later, I learned that Billy Graham had gone away from that meeting discouraged, mainly because a few pastors, zealous for their denominational distinctives, accosted him afterward and criticized him for not "preaching baptism." Well, I wasn't baptized until three years later, but I want you to know that God saved me that night, and I was just as much saved then as I was on July 11, 1948, when Rev. Dewey McFadden immersed me at the First Baptist Church in Whiting, Indiana.

$$\boxed{3}$$

After you become a child of God, what do you do next?

One of the first things I did was share my testimony at the Mission Covenant Church. Many of the people in the church family had prayed for me, including relatives now deceased, and the people in the congregation were thrilled to know that God had answered their prayers. When I told them I felt God had called me into the ministry, they were especially excited because my great-great grandfather, one of the founders of that church, had prayed that there would be a preacher of the Gospel in every generation of our family, and there has been. The church family was very supportive, and before long I found myself participating in various kinds of ministry.

One Lord's Day, between Sunday School and the worship service, one of the deacons stopped me and asked if I'd take the Scripture reading that morning. It was Luke 3:1-9, a passage heavily seasoned with words like "tetrarch," "Ituraea," "Trachonitis" and "Caiaphas." I didn't have a self-pronouncing Bible and was too dumb to borrow one, so I stumbled through the reading the best I could. It was embarrassing, but I learned two lessons from that experience: (1) never read the Scriptures publicly unless you're prepared, and (2) never draft anybody at the last minute to participate in a public service, unless the person feels he or she can do it.

As I look back and reflect, I can see how important it is for the new Christian to identify with a local fellowship of believers. The dear people in the Mission Covenant Church prayed for me, encouraged me, and gave me opportunities to serve the Lord and learn how to trust Him. I gave my testimony at street meetings. I began to use my magic tricks (not the cards!) as object lessons in Sunday School and in occasional YFC functions. I assisted in Vacation Bible School. It was an exciting time of discovering and developing the spiritual gifts the Lord had given me.

But the most fascinating thing was this: since my conversion, I had developed an insatiable appetite for the Word of God, and I wanted to study and understand the Bible more than anything else in all the world. In those early days of YFC, we didn't have follow-up material and study courses for new Christians, and Bob Cook's *Now That I Believe,* the standard YFC text for new believers, wasn't published until 1949. (Over a million copies would be sold and the book would be translated into twenty-seven languages. It's a classic.) The Bihls and Albaughs had the answer: they'd start a Thursday evening Bible study at 3724 Hemlock Street, and Mr. Bihl, a gifted teacher, would teach a book of the Bible.

The book he selected was the *Epistle to the Hebrews.*

So, every Thursday evening about 6:30 P.M., I'd leave 4216 Ivy Street and walk to 3724 Hemlock to join a sizable group of young people and adults who studied Hebrews for about an hour and then prayed for another hour. Much of what Mr. Bihl taught from Hebrews went right over my head, but enough stuck in my mind and heart to make me hungry for more. The book magnified Jesus Christ and told me that He was working for me up in heaven, and that's the assurance I needed.

I remember scanning the books in the Religion section of the public library, looking for something that would help me become a better Bible student. Most of the books were poisonous because they were slanted toward liberalism, but nobody told me that. By the providence of God, there on the shelf was a copy of *The Scofield Reference Bible,* and I checked it out. (It had never been checked out before.) Walking home, I went past "Forsberg row" on Parrish Avenue where three aunts, three uncles, and four cousins lived, and I met my cousin Louise who asked, "What in the world are you doing walking around with a Bible when it isn't Sunday?"

Eventually I bought myself a copy of *The Scofield Reference Bible,* and then a *Strong's Concordance.* My parents gave me a Christmas gift of *Cruden's Concordance, Smith's Bible Dictionary,* and *The Christian Worker's Commentary* by James M. Gray. I'd found the set listed in our Sear's catalog and asked them to order it for me. I read in a Christian book catalog that

D.L. Moody urged every Christian to read *Notes on the Penta-teuch* by C.H.M., so I sent away for the six-volume set and read it greedily. That set and *The Scofield Reference Bible* were my first serious introduction to what I'd heard Mr. Bihl call "dispensational truth." Those books became the nucleus of my library, which today numbers over 10,000 volumes.

My Uncle Simon occasionally preached at our church, and Ma would have him and his wife over for Sunday dinner or maybe coffee and cake. One day he brought me ten or fifteen books from his own library, including *The Crises of the Christ* and *Searchlights from the Word* by G. Campbell Morgan. Imagine my surprise a few years later to learn that Morgan had died on my sixteenth birthday, May 16, 1945, just a few days after I was converted. He has always been one of my heroes and has taught me much about the Word of God and the God of the Word.

If this were a sermon, I'd pause here and make a personal application of all that I've said, and it would be this: *If life is to have meaning, and if God's will is to be done, all of us have to accept who we are and what we are, give it back to God, and thank Him for the way He made us. What I am is God's gift to me; what I do with it is my gift to Him.*

For years, I'd been silently complaining to myself and to the Lord because I wasn't an athlete or a mechanic but had interests different from most of my peers. But after I became a Christian, I began to see that athletics and mechanics weren't in God's agenda for me. Miss Jablonski had been right: do a lot of reading and writing; spend your life with words.

And that's what I've been doing.

When I graduated from high school on June 11, 1947, it was announced that I was the class valedictorian. My brilliant academic rival on campus was Edith Gerkin, and the two of us had almost the same number of academic points on our records, so it was a toss-up which one should be valedictorian and which one salutatorian. Our principal, Frank Cash, made the decision and was quite up-front about how he reached it: he felt the valedictorian should be a boy rather than a girl in order to set a good example for the boys in the school to follow. A former coach, Mr. Cash's views of life were very masculine, and Edith took it graciously. We both knew she was smarter than I, even if our male-dominated administration wouldn't admit it.

At commencement, Edith walked off with the D.A.R. Citizenship gold medal and the Psi Iota Xi scholarship. I'd won the J.W. Lees Memorial Scholarship, which was a year's tuition at Indiana University's local Calumet campus on the East Chicago side of town. I'd also been offered a full four-year scholarship to Wabash College, "the Princeton of the Midwest," but had turned it down for two reasons: it was too liberal for me, and I didn't want to leave home. I'd lived in that house since the day of my birth and wasn't about to live anywhere else. A couple of times I'd been given Chicago Motor Club camp scholarships as rewards for my "faithful service" as a school patrol boy, but I always gave the prize to John Kail. I wasn't about to go to a strange place and eat food I didn't like cooked by people I didn't know, and I certainly wasn't going to waste a week of my precious summer doing things I hated to do, like playing baseball, making crafts, and rowing boats. Life was safer and far more comfortable in the Indiana Harbor public library.

But graduation brought with it a serious problem, serious at least to a young Christian who had a lot to learn about trusting the Lord for daily guidance. I'd been promised a job at the Edward Valve Company, where Ed, Tat, Doris, and Uncle Dave worked (guess how I got the job), and I was scheduled to start work the week after graduation. But I'd also promised to help direct the church's Vacation Bible School program that same week. If I kept my promise to the church, I might lose my job, but if I took the job, I might lose my testimony at the church. What a dilemma!

Whether I heard it in a sermon or found it in the course of

**The teenage magician.**

▲ **High school graduation (1947).**

◄ **My high school graduation picture.**

my Bible reading, Matthew 6:33 came to my rescue: "But seek ye first the kingdom of God, and His righteousness; and all these things shall be added unto you" (KJV). I couldn't have told you what "the kingdom of God" was, but the verse seemed to promise me that God would take care of everything material if I'd put His spiritual interests first. So, I decided to work at VBS and let God take care of the job. My sister told my prospective boss the news and he said, "Well, tell Warren we'll wait a week. The job's still his." More than once during these years of ministry, I've remembered that experience, and my faith has been strengthened.

Except for German class and Psychology 101, my year at Indiana University was boring. I got the impression that almost everybody in the freshman class was learning what they should have learned in high school. But I did enjoy German class because of my German ancestry and my personal delight in studying languages. I had enjoyed studying Latin for two years in high school and had even taught the class when Miss Brill was sick.

During my freshman year at Indiana University, I began to do some preaching here and there whenever an opportunity opened up. I think my very first sermon, preached as part of a church worship service, was delivered at the Hyde Park Methodist Church in Hammond, Indiana, where Ramona Mapes, now Mrs. Robert Reed, attended. It was Mona who engineered the invitation because the church service guild she belonged to was in charge of the service. That was August 4, 1946. On Sunday evening, November 30, 1947, I preached at our own church from Exodus 34:2-3. Years later, Mrs. Harold Carlson, one of the members who was there that night, sent me this excerpt from her diary:

> November 30th, Sunday. Feeling a little better today. I rested and went to church in evening. Warren Wiersbe preached; God's Spirit was felt. I know Warren is being and will be used of God mightily. I feel it.

With people like that encouraging you, how can you lose?

When classes ended in June 1948, I was uneasy about enrolling for the next year. I had been working part time at Edward Valve Company and had a full-time job promised for the summer, so finances weren't a problem. But I just couldn't see myself spending four years getting a liberal-arts education when what I really wanted to do was study the Bible and preach.

One day that summer, the Bihls had a party at their house for one of the YFC young people, and my friend John Cornwall was there. (Come to think of it, the party may have been for him.) John was older than the rest of us, had served in the army, and was a vibrant Christian we all admired. However, his witness had caused his family to turn against him, and he was now living with the Albaughs.

"I'm planning to enter Northern Baptist Seminary in Chicago this fall," he said to me over ice cream and cake. "Why don't you come along and we'll be roommates?"

At that time, Northern had a five-year program that combined college and seminary studies, and my credit hours from Indiana University could be transferred. The prospect of living with a disciplined Christian like John attracted me—I needed all the help I could get—and the school was only fifty miles from home. Thanks to the South Shore train, I could go home on weekends and even do some part-time work at Edward Valve.

After reading the seminary catalog, praying, and chatting with some friends about the decision, I sent in my application. I was accepted provided I was baptized and became a member of a local church.

I have to explain that at some point between high school graduation and my applying to Northern, I had left the Mission Covenant Church and was attending Central Baptist Church on the East Chicago side of town. The church was very evangelistic, and their many young people had backed East Chicago YFC enthusiastically. I thought things were dead at the Mission Covenant Church, but I was a young Christian, and I guess I got too critical.

Central Baptist didn't have a pastor at that time, but they arranged for me to be baptized by Rev. Dewey McFadden at the

First Baptist Church in nearby Whiting, Indiana, home of the oil refineries and a huge Lever Brothers plant. These arrangements weren't accidental, because Dewey McFadden was a close friend of D.B. Eastep who a dozen years later invited me to become his associate at Calvary Baptist Church, Covington, Kentucky, where I ministered for ten happy years. In the Christian walk, there are no accidents, only appointments.

My mother wasn't too happy about me leaving home and living in the heart of wicked Chicago, but there wasn't much she could do about it. Painful as it was, the time had come to cut the cord. She generously supplied me with some new clothes and I bought myself a suitcase, a desk lamp, and a briefcase. The dear folks at Central Baptist Church had a farewell party for me and gave me a set of *The Matthew Henry Commentary,* which I still have and use; sometimes I read the signatures on the flyleaf of the first volume and thank God for those precious people who prayed for me and helped get me started.

I think it was Pa and Doris who drove me to the campus at 3040 W. Washington where I moved into a monastic-like room on the second floor of Wilkinson Hall, the boys' dormitory. John and I each had a twin-size bed, a study table and chair, and a four-drawer bureau, and we shared a large bookcase. We put a couple of throw rugs on the floor, hung some curtains at the window, and called the place home.

Wilkinson Hall was to be my academic home for the next five years, and during those years, God would do some wonderful things for me in helping me build some important bridges.

# CHAPTER FIVE

### 1

U ntil that Labor Day weekend when I moved to the seminary campus, I had never been away from my family for any extended time, not even to spend a night with a friend, and here I was living in the geographic center of Chicago, the city of Al Capone and the mob. John Gunther's *Inside U.S.A* had been published the year before and in it he wrote, "Chicago is as full of crooks as a saw with teeth. . . ." Fortunately, my mother didn't read John Gunther's books, but she did read the newspapers and must have worried a lot about her little boy alone in the big city.

I was enrolled in the Th.B. program (that's bachelor of theology), a five-year course which was a composite of college and seminary, liberal arts and theology. Because I had transferred a year's credit from Indiana University, I should have enrolled as a sophomore. But for some reason, the registrar later decided that not all my I.U. credits were acceptable, so I ended up investing six years to earn a five-year degree. However, by the time I got to my fifth year at Northern, I was able to take a number of elective courses not usually open to undergraduate students, and this gave me a valuable exposure to serious theological study. The delay turned out to be a tremendous blessing.

One lonely evening, during my first days on campus, I began

to wonder about what lay ahead of me for the next five years and whether or not I'd make it. I reached for my new *Scofield Bible* and asked the Lord to give me a promise, not just any promise, but one that would stay with me for the rest of my life and ministry. I began reading in the Book of Psalms; and when I got to Psalm 16:11, I knew my prayer had been answered:

In Thy presence is fullness of joy, at Thy right hand there are pleasures forevermore.

Trusting the promise God gave me that evening has over many years brought me courage to face the battle, wisdom to know what to do, and confidence that God is with me accomplishing His purposes. That promise has been an anchor, a rudder, and a compass, and it's never failed.

# 2

I can't prove it and I won't debate it, but I believe that God put me in Northern Baptist Seminary at a time when the school was at its peak, both spiritually and academically. To be sure, day and night the Lake Street "el" rumbled past the school only a street away, and tons of Chicago pollution fell on the campus every day, but you got used to those inconveniences after the first week. Nobody worried about noise and dirt when we had the privilege of rubbing shoulders with people like Greek scholar Julius R. Mantey, church historian Peder Stiansen, archeologist and Old Testament scholar Arnold C. Schultz, Hebraist William M. Fouts, gifted homileticians* Faris D. Whitesell

---

*For the uninitiated, let me explain that homiletics is the science of preaching—how to study a Bible text and make a practical sermon out of it. I can still hear Dr. Perry saying, "Homiletics is the science of which preaching is the art of which the sermon is the product."

and Lloyd M. Perry, and Christian education expert (and amateur magician) W. Warren Filkin. It was a stellar faculty, and I haven't named all of them!

Dr. Charles W. Koller was our president. He was a conservative, a Texan, a loyal Baptist, an experienced pastor, a gifted preacher, and a man we all revered from a distance, not because he was remote or unfriendly, but because we didn't consider ourselves worthy to approach him in a casual manner. During my five years on the campus, I was in his office only once, and that was to hear his views concerning the campus newspaper the student council wanted me to edit. He wanted to be sure the publication didn't become a sounding board for some of the campus radicals. The short-lived newspaper turned out to be about as radical as a restaurant menu.

I thank God that Dr. Koller was at Northern during my student years because in two ways he made a lasting positive impression on my life and ministry. To begin with, he was a magnificent preacher, and whenever he spoke in chapel, it was an exciting event. In the pulpit, Charles Koller was everything all the ministerial students wanted to become. He was a master homiletician whose sermon outlines liberated the text from paper and ink and made it live in the hearts of the listeners. They say that preaching isn't taught, it's caught, and we certainly "caught" it whenever we heard our president preach.

But he was also a master teacher in the classroom. All the pastoral students were required to take his "Senior Preaching" course, which was a combination of hearing lectures on sermon preparation and ministerial life, reading hundreds of pages of homiletical literature, and preparing sermon outlines which he read and graded. In this course, Dr. Koller did much more than teach us how to study and preach. He also shared with us the kind of wisdom that comes only from mature experience and a close walk with God. When I graduated from seminary, I wanted to be able to preach like Dr. Koller. I'm still trying.

I've heard people say that it's dangerous to let your professors become your friends, and with many professors, that's probably true. But two of my professors at Northern became my close friends while I was on campus and have remained close friends since I graduated in 1953. Their friendships have not only enriched my life but they have strengthened my ministry.

On checking the Wilkinson Hall bulletin board, I discovered that my faculty adviser my first year was Dr. Lloyd M. Perry, who taught in the homiletics department. I'd heard from some of the older students that Dr. Perry was a bit acerbic and felt it his responsibility to whittle "preacher boys" down to size. He knew that some of the students believed what the people said about them in their home churches ("You're another Spurgeon! You're the best young preacher I've ever heard!") and he dedicated himself to prove the churches wrong. If the churches turned out to be right, so much the better.

Dr. Perry stood up to greet me when I walked into his office, something he didn't have to do since he was my superior. I said to myself, "I think I'm going to like this man." But the first question he asked clinched it: "Well, son, how's your devotional life?" I was able to reply, "Fine!" mainly because of what I'd learned from my roommate, John Cornwell. John was an early riser, so I became an early riser; at 5:30 each morning, we were both out of bed and at our study tables, reading the Bible and praying, a practice I've followed ever since.

During the next five years, I think I took every course Dr. Perry taught, including some courses that even the graduate students tried to avoid. Dr. Perry knew his material and he knew how to teach it. True, there were times when he was a bit caustic in his evaluations of our work, but I knew that behind those words was a loving heart that wanted us to do our best for the Lord. He didn't suffer fools gladly. The better I got to know him, the more I appreciated him and loved him.

During our first week on campus, the students were invited to attend a reception in Byrne Hall so we could formally meet the faculty and at least get started on a friendly footing. What happened after that was up to us. In that receiving line was a professor who was as new to the campus as I was, Dr. W. Warren Filkin. He had recently resigned from teaching at the Moody Bible Institute to become Professor of Christian education at Northern Baptist Seminary. I especially wanted to meet him because I knew he was an amateur magician, and I was still doing magic.

"You and I have two things in common," I said to him when we met. "My name is Warren, and so is yours, and I also do magic. I think you know my friends, the Irelands."

From that first handshake, our friendship was sealed, and we were devoted friends for forty-five years. Little did either of us realize that a quarter of a century later Dr. Filkin would join me on the pastoral staff at the Moody Church in Chicago and direct our senior adult ministries. He and I were friends from 1948, and never had a misunderstanding or a time when we didn't enjoy being together.

Let me interject a parenthesis at this point because it relates to Dr. Filkin. Early in the '50s, the General Director of the Greater Europe Mission, Noel O. Lyons, had a room in Wilkinson Hall, and he and Warren Filkin were very close friends. Noel's home was in California, but the mission office was in Chicago, which helps to explain why he occasionally stayed on our campus. It wasn't unusual for him and Dr. Filkin to knock on my door at 10 o'clock at night and invite me to go with them to Porter's, a local restaurant, and "have some fellowship." I suppose it wasn't kosher for a student to be running off at night with a professor and his friend, but nobody ever complained, and neither the food nor the hour seemed to hurt my academic career.

# Be Myself

In later years, Noel Lyons tried desperately to recruit me and my wife for missionary service in Germany, but it wasn't the Lord's plan for us. Noel was a great man who encouraged me much in my ministry, especially in focusing on the needs of a lost world. He went home to glory October 21, 1959. There has arisen a generation that knows not Noel O. Lyons, but I remember him with gratitude. His friendship was a rich treasure to us.

But back to Dr. Filkin. During my five years at Northern, I was able to take only two of the Christian education courses that he taught: "Older People and the Church" and "Using Audiovisual Aids." We had a student in the first course who was a bit strange. He came to class one day carrying a mail order cemetery monument catalog (I think he was selling tombstones on the side), and Dr. Filkin took one look at the catalog and said, "Jack, those people can't be helped by this course."

The first day of the audiovisual aids class, Dr. Filkin asked us each to give him a list of the audiovisual aids that most interested us, in order of priority. My list read:

1. Magic
2. Flannelgraph
3. Magic
4. Movies
5. Magic
6. Chalkboard
7. Magic
8. Puppets
9. Magic
10. Tape recorder

Dr. Filkin has a great sense of humor, and when he got to my list and started reading it out loud, he fell apart.

He was one of the most sought-after speakers on the faculty and often traveled long distances on weekends to preach and do his "Gospel magic." My guess is that he brought in more funds to the school, and developed more good will, than perhaps any other professor. It wasn't easy to teach from Tuesday to Friday, then drive or fly to a meeting, returning very weary on Monday. (We didn't have classes on Mondays.) Frequently in class, he'd complain because the last church service or banquet program was so long that he wasn't introduced until it was too late to say and do all that he'd planned, but he kept emphasizing that he never missed a date.

Another student and I decided to write Dr. Filkin a letter, inviting him to speak at a fictitious church, but we planned to have the letter delivered during a class session. He was sure to open the letter and read it. I got some canceled special delivery stamps from Joe Guthrie, manager of the seminary bookstore, wrote the letter, and arranged for one of the students to deliver it. Here's the letter.

---

## THE BEDLAM BAPTIST CHURCH
### MONTREAT, N.C.

Feb. 18, 1951

Dr. W. Warren Filkin
3040 W. Washington Blvd.
Chicago 12, Illinois

Dear Dr. Filkin:

Our church will be having a Sister and Brother Banquet Friday evening, March 23, at 6:00 P.M. and would very much like to have you speak and perform your magic. We understand that you never miss a date, and we appreciate this fact immensely. The last four speakers failed to show up after we sent them the program. This is the program:

6:00–7:00 — Supper
7:00–8:00 — Brief Singspiration and Testimony time
8:00–8:20 — The Deacons' Quartet will sing "Just outside
        the Door"
8:20–8:50 — Toast to Sisters by the church janitor

8:50–9:15 — Toast to Brothers by the pastor's wife
9:15–9:30 — A saw solo by the chief trustee
9:30–9:40 — Brief prayer for the speaker
9:40–9:55 — Introduction of speaker
9:55 —  Dr. W. Warren Filkin will speak and perform his amazing tricks

If this program seems a bit too long, we can arrange to have the offering taken during the introduction to your sermon. Most introductions don't say anything anyway.

You will find direct train connections to the church. In fact, we're meeting in an abandoned station just next to the tracks. Occasionally a train goes by, but that will not upset your program since we'll be watching you and not listening to you anyway.

Please let us know what your decision is. We earnestly want you to come and preach the Gospel to the heathen here in the South.

Sincerely,


(Signed) Montgomery Schmedlap
Pastor

---

Right in the middle of Dr. Filkin's lecture, there was a knock at the door and our messenger came in, apologized for the interruption, and handed Dr. Filkin the letter. It looked authentic and important and we urged him to open it right then and there and read it out loud. He did and that just about ended class for the day.

Dr. Filkin went home November 3, 1993; I miss him.

When Dr. Edgar Boss decided to seat his Old Testament survey students in alphabetical order, he didn't know what the consequences would be for one of them—me. I found myself seated next to an attractive brunette from Clinton, Wisconsin named Betty Warren. We thought it was quite a coincidence that my first name and her last name were the same and that she was Norwegian and I was Swedish. I was the only student in the class who had his full name read when Dr. Boss called the roll: "Warren—Wiersbe!" After a while, he didn't even bother to pause between the two names.

Betty worked three nights a week in the school library, and since I spent a good deal of time studying there, I saw her regularly. We both belonged to the William Carey Missionary Society and attended the Japan prayer fellowship. We also ended up as host and hostess at one of the tables in the school dining room, she at one end of the table and I at the other. It looked like something more than our names was starting to bring us together. But that first year and a half, we were only friends who enjoyed each other's company.

When I returned to campus the next fall, I found myself looking for her, and that told me I might be getting involved in something more than friendship. However, when you're getting interested in a girl, as I was, you've got to find out as much as you can about her and her family, so I had to figure out a way to visit Clinton, Wisconsin and covertly survey the situation.

There was a Youth for Christ ministry in Walworth County, which was near Clinton, so that was a possibility. Then Betty's pastor, Bert Iddins, asked me when I was available to preach at Clinton's First Baptist Church. (I think Bert suspected something, or maybe Betty's folks put him up to it.) So, we put the two invitations together, and on Saturday evening, February 11, 1950, I did "Gospel magic" and spoke at the YFC rally and the next day preached at Betty's home church.

# Be Myself

One of the local papers announced: "Theological Magician is Speaker Tonight for Walworth Co. Rally!" I'm not sure I know what a "theological magician" is — maybe a guy who pulls sermons out of hats — but that's what I was supposed to be that evening. The rally was held in the Williams Bay Tabernacle, where Torrey Johnson had preached many times, and where I was to preach often in later years when our family vacationed in Williams Bay.

I was scheduled for Sunday dinner with the Warrens and committed a monumental *faux pas* five minutes after I'd walked into their house.

"Where's the Sunday paper?" I asked. "I'd like to read the comics."

What I didn't know was that Clifford Warren didn't permit newspapers in his house on Sundays. If you wanted to read something after church, read the Sunday School paper. (Actually, he should have declared war on the *Monday* newspaper because it's printed on Sunday. The Sunday paper was printed Saturday night.)

However, Betty's seventeen-year-old brother Bob jumped at the chance to read the sports news, so we both got in the family car and drove to the drug store where I bought a *Chicago Tribune.* (We could have walked to the store because "downtown" was only two blocks away and two blocks long. The population of Clinton was probably 1,200 people.) When Bob and I walked in carrying that Sunday newspaper, I'm sure my future father-in-law was convinced that this "theological magician" — a.k.a. preacher — was a worldly upstart with no convictions at all about the sanctity of the Sabbath. Was it even safe for his daughter to know him?

Betty's mother was a small lithe woman with boundless energy and great personal concern for her guests. She was constantly jumping up and going to the kitchen to get something, or else she was passing a dish or refilling a glass. Maybe she was just nervous, wondering what klutzy thing I would do next. She sat at the edge of her chair, like an acrobat poised for action, and when she moved, it was as though she was propelled by springs. She was a superb cook and the meal was delicious. I decided that if Betty became anything like her mother as she grew older, at least I wouldn't go hungry, and she would certainly know how to entertain guests at the parsonage.

Betty had a younger sister named Dorothy who was the life of every party and the friend of everybody in need. A gifted musician, she played both the piano and organ beautifully and often sang in church services and at weddings. I suppose the best way to described Dottie is that she was a "free spirit" and her father was never able to clip her wings. In later years, whenever we told our children that Aunt Dottie was coming to visit us, they would slip into a holiday mood, because she would swoop in like a visiting movie star, keep on the go all the time she was there, finding happy things to do, and then leave in a blaze of glory. What Dottie brought with her was the combination of a revival meeting and a sideshow, and it was unforgettable.

When I returned to Chicago the following week, I wanted to tell Betty all about my visit to her hometown, and the cooks in the seminary kitchen helped me do it. At Northern, the main meal of the day was served at noon, when most of the students were on campus, but the evening meal was not as elaborate because many of the students were away at their jobs. One of the most dissatisfying supper menus concocted by our kitchen was corn bread and butter beans. Hot corn bread I like very much, but those butter beans—yuk!

That particular evening, Betty and I walked to our table in the dining room and saw the big pans of butter beans and the plates of corn bread; and I turned to her and said, "Would you like to go to Porter's for a hamburger?" She said yes and that was our first official date. I still don't like to eat butter beans, but I'm glad for the help they gave me in having my first date with the girl who is the most wonderful wife and helpmeet any pastor could want.

I know it isn't politically correct these days to say that marriages are made in heaven, but I believe that God prepared us for each other. The Lord knew how much I needed her because she provides everything that's severely lacking in my own life.

For one thing, I have no dependable sense of direction. Betty has built-in radar and is rarely confused about geography. I've been known to get lost five miles from home or even after walking out of Marshall Field's in downtown Chicago. Even today, when I drive to places alone, Betty has to draw me two maps: one to get me there and the other one to get me home. In more than forty years of ministry together, I've depended on her to plan the trips and call the signals, and she's never failed me, whether on the bumpy trails of Africa or on the wrong side of the road in Great Britain.

She's also very good at handling finances. People have asked me, "How did you ever find time to pastor churches, speak at conferences, and still write all those books?" and the answer is always the same: I have a wife who manages our household affairs wisely. From day one of our marriage, Betty has kept the books and balanced the budget. I endorse the checks and she takes it from there. Once when buying a car, I had to phone her to find out what my annual salary was because I didn't know!

I'm impetuous and want to get things done right now, but Betty is patient and helps to keep me from rushing ahead and saying or doing some dumb thing. It's strange how I can be so patient in ministry matters and yet lose my patience when a plane is delayed or we encounter a traffic jam on our way to a meeting. The familiar poster "Lord, make me patient—and do it now!" was designed just for me.

Whether it's from her years of living on the farm, or just her native talent, my wife is a good "jack-of-all-trades" and understands things mechanical much better than I do. The extent of my mechanical ability involves sharpening a pencil, putting a refill in my pen, and operating a computer, the latter with much fear and trembling. When the experts come to our house to make service calls, they're amazed at how much she knows about their equipment.

Best of all, she's a godly person, disciplined in her devotional life and walking with the Lord. When we started dating, we took time to pray together, and we're still dating and still praying! Our ministry has been a team effort and I couldn't have wanted a more understanding and dependable partner.

Betty and I became officially engaged on April 25, 1952, just before she graduated from Northern. (She was in the four-year Bachelor of Religious Education course. I should have graduated with her—well, I've already explained that.) I was the emcee at the annual seminary spring banquet that year, and when I announced our engagement to the guests, the applause and cheers were so enthusiastic you would have thought the Chicago Cubs had won the World Series. "We've gone together so long," I told the crowd, "that I've got to marry her for *my* money!"

Eugenia Price was the speaker that evening and I had the privilege of introducing her. She'd been a believer only a short time and was helping produce the new "Unshackled" radio program from the Pacific Garden Mission. I got the impression that she was "unaccustomed to public speaking" because she rambled quite a bit, but maybe it was just my euphoria at being engaged to the most wonderful girl in the world.

The music that evening was provided by the King's Karollers, the well-known ladies' trio that sang over the "Songs in the Night" radio program from the Village Church of suburban Western Springs, Illinois. Twenty years later, I would be working together with them as we produced "Songs in the Night" from the Moody Church. It's strange how people can touch your life tangentially and then one day become an important part of your ministry. In God's providence, no person we meet is unimportant and no contact is casual. At least, that's the way I interpret Romans 8:28 and Ephesians 2:10, and that's the way it's worked out in our lives.

Betty's commencement took place in Chicago's Orchestra Hall the day after my twenty-third birthday, and it was the largest class in the thirty-nine year history of the school, ninety-four students. The faculty awarded me the annual Heagle Scholarship, which helped to pay my tuition during my senior year. When Dr. Koller made the presentation, he said that the award was based on "scholarship, Christian character, ability, loyalty, truth, faithfulness *[Mr. Heagle must have been a Scoutmaster!]*, real piety, initiative, and sound judgment."

Uh-huh.

He should have said it was given to me *in spite* of the crazy notices I put on the bulletin board, the terrible jokes I used when emceeing banquets, the snide remarks about the food in the dining room, and the "Texas jokes" I told whenever I had an audience. ("I met a midget the other day. Well, he wasn't really a midget. He was a Texan with the wind taken out of him.") If Dr. Koller had heard about my Texas stories, I might not have received the Heagle Scholarship. To him, Texas was the doorstep to heaven.

Betty returned home to Clinton, Wisconsin and for the next year worked as bookkeeper in the local co-op. I returned to Hammond, Indiana, where my family was now living, and took up the work at Central Baptist Church where I was now serving as pastor. How that happened is the subject of the next chapter.

Occasionally someone will ask me, "Did you really get anything out of seminary?"

Did I!

To begin with, I was given tools for ministry that have served me well for over forty years. Mrs. Maude Groom and Dr. Douglas Stevens taught me the basics of Greek and Hebrew, and Dr. William Fouts (the man who made me stay in school an extra year) added to what they taught me. I'm not an expert in the biblical languages, but at least I can use the resources and not have to be the slave of the commentators. Dr. Donald Burdick, who later served long and well at Conservative Baptist Seminary in Denver, showed me how to study the New Testament and understand why each book was there. Besides being my friend and fellow magician, Dr. Filkin taught me how to know the difference between *principles* and *methods* in building an effective ministry in the local church, and how to use principles based on Bible truth. (He also taught me never to miss an engagement.) I've already mentioned the impact Dr. Charles W. Koller and Dr. Lloyd M. Perry had on my life and my approach to preaching. I gladly confess that I owe my "homiletical soul" to those two men.

I also found a wonderful wife at seminary, as many preachers have done, and during those years, Betty and I met some super people whose friendship has enriched our lives and ministry, people like Joe and Dorothy Guthrie, who managed the seminary bookstore. Betty and I had our engagement party in their apartment, and when the Guthries and Wiersbes were serving in neighboring pastorates in the Chicago area, we often got together and talked shop. I'm like the man who wrote Hebrews 11: time won't permit me to name all the friends whose lives impacted ours and encouraged us along the way.

My five years at seminary gave me time and opportunity to mature somewhat in the Christian life. Remember, I'd been a Christian only three years when I went off to train for ministry. Pastor Bill Taylor had taught me the books of the Bible, but I'd never read straight through the Bible and I didn't know how to interpret it. I'd attended church all my life but I'd never been exposed to a consistent teaching ministry of God's Word. Those five years in seminary were to this preacher what "boot camp" is to a soldier: they got me ready for the battles that still lay ahead.

Finally, those years at Northern helped me to build another bridge, this time into the challenging world of ministry. I met people who for years to come would be an important part of my life and work. I discovered how vast is the outreach of the church of Jesus Christ in this world. I got my hands on some tools for studying the Bible, an ancient book, and making it meaningful to people today.

It really wasn't important anymore that I wasn't an athlete or that I couldn't make things or fix things. What was important was the glorious fact that God had saved me, called me, and equipped me to serve Him. With Betty at my side, that's all I really wanted to do for the rest of my life.

# PART TWO
# Central Baptist Church

# CHAPTER SIX

$$\boxed{1}$$

I'm not proud of the way I left the church my great-grand-father helped to found and the denomination to which so many of my godly relatives belonged. I could have been more loving about my exodus, but I was a young Christian and the fervor of Youth for Christ made my home church seem dull. I was convinced that the Swedes weren't really burdened for us young people, so in March or April of 1948, I left the Indiana Harbor Mission Covenant Church and started attending Central Baptist Church on the East Chicago side of town.

A couple of years later, I visited the pastor of the Covenant church and apologized for what I had said and done. He was very kind about it and told me that, if I was going to be a pastor, I'd have to learn to take bruises like the ones I'd given him. He was right. Over these many years, I've had my share of bruises from parishioners who get their spiritual kicks from steady injections of TV religion, then criticize the pastor and leave the church for something more exciting.

In 1948, "East Chicago Youth for Christ" was officially chartered by Youth for Christ International, and I was appointed director. Johnny Hope, director of Elkhart, Indiana, YFC came to our rally to publicly present the charter. (In his pre-conversion days, Johnny had played the guitar for the Andrews Sisters

and was one of our brightest lights in YFC.) I didn't know the
first thing about directing a YFC rally, but somebody had to do
it, and the Albaughs and Bihls were a big help in planning
rallies and sending out promotion. Two years later, when the
local Calumet Region rallies merged into "Lake County YFC"
and Dave Breese took over, I lost my job as director and was
eventually elected to the local YFC board.

There were YFC programs in several of the northern Indiana
cities at that time—East Chicago, Hammond, Gary, Whiting—
and once a month we'd sponsor a "singspiration" and get
together in one of the churches after the Sunday evening service. This was a good way to get the members of local churches
to know each other and to work together in reaching teenagers. A "singspiration" was more of a religious pep rally than a
worship service and not every pastor approved of what we did.

It was through these "singspirations" that I had gotten acquainted with the believers at Central Baptist Church, and I
liked what I saw. The congregation was comprised mostly of
people from the south who had moved to the Calumet Region
to work in the oil refineries and steel mills. It wasn't an official
Southern Baptist Church, but the congregation used *The
Broadman Hymnal,* the young people attended B.T.U (Baptist
Training Union), and the ladies served baking-powder biscuits
and corn bread at church suppers. The choir used the *Waves of
Devotion* songbook and sang songs I'd never heard before, like
"He Will Set Your Fields on Fire" and "Waves of Devotion."

My new church family was different and was going to make a
difference in my life.

When I started attending East Chicago Central, Claude Williams
was the pastor, but he had resigned to enter full-time local

church evangelism, so I heard him preach only three Sundays. In the year that followed, we heard a number of guest speakers, mostly from the Moody Bible Institute, and a few pastoral candidates. Finally the church called Robert Johnson, an experienced, energetic, soul-winning pastor who came in March 1949 and revolutionized the church. The Sunday School grew, people were saved, and the church constructed an educational building to house the expanding ministry. The Johnsons ministered at Central only eighteen months, but what they did in that short time gave new impetus to the congregation.

Since I was already on location and preparing for the ministry, on October 11, 1950, the congregation asked me to serve as "interim pastor," a title I ended up holding for nearly two years. (I told a friend of mine at seminary that an interim pastor was a man who candidates at the same church every Sunday but never gets a call.) This was a big decision for me to make and everything seemed to encourage me to say no. I didn't own a car, I was a full-time seminary student, I was only twenty-one years old, and I'd been a Christian only seven and a half years. There were dedicated people in the church who'd been walking with the Lord longer than I'd been alive! Furthermore, what did I know about shepherding a flock?

I prayed for God to guide me, and He did. During the course of my systematic reading of the Bible in my daily devotions, I was struck with Psalm 75:2, "When I shall receive the congregation I will judge uprightly" (KJV). The Lord seemed to be assuring me to accept the call and trust Him to give me what I needed.

If I'd been using the *American Standard Version,* I would have read, "When I shall find the set time, I will judge uprightly," which is apparently an accurate translation. We didn't have the NIV in those days, and the RSV Old Testament wasn't published until 1952. However, the Lord used that verse to direct me to say yes to the church, and I believe my decision was in the will of God.

In the course of these memoirs, you'll find that often the Lord gave me and my wife guidance through our daily systematic reading of the Bible. I'm not talking about "religious roulette" where you open the Bible at random and point to a verse. I'm talking about the daily reading of Scripture in a systematic way, with hearts open for the Spirit of God to teach us. Throughout our marriage, each of us has had a private time with the Lord each morning, and from day one, we've prayed together after breakfast each morning and before retiring at night.

On January 12, 1951 the church ordained me, mainly because the leaders felt that only an ordained minister should serve the Lord's Supper and baptize. The examination was on January 5 and was presided over by Dr. Donald J. MacKay, pastor of Central Baptist Church in Gary. I prepared for the interrogation by studying Henry C. Thiessen's *Systematic Theology* and praying that my Baptist inquisitors would get so involved discussing the fine points of theology among themselves that they'd forget I was even there. They didn't.

On a scale of one to ten, my answers may have rated a seven. When asked to define "the invisible church," I replied, "That's what meets on Wednesday nights." The scowls I beheld taught me that some preachers don't have a sense of humor. I didn't do so well when the moderator asked what I thought about fundamental churches joining with liberal churches in evangelistic meetings. (Billy Graham's "cooperative evangelism" was a hot issue in those days.) "If God could use an unclean raven to feed Elijah," I said, "maybe He could even use a liberal." The moderator's only response was to advise me to study up on the biblical doctrine of separation.

Dr. MacKay later left the GARBC and became a part of the Conservative Baptist movement. Over the years, I admired him and his ministry very much, and we were good friends. Whenever my conference ministry brought me close to where he was living, he'd usually attend at least one meeting and always leave me with a warm word of encouragement. He never asked me if I'd studied up on biblical separation.

I was still living at home with my family, so the church didn't have to worry about supplying a parsonage. Since I'd be away at school only four days a week, I could still do my pastoral work from Friday evening to Monday evening. The South Shore

## Chapter Six

Line electric train ran from Chicago's Randolph Street station to downtown East Chicago, just a block away from the church, so I had no transportation problems and could even come in to lead the midweek service.

So, for the next two and a half years, my life fell into a pattern. On Wednesdays, I'd leave school about 4 o'clock in the afternoon, take the Lake Street "el" to the Loop, then grab the next train to East Chicago. I'd eat supper in the East Chicago Restaurant, then go to the church and get ready for the mid-week service. If we ended on time, and we usually did, I'd catch the 9 o'clock train back to Chicago and take the "el" or the bus back to school. On weekends, I'd take an earlier train home on Fridays and, carrying a suitcase full of dirty clothes, walk over to the Edward Valve parking lot where I'd meet Tat and Doris and go home in Tat's car. On Monday evenings, I'd pack clean clothes and eat supper, and then either Pa or Tat would drive me to downtown East Chicago where I'd get the train back to Chicago.

I did a lot of reading and studying while traveling to and from school, maybe as much as I would have done if I'd stayed in Chicago. One evening, I was studying my Hebrew vocabulary cards on the train, getting ready for an exam, and the lady sitting next to me asked me if I was studying Chinese. If there was an emergency in the congregation while I was at school, somebody would call Ma and she'd get word to me. More than once I had to cut classes and go to East Chicago to conduct a funeral or help a family with a crisis, but for the most part, I learned to live with that hectic schedule and things went fairly well.

As I look back, I realize that I'd bitten off a big chunk of responsibility, something nobody in his right mind would have done. But I was young and didn't know any better and I seemed to have inexhaustible stores of energy, some of which I wish I had now. My experience in YFC had convinced me that nothing was impossible with God, and after all, hadn't my Swedish ancestors prayed for me long before I'd arrived on the scene? With that kind of support, I was invincible!

The church paid me $37.50 a week. I think they could have

offered to pay either my travel expenses or some of my school dormitory expenses, but nobody suggested it and I wasn't about to bring it up. After all, they weren't having to worry about either parsonage expenses or car expenses for a resident pastor, and this was saving them money. On the other hand, they had called an inexperienced part-time minister whose preaching wasn't that sensational and who still had a lot to learn. Some of the members probably thought I was being over-paid, and they may have been right.

# 3

Central Baptist Church had been founded in August 1930 by a small group of believers who felt the need for an evangelical Baptist church on the East Chicago side of town. I'm sure they were also interested in maintaining some of their "southern traditions" as aliens in Yankee territory. After meeting in various rented facilities, in 1934 they built a thirty-by-sixty corrugated sheet metal tabernacle ("our little tin church") on a leased lot that they eventually purchased. The tabernacle was dedicated November 11, 1934. Twenty-two years later to the day, we dedicated a lovely new sanctuary on the same location.

The church had been unaffiliated until Pastor Johnson's arrival, and he encouraged them to fellowship with the GARBC, "The General Association of Regular Baptist Churches." This was a growing fellowship of churches that in 1932 had withdrawn from the Northern Baptist Convention (now the American Baptist Convention) because of what they considered growing liberalism in that denomination. Their leader was Dr. Robert T. Ketcham, a gifted, self-taught preacher who had pastored Central Baptist Church in nearby Gary, Indiana. There were perhaps a dozen GARB churches in the Calumet Region, and many more in the state of Indiana, and it seemed wise for

East Chicago Central to be a part of a fellowship bigger than itself.

But when the church called me to be their interim pastor, nobody stopped to consider that I was attending an American Baptist seminary while pastoring a GARB church! The American Baptists were supposed to be the "bad guys." Being a relatively young believer, this was my first exposure to religious politics, and I was mystified.

For one thing, First Baptist Church in nearby Hammond was at that time an American Baptist Church, and its pastor Owen Miller was a godly, soul-winning preacher who was seeing the work prosper in every way. Owen was a great encouragement to me in those days, and I appreciated him. He even invited me to become one of his assistants and pastor the young people. My American Baptist friends at seminary were all saved people who sought to serve the Lord for His glory, and not a one of them — seminary administration included — ever treated me as a second-class Christian because I wasn't pastoring an American Baptist church. In fact, they even awarded me a scholarship!

Without realizing it, I had built another bridge, an important bridge that for the rest of my life would influence my ministry and make for me both friends and enemies. *I had decided to be a Christian first, a pastor second, and a Baptist third.* I wasn't going to make denominational affiliation a test of spirituality or fellowship. My ecclesiastical home has been with the Baptists, and I've tried to live apart from anything that dishonors the Lord, but I don't think there's a drop of denominational blood in my veins. In more than four decades of ministry, I've preached in Christian churches of many denominations and no denomination; I've discovered that Bob Cook was right when he said, "I've learned that God blesses people I disagree with."

Just think of it: I attended an American Baptist seminary, was ordained by a Regular Baptist church and for ten years pastored a Southern Baptist church, and have lived to write about it! Of course, to some people this smacked of compromise, and they attacked me as a "liberal" or a "neo-evangelical."

I must add that when I was ordained to the ministry, the *Baptist Bulletin,* official magazine of the GARBC, not only included an announcement of my ordination in their news section for March 1951, but they even printed my picture *and said I was a student at Northern Baptist Seminary!* How's that for a true Christian ecumenical spirit?

I'm not going to try to impress you and say that those two and a half years were easy because they weren't. As a pastor, every week I had to prepare two Sunday sermons, a Sunday School lesson (I taught the young people) and a midweek Bible study, plus do all the other things a pastor is expected to do, like visit the sick and needy, win the lost, counsel the confused, attend board meetings, and oversee the general ministry of the church, none of which I really knew how to do well. As a seminary student, I had to read thousands of pages of text, write term papers, take examinations (and I was taking both Greek and Hebrew), and participate as much as possible in campus activities. I spent many hours a week on public transportation, and occasionally did have to sleep, eat, spend time with my girlfriend, and be a visible part of the Wiersbe family.

When I look at the sermon outlines I prepared in those years I was groping my way along in the pastorate, I hang my head in shame and wonder why God ever let me open my mouth. I confess that there was many a Saturday evening, after a hectic week at school, when I didn't know what I was going to say the next morning. The last thing I did each Saturday was to mimeograph the church bulletin in my little "office" at home, and many a generic sermon title was put on page 2 because the preacher didn't quite know what his text would be or what he would do with it!

I had neither a driver's license nor a car, so I depended on shoe leather and public transportation for doing my visiting.

We had members not only in East Chicago, near the church, but also in Hammond and on the Indiana Harbor side of town, and I got to know the bus schedules pretty well. Fortunately for me, we had only two hospitals, St. Catherine's near my boyhood home in the Harbor, and St. Margaret's in Hammond. Occasionally a patient was sent to a Chicago hospital, but that just made it easier for me to visit them.

Because I'm more a right-brain person than left-brain, I don't enjoy board meetings or committee meetings where you discuss the details of the heating system or the plans for the church picnic. (I don't like picnics anyway!) I'd rather shovel snow than spend an hour debating over who will tell the janitor to paint the back door. Some people revel in committee meetings, but I'm not one of them. I was encouraged to discover that one of my homiletical heroes, G. Campbell Morgan, felt the same way. He once said in a sermon that he'd "prefer to preach three sermons a day rather than spend half an hour at a deacon's meeting discussing who ought to keep the keys to the doors."*

As a young man and a young Christian, I was intimidated by the older Christians in the church, so the monthly deacon's meetings always frightened me. What if they wanted a report on how many pastoral visits I made? What if a member in the hospital had been overlooked or a shut-in at home neglected? Did they think they were getting their money's worth out of my ministry? Would they ask me about my future plans for the church? At deacon's meetings, I didn't feel like the shepherd of a flock; I felt like a criminal on a witness stand.

Not that the deacons were critical or unkind, but they didn't always understand or appreciate the demands being made on their pastor. They were a diverse group of honest, serious blue-collar workers who wanted to be sure other people worked as hard as they did in earning their daily bread. They were good men who served the church faithfully, but I didn't feel as close to them or as comfortable with them as I would in later years.

---

*See Jill Morgan, *Campbell Morgan: A Man of the Word* (Grand Rapids: Baker Book House, 1972), 198.

# Be Myself

After Betty and I were married and I was on the field full time, one of the professors at Northern asked me to teach his Old Testament survey class for four days while he ministered elsewhere. Since there were plenty of graduate students on campus he could have turned to, I thought it was quite an honor to be asked, and I told him I'd do it. All it involved was driving to Northern four mornings, teaching for an hour, and then driving home. And, after all, the morning hours belonged to me as my usual time for sermon preparation. I'd just have to give up a couple of days off plus some evenings and work ahead in preparing my messages. Betty would probably suffer more than I would.

In retrospect, I suppose I should have consulted with the deacons and asked for their approval, but I didn't. After all, I wasn't in the habit of asking their permission to speak and do magic at banquets or YFC functions, and maybe I was fearful they'd say no and start controlling my calendar.

We had a deacon's meeting scheduled for the Wednesday evening of the week I was teaching at Northern. The only thing on the agenda was the peculiar behavior of one of the young men in the church who frequently left the service and went to the church basement. After we'd decided who would follow him the next time he did it, the men brought up my extracurricular activity of the week. They didn't say, "Pastor, we're proud of you for being asked to teach at your alma mater. We had no idea you were so respected by your professors! Feel free to do it any time they call." They didn't ask for an explanation or even for a defense. All they said was, "If you have any spare time, we suggest you spend it here, serving the church."

I was devastated and felt like resigning the next Sunday. If some of the members of the church had known what the deacons had said, the fire would have hit the grease, but I kept my mouth shut, prayed a lot, and eventually got over it. I was surprised to learn that my hero Campbell Morgan had gone through a similar experience with a board of deacons at his first church.

"The Deacons," they wrote Morgan, "having received several strong complaints concerning the Pastor's repeated absence, and one of these having taken a formal shape, they are constrained to desire Mr. Morgan not to accept any further invitations to leave his pastoral duties *without their consent,* as they are fully convinced such repeated absences are weakening and dividing the church."*

In later years, when the famous Dr. G. Campbell Morgan was minister at Westminster Chapel, London, a visitor remarked about Morgan's absences from the pulpit, and one of the members replied, "Oh, we'd rather have Dr. Morgan *part* of the time than anybody else *all* of the time!" So there, deacons!

Churches have to learn that the pastor is a gift *to the whole church* and not just to one local congregation. Dr. D.B. Eastep, my godly predecessor at Calvary Baptist Church, Covington, Kentucky, was in great demand as a Bible conference speaker, and occasionally a member would complain because he was away. Dr. Eastep would smile and say, "Well, there's a simple solution to the problem: call a pastor nobody else wants to listen to!" And when I accepted the call to the Moody Church in Chicago, the chairman of the elders said to me, "We expect the pastor of Moody Church to minister in other places." But it wasn't that way at Central Baptist Church in East Chicago, Indiana.

The church constitution called for monthly business meetings at which all reports were read to the assembled saints, pondered, discussed, and approved, including the treasurer's report. I didn't mind listening to Sunday School statistics or a summary of how far the Ladies Missionary Society had progressed in making their latest quilt, but the financial report

---

*Morgan, 69.

aggravated me. We were told the *totals* on the income side of the ledger, but *every single item of expenditure* was read from the debit side!

To the church, this procedure was both biblical and reasonable. Every member had a right to know how their tithes and offerings had been dispersed the previous month, including how much was spent on postage, mimeograph paper and stencils, heat and light, the repairing of the hole in the wall in the men's restroom (we found out why the fellow was going downstairs), and even the pastor's salary. Nobody else in the church got up and announced to the world how much money they made, but my salary was read four times at each meeting and sometimes five: "Pastor's salary, thirty-seven dollars and fifty cents." (After Betty and I were married, they generously increased it to "Pastor's salary, sixty-seven dollars and fifty cents.") It embarrassed me, especially if visitors were present, but there wasn't a thing I could do about it.

Like every young pastor, I needed mentors and counselors, and the Lord was good to supply me with some godly men with tender hearts and strong shoulders: Ken McQuere, who with his wife Thelma served the First Baptist Church of Hobart, Indiana; Sam McDill, pastor of Christian Fellowship Church in Hammond; Al Colwell, State Representative for the GARBC in Indiana; and Dewey McFadden, who had baptized me at First Baptist Church, Whiting, Indiana.

I recall phoning Dewey McFadden and sharing a church "authority conflict" problem with him. ("Authority conflict" is a polite way of saying that the pastor wanted it done one way and somebody else in the church had a brother-in-law who could do it cheaper.) In his quiet way, Dewey said, "Well, Warren, somebody in the church has to be the leader, and if it isn't the pastor, it'll be somebody else. If it's somebody else, the church may get the idea they don't need the pastor."

One day I asked Dewey if he knew anybody who would be willing to come to our "little tin church" and conduct a Bible conference. "Sure," he said, "my old roommate at Southern Baptist Seminary, D.B. Eastep. He's pastor of Calvary Baptist Church in Covington, Kentucky. He's a busy man, so you may have to schedule him a couple of years in advance."

I wrote to Dr. Eastep, explained our circumstances, and asked if he could fit us into his future schedule. I'm sure it was Dewey McFadden's name that did the trick—for all I know, Dewey may have phoned him—but Dr. Eastep agreed to come for a Sunday-through-Tuesday conference in September 1954. He stayed with me and Betty in our apartment/parsonage and brought the benediction of the Lord to our humble home. He was gentle but powerful in his preaching, and what he taught our people made a difference in the church, especially his message "The Scriptural Responsibilities of a Church to Its Pastor." The deacons even voted to start paying me a car allowance!

Betty and I didn't know that during that conference, we were being scrutinized and measured for another place and that seven years later we'd be moving to Covington to assist Dr. Eastep.

I feel sorry for young preachers today who don't have an older pastor to talk to and pray with as they face conflicts and demands in ministry. The tendency today is for a young pastor to find a "guru" and become his disciple, reading his books, listening to his tapes, attending his seminars, imitating his methods, and trying to copy his ministry. It won't work. God doesn't want me to *duplicate* myself; He wants me to *reproduce* myself. In all the years of my ministry, I've never been any man's disciple, and I've never asked anybody to be my disciple. I learned a lot from my pastor friends, and they were wise enough to let me be myself as I worked out my own ministry.

According to a Sunday bulletin in my file, dated September 28, 1952, the church called me to be their *official* pastor on October 8 at their regular monthly business meeting. The transition from "interim" to "official" went unnoticed and I kept on doing all the things I had been doing. But perhaps it made a difference for the future. The Lord willing, I would be graduating from seminary in May and would get married in June, so maybe it was better to be "pastor" instead of "interim pastor." The dictionary defines "interim" as "a temporary or provisional arrangement," and that wouldn't be the greatest foundation either for ministry or marriage. Both of my "engagements" would terminate at about the same time.

# CHAPTER SEVEN

On May 19, 1953, after six long years that should have been only five, I finally graduated from seminary. A month later, on June 20, Betty and I were married at First Baptist Church, Clinton, Wisconsin. It was a hot day in Wisconsin, over 100 degrees, and in those days, very few buildings were air conditioned ("refrigerated" they called it then). When I woke up on the morning of the wedding, I was drenched with perspiration. I was sure I'd caught some mysterious disease and that the wedding would have to be postponed. But it was only the heat, and soap and water took care of my malady.

Ed was my best man, and during the ceremony, the perspiration dripped off the end of his nose like drops of water from a leaky faucet. His daughter Corinne, who was nearly five, was very upset about the wedding and kept saying, "But I don't want a new mommy!" It was finally explained to her that she wasn't getting "a new mommy," she was getting a new aunt, and that calmed her down.

My Uncle Henning, who traveled a lot and knew all about hotels, had suggested that we spend Saturday night at a quiet residential hotel in Milwaukee, so we got reservations. The hotel was residential but it wasn't very quiet. A poker game and beer party were in progress next door, and all we heard all night was loud talking, the snapping of cards on the table, and the flushing of the toilet. Considering my ability with a deck of cards, I could have joined them and might have made enough money to pay for another week of honeymoon. But then the deacons would have heard about it and I'd have been in trouble again. That was no way for a preacher to start married life.

Things didn't improve the next morning, because we couldn't find any restaurants open for breakfast. I got the impression that the whole city of Milwaukee had gone into hibernation except for the poker players. We finally found a drug store where a nice lady served us orange juice, English muffins, and coffee, and then we went off to attend the morning worship service at the Garfield Avenue Baptist Church, which was pastored by Bill Kuhnle, one of the leading GARBC preachers. It was Father's Day and he preached on the theme "A Pop Who's Tops." (Memory is a funny thing. I can't tell you where the church was located but I remember the sermon title.)

We honeymooned in Door County, Wisconsin, along with millions of mosquitoes who managed to show up every time the moon rose and we were feeling romantic. Instead of strolling hand-in-hand along the beach, we sat side-by-side in the front seat of the car and kept the windows closed. The mosquitoes perched expectantly on the windows, staring at us and daring us to open a door or window even a crack. I didn't own a car during our dating years, so this may have been the Lord's way of showing us that we hadn't missed a whole lot.

Door Country was a special place to me and Betty because each of our families had often vacationed there, and the county was populated by Swedes and Norwegians, probably two Scandinavians for every mosquito. During the week, we did our own cooking in our cottage on Sturgeon Bay; but one evening we decided to splurge and have dinner at Samuelson's, a local restaurant especially famous for Scandinavian cuisine and mile-high pies.

"Don't drink so much coffee," Betty warned me several times during the meal. "It'll keep you awake."

"It won't bother me," I assured her. "We Swedes aren't affected by caffeine. Why, I had coffee in my formula when I was a baby! Just watch; I'll sleep like a log."

That was the first of innumerable times in our marriage when my wife was right and I was wrong. I don't know anything about feminine intuition, but over the years, I've learned to respect Betty's warnings, and sometimes I heed them. When I don't listen and things get bungled up, she's very kind about it and patiently waits for the proper time to smile and say, "I told you so." In recognition of her uncanny ability to anticipate my self-inflicted calamities, one Christmas I gave her some note pads carrying the following statement: "All men are created equal—all women are created superior."

## 2

The church rented a five-room upstairs apartment for us at 4852 Indianapolis Boulevard, just a few short blocks from the church and next door to a Dairy Queen and a filling station. The filling station was a convenience, the Dairy Queen a temptation. At the close of each season, the manager would unload his surplus toppings on us, and we'd spend the winter gaining weight. We lived at that location until February 1958, when we moved to Wheaton, Illinois.

Indianapolis Boulevard was—and is today—a very busy street since it's one of the few main thoroughfares to south Lake County, Indiana. Traffic is usually heavy and people are always in a hurry. On more than one occasion, we'd hear the screech of brakes and the sound of fenders and bumpers getting acquainted, and we'd routinely reach for the phone and call the police. Then we'd stand at the dining room windows and watch the excitement.

Until our son David joined the family July 6, 1955, I was able to use the back bedroom for my study, but when we turned it

**Seminary graduation photo (1953).**

**Our wedding, June 20, 1953. Back row left to right: Bob Warren, Ed Wiersbe, Warren, Joe Guthrie. Front row left to right: Dorothy Svedin, Betty, Dorothy Warren, Doris Wiersbe.**

into a nursery, I moved my books to the dining room. When we finished our new church building in 1956, I at last had a study of my own, and Betty repossessed her dining room. I've always appreciated her gracious attitude concerning my books as over these forty plus years she's watched my library grow from a few hundred volumes to more than 10,000. When Baker Book House published my book *Giant Steps* in 1981, the dedication read:

> To my wife
> Betty
> who has lovingly accepted me as I am (a
> bookworm), has never complained as
> the library grew, and who has been my
> greatest encouragement in my ministry
> of preaching and writing.

Benjamin Franklin had "Poor Richard" say that there were "three faithful friends: an old wife, an old dog, and ready money." I had a young wife, no dog, and not a great deal of ready money, but that autumn, God gave us two faithful friends in Bruce and Verla Love. They'd been married in August, were our age, and had come to direct the ministry of Lake County Youth for Christ. Even though they lived in Gary and we in East Chicago, that didn't prevent us from seeing each other often and doing things together.

During my last two years in seminary, I'd lost close contact with the local YFC ministry (I was usually preparing sermons on Saturday evenings), but Bruce made sure I started getting involved again. He frequently asked me to speak or do magic at one of the many high school YFC clubs, a few of which had several hundred students attending. God was blessing the Saturday night rallies and the club program, and young people were coming to Christ week by week.

The YFC "Bible Quiz" program was in full swing then, keeping the young people busy studying and memorizing Scripture and bringing to the Saturday night rallies the excitement of a basketball tournament. I was often one of the "judges" for the competition, helping to determine who jumped up first and sometimes deciding whether the answers were correct. Eventually, I ended up on the Lake County YFC board, serving along with a dozen or so pastors and businessmen who had a burden to reach the teenagers in Lake County with the Gospel.

But as time went on, I was to discover that my local YFC ministry involved much more than just our friendship with Bruce and Verla. God had surprising things in store for me and Betty.

Central Baptist Church was growing. Every young couple I'd marry meant that within a year or two we'd have another baby in the church family. Our people were a praying people and a friendly people, and more than one stranger who came to visit returned to worship. The visitation program discovered people in the neighborhood who needed Christ, and some of them did become Christians and join our church family.

But we desperately needed a new church building. As much as the people loved their "little tin church," they knew that one day it would have to be replaced. However, whenever I'd mention the subject of building, somebody was bound to say, "Well, we'd better wait. There's going to be a strike and people won't have any money to give."

In the Calumet Region back in those days, one union or

another was always threatening to strike, usually the steelworkers or the refinery workers. That was the era of strong unions and sometimes bitter enmity between labor and management. Newspaper columnist Westbrook Pegler could get away with writing in 1943, "When I get to thinking about this dangerous union thing, this empire of the irresponsible which President Roosevelt has set up in this country, I find that I am more afraid of that than of Hitler." Most of the men in our congregation belonged to a union, some of them were officers in their unions, and all of them knew what would happen to the area's economy if there happened to be a long strike.

The church did have a Building Fund and every fourth Sunday of the month was "Building Fund Sunday" in Sunday School, an opportunity to bring an extra gift toward future expansion. The new educational building Bob Johnson had prayed up was paid for and, during a building program, could provide crowded but adequate facilities for church and Sunday School. The real problem wasn't space or strikes; it was unbelief. We just didn't believe that God was able to help us do what we knew needed to be done.

I think it was the chairman of our trustees, Joe Moore, who first suggested that we forget about strikes and start doing something positive toward building a new sanctuary. Joe Moore had been saved just a few years before at an Easter Sunday service, the first time he'd ever attended the church. Until that Sunday, he would bring his wife and family to church and sit in his car reading the Sunday paper, but the Lord got hold of him that Easter Sunday; he came into the church building, listened to the Word, and trusted the Lord.

As you now imagine me contemplating a building program, you must remember that I almost failed wood shop in high school, I can't read a blueprint, and even today I couldn't construct a bird house or a model airplane from a kit, no matter how simple the instructions might be. If we moved into a building program, the church would save money by being its own contractor, but that would mean extra work for me in doing things I was totally incapable of doing.

In June 1954, the church officially set up a Building Committee and authorized it to get plans drawn for a new church edifice. I was both excited and frightened. Maybe it was time for me to resign and go to another church and make room for a more experienced pastor who could oversee the building program with skill. But once again the Lord gave me a promise to carry me through. In the course of my regular daily Bible reading, I came to 1 Chronicles 28:20, David's words to Solomon concerning the building of the temple:

And David said to Solomon, his son, "Be strong and of good courage, and do it: fear not, nor be dismayed; for the Lord God, even my God, will be with thee; He will not fail thee, nor forsake thee, until thou hast finished all the work for the service of the house of the Lord."

In the months that followed, I don't know how many times I reminded the Lord of that promise. I quoted it frequently in my morning devotions; occasionally I silently brought it to His attention at Building Committee meetings when all of us were running out of patience; and more than once I rested on it when I woke up at night with a tightness in my stomach. I almost worried myself into an ulcer.

During those months of planning and construction, I learned a great deal about reading blueprints, studying specifications, and working with contractors, but the greatest thing I learned was that God keeps His promises and answers prayer.

## 5

The first thing we had to do was find somebody qualified to design the building, draw the plans, and get them approved by the city and state officials. At this point, Bruce Love came to the rescue. He knew a man in Gary who had worked with a number of area churches on construction projects and could do everything we needed for a reasonable fee. Frank Schutt turned out to be a quiet man who listened a lot, spoke softly, and did his work well. As we met with him from month to month, little by little the design of the new sanctuary took shape and the church began to get excited.

At one of those committee meetings, I learned a good lesson about both architecture and theology, something they'd not taught us in seminary.

"Why do we need such an expensive high ceiling in the auditorium?" I asked Mr. Schutt. "We're not building a cathedral. Why not just build an auditorium with a flat roof and then put a church facade in the front of the building?"

In his quiet way, Mr. Schutt replied, "Pastor, the building you construct reflects what a church is and what a church does. You don't use facades on churches to fool people. That's for carnival sideshows. *The outside and the inside must agree.*"

There must be integrity in church architecture as well as in church ministry. It was a valuable lesson and I'm glad I learned it early, because in later years I'd go through another church building program as well as two remodeling programs.

The congregation approved the plans in January 1955. Now we had to secure financing. This was a whole new world for me because I grew up in a home where my parents paid cash for everything, including the family car. (After Pa's retirement, they tried to get credit cards and were turned down because they had no credit rating! Boy, did my father and mother vent their German and Swedish wrath on the economic system!) When Betty and I set up housekeeping, my savings bought the car and her savings the basic furniture we needed, but we bought the furniture "on time" so we'd establish a good credit rating. But when it came to dealing with banks about thousands of dollars for building construction, I was completely out of my element.

I saw an ad in a Christian magazine offering the services of an investment firm that would evaluate a church's financial resources and give "professional counsel" concerning the advisability of building. With the approval of the deacons, I wrote the firm and shared our current financial picture. Our income for the previous three years (1952–54) had been $58,080.69 and our total expenditures $41,639.98. Our membership had grown from 206 to 275, and our property was valued at $18,500. We had $16,910.43 in the Building Fund and the church was debt free. What did they think we should do?

Their reply a week later was not at all encouraging: it was their professional opinion that we didn't have the resources necessary for building. First of all, we needed to set up a pledge system and invite a professional fund-raiser to come to the church and challenge the members to give an additional $20,000 a year. (They said nothing about the possibility of a strike.) This would mean delaying construction until we had more money in the bank.

But it meant something else even more fundamental: it meant changing the whole financial philosophy of the church. Our people believed in bringing "the Lord's tithes and offerings to the Lord's house on the Lord's Day" and trusting God to meet the needs week by week, and He had never failed them. Our faithful church treasurer, Scott Porter, often reminded us of the words of Hudson Taylor: "When the Lord's work is done in the Lord's way for the Lord's glory, it will never lack the Lord's support." Central Baptist Church wasn't about to accept the financial schemes of a fund-raiser when they had proved the promises of God for twenty-five years.

We met with the loan officers of several area banks and savings and loan associations, only to be told the church wasn't a good risk. We had no "moneyed people" in our congregation of about 200 people, and most of the wage earners were blue-collar workers who might go out on strike any time. The specter of a strike always loomed large over our city, even to wealthy bank officers.

Finally, we found a savings and loan association in Hammond that was friendly to our cause. In contrast to the other institutions, this one said that they found churches to be excellent risks because people were devoted to their churches and saw to it that the bills were paid. With the money we had in the Building Fund, the money that would come in during construction, and the money available from the loan, we'd have what we needed to build and furnish the new sanctuary, and the church could easily be able to make the mortgage payments.

As pastor, I wasn't punching a clock like the other men on the Building Committee, so it became my responsibility to deliver the blueprints to the subcontractors, get their bids, and deliver them to the committee for their study and approval. A few of our members thought we should have only believers working on the church, but when we checked with people who had used the services of some of these professed Christians, we found that the customers weren't at all satisfied with their work. In fact, a few of these so-called Christian contractors turned out to be hypocrites. Over my years of ministry, I've learned to be wary of the salesman or contractor who comes to a committee meeting and says, "Now, I'm born again, and I know just what you're looking for!" The person who's born again proves it by faithful work on the job, not by a religious speech in the board meeting.

After the morning service on Sunday, July 31, we had our official groundbreaking for the new building, and on Monday, the men from the First Mexican Baptist Church in Indiana Harbor drove up in their trucks and began to take the building down. They worked for several days hauling away lumber, sheet metal, and other materials to be used at their own church site where they needed another building. The pastor apologized to me for not having more men on the job.

"Some of our men are 'lily Christians,' " he explained; seeing that I didn't get the point, he added, "They neither toil nor spin." But every church has people like that.

The occasion of dismantling the old building was not unlike what Ezra experienced when he began to rebuild the temple (Ezra 3). Some of our people openly wept as they saw their "little tin church" coming down, and this was to be expected. Some of them had found Christ in that building; others had been married there, and many of them had said good-bye to loved ones in that humble tabernacle. It's not easy to watch your memories being dismantled and hauled away.

But others of us, especially this preacher, were very happy that the old building was no more, and while the older folks were weeping, we were rejoicing inwardly. The building was hot in the summer and drafty in the winter. The huge heat registers in the center aisle were inefficient, dirty, noisy, and somewhat dangerous.* In the hot summer, we had to use two large electric fans to "cool" the auditorium, and it was difficult to preach over all that noise. I was embarrassed that we had no baptistery and had borrowed the use of the baptismal facilities at other area churches. We had to schedule our baptismal services either on Sunday afternoons, which was very inconvenient, or after church on Sunday evenings, which wasn't much better.

While on the subject of baptism, I must tell you about the bid we received for the baptistery tank from a local steel fabricator. Apparently the man had never seen baptism by immersion and had no idea how the tank would be used. He ended up designing *a completely enclosed tank with two stairways inside!*

"Explain this tank to me," he said when I stopped to pick up his bid. "What are these stairways for?"

"For people to go in and out of the tank," I explained.

He was puzzled. "But how do they get in to begin with?"

It was then that I realized he'd designed a tank for storing liquids and not for baptizing people. When I explained his error, we had a good laugh, and he went to work making a new set of prints for a tank that was user-friendly.

Whenever a church family goes through a building program, there are usually internal stresses and strains that try their pa-

---

*There's a story, probably apocryphal, about a lady who got her heel caught in a similar heat register in her church as the choir marched down the center aisle. The man behind her reached down to retrieve her shoe, only to dislodge the register cover; and the man behind him stepped right down into the heat duct. This could never happen at Central Baptist Church because we never did anything as liturgical as having the choir march down the center aisle. We came into the choir loft from the basement.

tience and test their sanctification, and you really can't blame them. During a building program, we all have to sacrifice more time and money, and we don't like to have our Sunday School classes moved or merged with another class. We like everything to remain "as it was in the beginning" because changes are a threat to us. Sometimes the Building Committee makes decisions we don't approve of and we wonder why we weren't consulted.

There are always delays and extra demands that nobody can anticipate. Whenever a pastor tells me his church is in a building program, I say, "Well, plan to add 25 percent to the budget and three months to the schedule, and be sure to do a lot of praying!" Often they phone me months later and say, "You were right on target!"

At East Chicago Central, our Sunday morning ministry, once housed in two buildings, was now crammed into one building; and things weren't too comfortable. Until we moved into the new sanctuary, I taught a combined adult Sunday School class in the main assembly room of the educational building, but we tried to keep the classes distinctive for the sake of between-Sundays ministries like caring for the sick, following up on visitors, and contacting absentees. The age limits for our adult classes were always blurred, and sometimes visitors found themselves inundated with visits, phone calls, and mail from members of several classes. Granted, it's better to be noticed by three Sunday School classes than not to be noticed by one, but some people got the idea we were being just a bit pushy. It was a tough time for all of us.

For some reason, one of our best officers wasn't happy with the building program and showed little enthusiasm. When the Building Committee discovered that we had carelessly (but innocently) signed a contract with a contractor who didn't have a union shop, this officer became very upset and hinted that, if he wanted to, he could have the church picketed and stop the whole enterprise! He wasn't a bad man; he was a good man who'd gotten something stuck in his craw and temporarily wasn't getting enough spiritual oxygen.

The husband of one of our good members was a union representative who had always been friendly toward our church, even though at that time he himself wasn't a believer. His wife was one of the best cooks in the church, and Betty and I had often been in their home and enjoyed fried chicken, corn bread, and all the trimmings. I went to see him, explained our mistake, and told him our problem, without naming the man who'd caused it. I tried to be as wise as a serpent and as harmless as a dove.

He was shocked. "Why, never in my life have I ever heard of a union picketing a church!" he said. "You've got to fulfill your contract because you signed it, but don't worry about any union interference. I'll see to that." And he did.

The unhappy church officer had planned to come to the next monthly business meeting and air his grievances, which certainly was his privilege, but that night *he was in the hospital.* A few days later, when he came out of the hospital, he was a subdued man, so I assumed that the Lord as well as the doctors had worked on him. After the building was completed and we were happily using it, he came to me privately and apologized for his attitude. I appreciated that. Like I said, he wasn't a bad man; he was a good man who had temporarily lost his perspective.

On September 9, 1956, we worshiped for the first time in our new sanctuary, with a grand piano and a Baldwin organ to assist us! It was a high and holy day and we praised the Lord from hearts that were full of gratitude. The official dedication was held November 11, 1956, twenty-two years to the day since their first church building was dedicated.

First Chronicles 28:20 had worked, and I was grateful to the Lord for His faithfulness.

# CHAPTER EIGHT

$$\boxed{1}$$

I just came from the dedication service for a new church building," Vance Havner said at a Bible conference. "The people thought it was a milestone, but it may turn out to be a millstone."

That wasn't what happened at East Chicago Central Baptist Church after we moved into our new building! Whether it was because of the burden of the debt or the blessing of the new facilities, the people united in giving, working, and praying; and the church experienced growth. We enjoyed making use of the new baptistery as people trusted Christ and identified with the church family. The neighborhood sat up and took notice that the old tin building was gone and in its place stood a modest but attractive brick building with crosses on the tower and people in the pews.

At last, I had a private study where I could set up my bookcases and fill them with my ever-growing library. My practice was to walk to the church early each morning and have my devotional time in my study, and then return home in time for breakfast with Betty and David. One of the first times I did this, I was interrupted by our part-time custodian who happened to be driving past on his way to work. When he saw a light on, he was sure somebody had broken into the building, so he rushed to the rescue. If the discipline of my devotional life impressed him, he never mentioned it. Maybe he thought Betty had thrown me out and I'd spent the night in my study.

We had an especially happy Christmas in 1956. There were no stressful Building Committee meetings to attend, the new church sanctuary was completed, and we were anticipating an addition to our family sometime in March 1957. The church was going well; we were enjoying the people and the ministry very much and had every reason to believe we'd be staying at Central for several more years.

Beside that, I was enjoying being near my family and would often stop to see Ma whenever I was driving near 7113 Baring Parkway in Hammond. I knew she always had the coffeepot on, and there was probably Swedish coffeecake in the bread box. Those half-hour chats over coffee meant a lot to me, and Ma was always interested in the progress of the church. She and Pa had been very generous in their giving to the building program and were now attending Central Baptist on Sunday mornings.

But there was an unrest in my heart, a slow but steady feeling of detachment from the church and the people. This was the first time I'd felt it, although I would experience it several more times in the years to come. Each time it began, I knew that the Lord was preparing us for a move.

Whenever pastors share with me their concern about staying or moving, I remind them that God's servants don't *leave* a place; they *go to* a place. There are always enough problems in any local church to make the pastor want to leave, but that's not the test. (I heard about one pastor who carried an undated resignation in his pocket just in case the next church crisis turned out to be God's green light.) But if there weren't problems and challenges in our churches, they wouldn't need pastors! When Titus offered to hand in his resignation, Paul wrote him, "The reason I left you in Crete was that you might straighten out what was left unfinished" (Titus 1:5, NIV). Each pastor has a work to do and he'd better not leave the field until he's finished it. If God wants you to leave, He has the place for you; but if He wants you to stay, He has the grace for you. Let Him tell you what to do.

Even before we met, Betty and I had been burdened for foreign missions and had even made preliminary application to a mission board. The board wanted me to get more education (in spite of my degree), and in the fall of 1954, I'd spent a semester at Roosevelt University in downtown Chicago, starting my work toward a master's degree in history. Once again I was riding the South Shore, this time once a week, and studying on the train. I won't relate the details, but the Lord slammed that door in a hurry, and we got the signal loud and clear. Our work was to pastor a local church at home and not to go to the mission field.

**In the new pulpit and new sanctuary at Central Baptist Church, 1957.**

Betty and I will never forget the winter of 1955. One evening in late January, I spoke at a banquet sponsored by Christian Fellowship Church; and the pastor and his wife, Sam and Lois McDill, picked us up and drove us to the restaurant. It was a cold night and the heater wasn't working in Sam's car. Sitting in the back seat, Betty and I had to use blankets to keep warm.

The next day, Betty had a swelling in her neck, which we thought was caused by the frigid drive of the previous evening, but it turned out that she had the mumps! And she was pregnant with our first child, David, who was born July 6. She had to stay in bed for several weeks, which left me to do the shopping, cooking, and other household duties that I had always taken for granted. Believe me, the Lord never made me for domestic ministry.

But that's not all. February was cold and icy; and one Sunday evening, I slipped on the ice in front of our church building and injured my right ankle. Being a martyr, I led the service; but the longer it went, the more my ankle swelled and the pain increased. I ended up preaching while sitting on a kitchen stool, and when the meeting ended, two of the deacons had to carry me out of the church to my car because I couldn't walk. I was glad it was the evening service instead of the morning service, because the neighbors probably would have said, "Well, Central Baptist Church is getting rid of another pastor!"

One of the men drove my car and two of them helped me up the back stairs to our apartment. Hearing all the noise and wondering what was going on, Betty was shocked to learn that I'd been injured; but she didn't dare get out of bed to help. The next morning, Ed drove me to the hospital for x-rays; and the doctor told me to stay off my foot for two weeks.

So there we were, two casualties, both out of commission. Our dear friend Katherine Howard* came to the apartment to help us; when she saw Betty languishing in bed and me on a stool, washing the breakfast dishes, she just stood in the door and laughed. I guess it was pretty funny. However, one good thing came out of our afflictions: we were able to tune in WMBI and listen to many of the "Founder's Week" speakers from Moody Bible Institute, including J. Vernon McGee, Charles Fuller, Alan Redpath, Paul Rees, and Bernard Ramm. It was sort of an enforced vacation and I guess we needed it.

---

*Dee and Katherine Howard were two of our greatest encouragers during our years in East Chicago, and Betty and I often found refuge in their home. During our dating years, whenever Betty could get away from school and spend a weekend with us at the church, she stayed with Dee and Katherine.

Along with my pastoral work, I was still actively serving on the Lake County YFC Board and speaking to YFC Clubs and rallies here and there in the Calumet Region. During the annual Youth for Christ International convention at Winona Lake, Indiana each July, Betty and I would drive down for one day and catch some of the fervor and flavor of what the Lord was doing in YFC around the world. Some of the conference sessions were broadcast over WMBI, the Moody Bible Institute radio station in Chicago, and we'd listen as often as possible. But to be there with thousands of other people and share in the excitement of world evangelism was an experience that did our hearts good.

One day Bruce Love casually asked me, "Warren, have you ever thought about ministering full-time in Youth for Christ?"

"I'm a pastor and a Bible teacher, not a youth leader," I replied. "What would I do?"

"Preach, teach, write, encourage — all the things you're doing right now, only you'd be sharing your gifts with a lot more people," Bruce said. "Believe me, YFC needs pastors as well as youth experts. Pray about it."

We did pray about it, but we kept our prayers to ourselves lest we upset things at the church. Then one day I got a letter from Bob Cook, President of Youth for Christ International, asking if I would come to Wheaton to chat with him about a possible future ministry with YFCI. Whether Bruce was behind this invitation or not, I never found out, but Bob had preached for us at Central and I'd met him at different YFC functions, so we weren't strangers.

It was Valentine's Day, February 14, 1957, when I kept that appointment and drove to the YFCI headquarters building at 109 N. Cross Street in Wheaton. After Bob closed his office door and sat down behind his desk, he asked me a strange question: "Would it make any difference to your future in YFCI if I weren't president of the organization?"

I thought he was asking me a hypothetical question, the kind you hear from ordination councils. Then Bob told me that he'd resigned that very day as president of YFCI to become vice president of Scripture Press, also located in Wheaton.

Pause here for a bit of history. At the 1948 YFC convention, Torrey Johnson had asked not to be renominated as president, and Bob Cook was elected to replace him. This turn of events didn't please everybody in the organization. Bob and Torrey were brothers-in-law and the whole thing looked like evangelical nepotism (it wasn't). Critics said that Torrey would run the ministry through his brother-in-law (he didn't) and that YFC would soon fall apart (it hasn't). Under the anointing of God, Bob Cook proved to be exactly what YFC needed at that hour, and he served faithfully until that day in February when he felt God telling him to pass on the mantle.

Back to 109 N. Cross Street. When I found my voice, I said: "Bob, if God wants me here, I think I can work under the leadership of another man, but I'd sure like to work with you. Do we know who the new president is?"

"Yes," he replied. "The board has named Ted Engstrom acting president until the Winona convention, and at Winona, he'll no doubt be elected president."

In those days, the name "Ted Engstrom" wasn't as widely known as it is today. Anybody who knows what's been going on in the Christian world recognizes Ted Engstrom as the man who, after serving as president of YFCI for six years, went on to minister with incredible skill and blessing at World Vision and then become president of that ministry following Dr. Stanley Mooneyham. During his fruitful life, Ted's written a shelf of books, mentored dozens of young Christian leaders, preached all over the world, raised millions of dollars for world missions and world relief, instructed thousands of Christian workers in leadership seminars, and set an example for spiritual leadership and administrative skill that has inspired two generations of Christian workers.

But we in YFC knew Ted primarily as the Executive Director of the organization, the man who sat in the Wheaton office and kept the complex machinery working while Bob Cook criss-crossed the North American continent and circled the globe preaching the Gospel and extending the ministry of YFC. Ted is a genius at organization and administration, a tenderhearted man of God who seeks to manage God's work on biblical principles. Prior to coming to YFCI in 1951 to assist Bob Cook with administrative duties, Ted had served as editor-in-chief at the Zondervan Publishing House in Grand Rapids; and maybe that was one reason the Lord wanted me to be at YFCI when Ted was at the helm. Ted was going to teach me a lot of what I needed to know about writing, editing, and publishing.

Bob Cook and Ted Engstrom were in many ways opposites; I privately wondered what direction YFCI would take after Ted took over. Ted is more a left-brain kind of person, a man who masters details and lives and breathes, "Let's get down to business!" Bob was certainly an efficient administrator, but he came out of the pastorate and not the business world. He was more of a charismatic kind of leader who saw the big picture and challenged you to be a part of it. Over the years, I don't know how many pastors and missionaries in different parts of the world have told me they got their impetus for serving Christ from Bob Cook. He certainly enriched my life.

Bob Cook went home to be with Christ on March 11, 1991, after a long battle with cancer, and I miss him. He ministered the Word at each of the three churches I pastored and I in turn often preached to the students at The King's College during Bob's twenty-three years of ministry there as president. It was a special privilege to live with Bob and Coreen in the President's Mansion at Briarcliff Manor, New York, while ministering to the college family. In all the years I knew him, Bob was never too busy to take time to write me encouraging letters. When we'd meet, I'd say, "And how is our Fearless Leader?" and he'd reply, "Greetings, O Seraphic Scribe!" How that got started, I can't remember, but it was a distinctive Bob Cook touch. Bob had a way with words. I think he's the originator of the phrase "easy believe-ism," and I can still hear him signing off his radio program with "Walk with the King today, and be a blessing!"

Bob and Ted must have gotten together and worked out the details of my job description, because in a few weeks I received an official invitation to join the staff of Youth for Christ International as "Director of the Literature Division." It would be my responsibility to produce all the promotional materials, write, edit, and publish books for teenagers under the YFCI imprint "Miracle Books," write regularly for *Youth for Christ Magazine* (now *Campus Life*), and when not doing all that, preach wherever the doors opened. It turned out to be three jobs, but in those days, that was true for everybody in YFC. Three jobs, one salary—and I had to raise the salary myself!

Betty and I prayed about the call and decided it was God's will for us to accept it. Saying yes was a gigantic step of faith for us because we now had two little children (Carolyn had been born on March 7), very little savings, and a car to pay for; and going to YFCI meant buying a house in the Wheaton area and trusting God to bring in funds to pay my salary month by month.

# PART THREE

# Youth for Christ

# CHAPTER NINE

I n May, I told the deacons how God was leading in our lives, and one Sunday morning, I read an official letter of resignation to the church, to take effect September 15. As I look back, I can see that it was unwise for me to be a "lame-duck" pastor for four months, but it did give the church time to find my successor, Allen Vine, who began his ministry September 22. Since the Vines would be moving into a house near the church, Betty and I could stay in the apartment until we found housing in Wheaton, and she could continue to worship at Central when I was out preaching on Sundays.

In all my years of ministry, I've always been fortunate in my predecessors and my successors. In only eighteen months, Bob Johnson got Central Baptist Church ready for new things before I was called to succeed him, and Allen Vine kept the ministry of the church healthy and growing after we left. Dr. D.B. Eastep's thirty-five years of ministry at Calvary Baptist in Covington, Kentucky prepared the way for us so beautifully, and after I left for Moody Church in Chicago, Galen Call became senior pastor at Calvary and accomplished great things for God.

Dr. George Sweeting preceded me at Moody Church, a gifted evangelist, preacher, and leader who was mightily used of God to guide that great church out of a period of decline. George preached his last sermon as pastor of Moody Church on August 29, 1971, and I began with the midweek service three days later on Wednesday, September 1. (This was something new for some of the Moody Church people. During much of their church's history, there had been prolonged intervals between pastors.) I was followed by Dr. Erwin Lutzer whose long ministry at Moody Church has effectively impacted the city with the Gospel.

As Bob Cook would say, "Small thought here": *The kind of successor I get may depend a great deal on the kind of predecessor I've been and how I've related to my own predecessor.* To reject the past and ignore the future while thinking only of *my* ministry in *my* era, is both selfish and foolish, but I've seen more than one Christian leader do it. Maybe that's why the Lord called me to be a bridge-builder: I've learned to thank God for those who have labored before me, and I don't think I've ever tried to make myself an "institution" and get in the way of those who followed me.

But, back to Youth for Christ.

# 2

At Beatenburg, Switzerland in 1948, YFCI had held its first World Congress on Evangelism, consisting primarily of YFC leaders from around the world who met to pray, encourage one other, and plan strategy for world evangelism. Subsequent congresses, much larger and involving local Christian leaders, would be held in Cannes, Brussels, Winona Lake, Belfast, Tokyo, Sao Paulo, Caracas, Copenhagen, Mexico City, and Madras. During my YFC years, I attended only two: Copenhagen and Mexico City.

The Copenhagen Congress was scheduled for August 5–10, 1957, followed by two weeks of evangelistic meetings during which the delegates would disperse into scores of towns and cities in Denmark and neighboring countries and conduct Gospel meetings. Since I was soon to become a member of the YFCI Wheaton staff, the powers that be thought it would be a good idea for me to attend the Congress. It would not only be a great opportunity for ministry, but I'd be able to meet many of the YFC people from around the world whom I needed to know.

Bruce Love was planning to attend the World Congress and was especially anxious for me to go along. Fine. But where would I get the thousand dollars needed for all the expenses involved? And what right did a pastor have to take nearly a month off and run around Europe just before he's about to leave his church?

As for the second problem, thanks to a pep talk from Bruce Love at a Singspiration held in our church, the deacons and church family saw no reason why I shouldn't go. I think they were weary of a lame-duck pastor anyway, and I may have had some vacation time coming. I didn't like the idea of leaving Betty and Carolyn and David that long, but she assured me they'd get along fine. The church family would be near and she planned to drive to Clinton and spend time with her folks.

As for the financial problem, one of the ladies in the church phoned me after the Singspiration and said she'd count it a privilege to give me the thousand dollars needed for the trip. In her younger years, she'd wanted to serve as a missionary but for a number of reasons wasn't able to fulfill the vision. Maybe this was one way she could ease her own heart and also help me get a running start in my new ministry.

Bruce and Verla were at our apartment when my benefactress called and he was glad his "pep talk" had been so effective. My next step was to phone Sam Wolgemuth, Overseas Director for YFCI, and get my name on the reservation list, and Sam would do all the rest. "But do it right now," Bruce urged, "because I think the deadline for reservations may be this week."

I may be wrong, but I suspect that while Bruce was saying all those helpful things, he was thinking, *I'd better get this amateur traveler committed to go before he looks at a map and changes his mind.* Before he and Verla were married, Bruce had ministered several months in Europe with a Gospel team, so things like packing and traveling and getting homesick never bothered him. But in my entire life, I'd been in only four states: Indiana, where I was born; Illinois, where I went to school; Michigan, where I reluctantly visited my farmer relatives; and Wisconsin, where I got married, spent my honeymoon, and visited my in-laws. If ten years before, it had been tough for me to leave my parents and go 50 miles to Chicago, what would it be like to leave my wife and two little children and fly 2,000 miles to Denmark!

The operator gave me Sam's phone number, and I called him and gave him the word that I wanted to go to the Copenhagen World Congress. He was delighted and told me what to do to get a reservation on the chartered plane. He also told me about passports, shots, wash-and-wear clothing, and sermons that didn't reek of American idioms and untranslatable alliteration. Had I known about all those things before the Singspiration, I probably wouldn't have allowed Bruce to make his speech.

The next week was a busy one with seeing the doctor, shopping for clothes, getting a passport, deciding what sermon outlines to take, and arranging to have preachers fill the pulpit the Sundays I'd be gone. There wasn't time to get cold feet. Finally the day came when I had to kiss Betty and the kids good-bye and head for New York City and then Copenhagen. It wasn't easy and it wouldn't get any easier in the years that followed when I traveled so much either for YFC or in conference ministry. No wonder our daughter Carolyn's first sentence was, "Where Daddy go?"

# 3

Before taking that trip to New York City, I'd flown only twice in my whole life, and that was to and from Grand Rapids, Michigan, where I'd spoken at a GARBC weekend youth conference. The flights were only across Lake Michigan on a Capitol Viscount plane, so it was hardly a pioneer effort. Now I was on a much larger plane and going much farther away, and I felt every air mile right in the pit of my stomach.

New York City overwhelmed me. Whenever I left the hotel, which was near Times Square, I stayed very close to the YFC crowd so I wouldn't get lost, robbed, or killed. (I get lost in a parking lot.) I latched on to Don Engram, director of Voice of Christian Youth in Detroit, and his VCY Club Director, Al Kuhnle, both of whom have been good friends ever since. Even today, if I want to get Al laughing, all I have to say is, "Kerteminde." I'll tell you why later.

Don and I decided to take a bus tour of the city that took in all the major sights. During this tour, I bought a leather wallet for my passport and other travel paraphernalia, and I'm still using it! The tour guide was a university student who had a bizarre sense of humor. He not only showed us the important buildings and monuments, but he pointed out places where famous crooks were shot, either by other crooks or by the police. Having come from East Chicago, I was able to identify with what he said.

That evening, Ted Engstrom gathered the whole delegation together for an orientation meeting. The first item on the agenda was a lecture on Scandinavian languages given by Phil and Louie Palermo. They were very popular Italian-American musicians who had married Swedes, all of which qualified them to lecture on the Danish language. Phil and Louie had attended every World Congress from 1948 on and were known by YFC-ers around the world as fun-loving, soul-winning musicians (accordion and guitar), who used every opportunity to talk to people about Christ. The first book I would edit and publish in my new YFCI ministry would be *Life with the Palermos* by *YFC Magazine* editor Mel Larson.

But back to the lecture: it was supposed to be helpful but it turned out to be hysterical. To begin with, unless they're very well-prepared, no two people can lecture together about anything, especially Phil and Louie, who occasionally had problems

even singing together. They started joking around and soon
they had all 120 delegates laughing. When you remember that
they were addressing a gathering of YFC leaders, all of whom
were amateur comedians, the situation isn't hard to imagine.

The evening of July 31, we had a grand send-off by Billy
Graham at the Crusade meeting. The next day we boarded our
Flying Tiger chartered plane and headed for Gander, New-
foundland, where we'd refuel and then leave for Copenhagen,
where we were scheduled to arrive at 10:00 on Friday morning,
August 2. As I sat on the plane, remembering my loved ones
back home, I started having second thoughts about the wisdom
of this venture, but it was too late. Maybe Abraham felt the
same way when he left Ur of the Chaldees and, as Halford
Luccock puts it, "marched right off the map."

Our refueling stop at Gander turned out to be a twenty-four
hour delay and we didn't arrive at Copenhagen until Saturday,
August 3.

Our four-motor Super Constellation had taken off beautifully
and we were out over the ocean when one of the motors quit
and the pilot said we'd have to return to the field. This meant
ditching the fuel so the plane wouldn't be too heavy for land-
ing. It's quite an experience to be in a plane climbing over the
ocean as you watch hundreds of gallons of fuel being poured
out into the water. You wonder if maybe a stray spark will
change your travel plans.

We landed safely, praise the Lord, and then the mechanics
discovered that they didn't have the part that was needed to
repair the motor. It would have to be flown in from New York
the next day.

I don't know what Gander is like today, but back in 1957 it

was primarily an Air Force base with not too many facilities available for travelers. (One of the YFC delegates called it "a cemetery with lights.") But you can't blame the airport personnel. It isn't easy to have 120 overnight guests drop in on you unexpectedly.

Phil and Louie had the baggage agents get their musical instruments out of the hold of the plane and they set up shop in the terminal. There were some waiting passengers in the terminal as well as numerous military people around, so in true YFC fashion, we decided to evangelize them. I don't recall that anybody got upset or angry either at our music or the personal witnessing. Our presence was probably the only bright spot in Gander that day.

Ben Weiss discovered a group of German travelers and witnessed to them in German. Since I'd studied German at Indiana University, I did my best to share the Gospel along with Ben. Of course, there isn't a lot you can say about salvation when your German vocabulary grew out of *Grimm's Fairy Tales* and *Drei Kameraden,* but I did the best I could.

You may recall that Ben Weiss was the man who organized Billy Graham's 1949 Los Angeles crusade and also founded the Christian Educator's Fellowship. Ben and I got acquainted during that Gander delay and became good friends. He's home with the Lord now where he's met a lot of people who came to Christ because of his personal witness and his ministry with various Christian organizations.

After many hours of waiting and occasionally trying to get some sleep, we got the good news that the part for the motor had finally arrived. The mechanics installed it and we packed up to leave for Copenhagen. We had lost the extra day we so desperately needed to help us get over the weariness of the flight, and we were all very tired and anxious to get to our Copenhagen hotel rooms. As I napped on the plane, I dreamed of showering, taking a nap, putting on clean clothes, and then finding something very special to eat. (Phil and Louie had told us that the food in Denmark was excellent. How that got into a lecture on the Danish language, I can't remember.) Only the Lord knows why we were delayed and what fruit came from our witness, but better the motor failed right over the airport than halfway to Denmark.

We were thinking about food and rest, but the Danish Congress Committee had other plans in mind. When we finally arrived at the Copenhagen airport on Saturday, we were met by committee members with the news that were scheduled to go on a tour of Zealand Island. The tour had already been lined up and if we had backed out, we would have hurt the feelings of our new Danish friends. I was so tired I went to sleep on the bus and had to be awakened at each stop. (A month later, before leaving Denmark, I bought a set of slides so I could see what I'd missed when I was sleeping.) When I finally got to my hotel room, I didn't take time to shower; I fell on the bed and went sound asleep.

That Saturday evening was supposed to be a free time for the delegates, but the American delegation had to catch up on the orientation sessions they'd missed; so we had a meeting. I slept so long and so hard I almost missed it.

I'm grateful that Bruce and Verla Love were at the Congress, along with Wendell ("Wendy") and Norma Collins, Bruce and Verla's close friends whom I got to know during the Congress and who have been our good friends ever since. All four of them were experienced in cross-cultural ministry situations and were a big help to a beginner like me.

Delegates from twenty-seven different nations were there, including the winners of the Teen Talent Contests held at the July Winona Lake Convention. Each of the adults in our group was assigned to shepherd one of the teens, and I was given a fine fellow named Gary Fagan. I guess I wasn't a very good shepherd because Gary got sick and I got blamed for it. In front of several of my new YFC friends, Engstrom gave me a lecture that reminded me of my duties, and I was just tired enough and frustrated enough to be tempted to pack up and go home. But I stuck it out. "Count it all joy."

During the week of the Congress, evangelistic teams spread out all over Copenhagen to conduct street meetings and rallies. In spite of the fact that a group of "rock and roll" teenagers had recently caused near riots in the Town Square, YFC got permission from Lord Mayor Clausen to hold two huge outdoor meetings featuring Phil and Louie Palermo. The police were impressed with the behavior of the teenagers, and many people who stopped to listen or to scoff remained to pray.

**YFC Banquet—Bob and Verla Love, Warren and Betty Wiersbe.**

My hotel roommate during the Congress was Victor Manogarom, director of YFC in India. Except for occasional visits to my Swedish relatives, this was my first opportunity to spend time with somebody from another culture, and Victor taught me a lot about India and the United States and myself. I learned that God wanted me to be a Christian first and an American second and that I shouldn't relate to delegates from other parts of the world as though Americans were superior to others. In the years that followed, as Betty and I have ministered in different parts of the world, this has been valuable counsel to follow.

When YFC is in town, anything's liable to happen from a street rally to a formal wedding. British YFC leader Dave Foster and his fiancée Susan Harmer were married at the Congress! I wasn't invited because I didn't know Dave and Susan then, but we eventually got acquainted. A few years later, Dave conducted a youth crusade for us at Calvary Baptist Church in Covington, Kentucky. Dave has traveled the world in evangelism and few people know the European religious scene as he does.

During the week, we were given speaking assignments in various places around the city. This was the first time I'd ever preached through an interpreter and it took me a little while to get accustomed to the pattern. I was careful to avoid American idiomatic expressions and alliterated outlines that couldn't easily be expressed in another language. In later years, I found it a challenge to preach through an interpreter, and some of them have really improved my sermons.

All of us in the U.S. delegation were assigned to a "Gospel team," and after the Congress we took off for our appointed cities and towns. My first assignment was in a town west of Copenhagen called Kerteminde. It was near Odense, the birthplace of Hans Christian Andersen. This time I didn't have anybody to help me as I traveled, and I prayed constantly that I wouldn't get lost, because the trip involved both a train and a huge ferry boat. My male ego makes me hesitate to ask for directions, and I wasn't sure I'd be asking people who understood English. I didn't want to look or act like the typical tourist.

## Chapter Nine

My pocket guide to Denmark had this to say about Kerteminde: "This quaint and picturesque fishing town has an idyllic situation, glorious air, splendid bathing facilities, and offers delightful walks in the surrounding woods which extend to the extreme point of the peninsula." It had a population of 3,795, most of whom never came to our meetings. The people were politely suspicious of the visiting evangelistic team, for hadn't all of them been properly baptized and catechized in the state church and thereby assured of salvation?

My team associate was Jackie Schultz, a delightful single young man from South Africa, and during that week (August 12–18), we lived quite comfortably with the local Danish Lutheran pastor and his family. I don't recall that either the pastor or his wife ever attended any of the evening evangelistic meetings. The ministry of the YFC team was the best kept secret in town. To promote the meetings, the Copenhagen office had sent ahead 1,500 leaflets and 30 posters, but they must have gotten lost in the mail, because I don't recall seeing them.

During the week, I learned that our host pastor was involved in ministerial responsibilities that seemed strange to me. For one thing, he was in charge of recording births and assigning cemetery lots, and he seemed to devote a lot of time to civic duties that in the United States would be handled at the city hall. He could read and speak English quite well, and when he discovered that I enjoyed reading detective novels, he came alive, especially when he learned I had a few paperback novels with me. During that week, he was often seen lounging on the sofa reading an Ellery Queen mystery. If he wasn't prepared to preach that next Sunday, it was my fault.

YFC had also sent ahead song sheets containing fifteen familiar Gospel songs and choruses translated into Danish. One evening I'd lead the singing and Jackie would preach, and then we'd switch "ministries" the next night. I'm not a musician, and I know very little about leading congregational singing in English, but trying to do it in another language was one of the wildest things I've ever attempted. By singing three songs and an invitation hymn each night, we soon used up the best songs on the sheet and had to start repeating. For weeks after I'd arrived home from the Congress, I'd wake up in the morning with "Himmelske Solskin" going through my mind. (For the uninitiated, that's "Heavenly Sunshine" in Danish.)

Our interpreter was an evangelical missioner from a neighboring village, a fine young man who did his best to bring to the meeting the life that was needed. He even got me into the local grade school to talk about life in America, but I wasn't really prepared and didn't do too well. The children applauded me at the end of my talk, but that was mainly because they were glad for the respite my talk gave them from their regular studies.

One day I decided to do a magic trick in the evening service, hoping it would liven things up a bit. I went to the local hardware store searching for soft cotton rope, but nobody in a Danish fishing village needs soft cotton rope. The fish laugh at it. I finally had to purchase a hank of rope so tough it was like a cable, and I borrowed a wicked-looking knife to cut it with when I did the trick. However, the rigid rope didn't respond to my subtle manipulations the way cotton rope would, and halfway through the lesson, my presentation was so pathetic that I felt like hanging myself with the rope or stabbing myself with the knife. Why would a guy try to do magic through an interpreter?

I was learning a painful lesson: no matter how successful I'd been in my pastoral work at home, I wasn't equipped to do the kind of creative evangelism that other YFC people could do, people like Wendy Collins and the Palermos and Bufe Karraker and Al Kuhnle. I was a *pastoral* evangelist, a Bible teacher, and I had a lot to learn about holy boldness and faith.

From a human point of view, the meetings in Kerteminde were not a success. The crowds were small, the singing was dismal, and the response nil. The only time we made any dent on the community was one night when Al Kuhnle showed up with his Teen Team and helped attract a bigger crowd and produce better singing. Kuhnle started calling me "The Kerteminde Kid." Even today, decades later, we both have to laugh at the mention of the word "Kerteminde."

My next assignment was in Esbjerg, the fifth largest city in Denmark. It was located on the North Sea and the author of my guidebook didn't recommend it too highly. "Except in passing through this gateway on entering or leaving Denmark by sea for Britain, I hardly think it need detain you. . . ." It detained me for a week.

My associate in ministry was a young man from Holland named Adrian Van Der Bijl. Since he didn't consider himself a speaker, I did all the preaching and he handled the music. We lived with an Apostolic Church pastor who did everything he could to promote the meetings and make our stay a comfortable and profitable one.

Unlike Kerteminde, Esbjerg was a populous city that offered a greater variety of churches and people, and the attendance and the spirit of the meetings were light years ahead of what I'd experienced the week before. We had excellent cooperation from the local Salvation Army staff and held our meetings in their citadel. Adrian and I didn't set the city on fire, but we had a good week and a few sinners came to the Lord.

At the end of the week, the train that took me across Denmark and back to Copenhagen didn't move fast enough, nor did the huge ferry boat that carried both train and passengers across the water that separated Fyn from Zealand where Copenhagen was located. When I arrived in Copenhagen, I went to the Viking Hotel, where I'd stayed before, and then I went to the Congress office to see if any mail had arrived from home.

It was then that I discovered the bad news that our delegation wouldn't be leaving for the United States in two days as planned. The SAS plane we were scheduled to take to New York was needed elsewhere in Europe to "rescue" a group of Boy Scouts who had been stranded and needed to get home right away. That meant another delay. Most of us had reservations at our hotels for only two days, but after that, the SAS people were kind enough to give us free hotel rooms and even daily spending money. Granted, we'd rather have been home with our families, but if we had to be delayed, better that somebody else was paying the bills.

Thanks to the generosity of SAS, I was able to tour the city and see some of the sights: the zoo, with its circus band; the waterfront, with its Little Mermaid; and at the top of the list, Tivoli Gardens, Copenhagen's ancient sophisticated amusement park that offers you everything from a flea circus to a ferris wheel, with delicious meals as well. Years later, when my wife and I were ministering at a Child Evangelism Fellowship conference in Denmark, we took a few extra days to see Copenhagen. Except for the noisy and embarrassing presence of gangs of American college students, active in the "rock and roll" and drug culture, the city hadn't changed from when I'd first visited it in 1957.

We finally left Copenhagen and had an uneventful flight to New York City where we found Idlewild jammed with Labor Day weekend travelers and the people seeing them off. When going through U.S. Customs, I was asked, "And what have you brought home with you from Denmark?" I mentioned the inexpensive gifts I'd bought and then added, "I have some books."

Immediately the agent asked, "What kind of books?" I showed him my guidebook to Denmark and two volumes of Hans Christian Andersen's fairy tales which I'd purchased for my niece. He was looking for pornography, of course, and we'd seen plenty of it displayed in Denmark. The books he thought I was smuggling in can be purchased today in bookstores, drug stores, and supermarkets in almost any city in America, and you can rent videos to go with them.

My plane reservations from New York to Chicago had been canceled and I had no idea what to do next to get home. While pushing my way through the crowd and going nowhere, I providentially ran into YFCI's business manager, Peter Quist, who shepherded me through the crowd and got me tickets for the same flight he and Ted and several of the other Wheaton staff men were taking to Chicago. We were practically the only passengers on the plane. I caught up on my sleep.

Many of the other Gospel teams reported greater success, so the Congress wasn't a failure. In the Danish town of Bogense, population 3,000, 46 teenagers were converted, and the next week, 30 of them cycled to the next town to give their testimonies. In Berlin, 30 young people who had come from East Berlin walked into the prayer room to receive Christ. In Ahlborg, Denmark, over 100 people came to Christ and the local committee insisted that the team remain another week. The team did remain but had to move the meetings to the largest auditorium in town because the crowds were so large.

The final summary showed that over 800 people recorded decisions for Christ in the post-Congress evangelistic crusades, and another 200 made dedication commitments to serve the Lord. By today's standards, those may not be exciting statistics, but if you remember that we were ministering in some pretty tough places, where "religion" had blinded people to the simple truth of the Gospel, those numbers represent a miracle of God in response to prayer and faithfulness.

I didn't have any remarkable stories to tell when I got back to East Chicago, but I had learned some great lessons and met some great people, many of whom are still beloved friends. For one thing, I learned that, when it came to spiritual ministry, I was a better pediatrician than obstetrician. I didn't have the gift of an evangelist. In my pulpit ministry, I'd always sought to preach the Gospel clearly, and in private, I'd tried to be a good witness. But after being involved in three weeks of intensive evangelism, I learned that I was basically a pastor-teacher who could counsel and encourage the saints better than he could deliver the babies.

I also learned to accept and appreciate people from other

cultures who did things differently from the way we American Christians do them. YFC people didn't make ministry methods a test of fellowship or spirituality. This doesn't mean they were unbelieving pragmatists ("If it works, it's right!"), because they stayed close to the Word of God. But they weren't afraid to try new methods if some of the old approaches weren't succeeding. True to their slogan, they were "geared to the times but anchored to the Rock."

During the Congress ministry, I'd seen once more how much YFC depended on prayer. Of course, I already knew that, but it came home with new power when I saw prayer turn battlefields into harvest fields. Maybe that's why my own ministry had been so seemingly fruitless in Kerteminde and Esbjerg: we hadn't spent enough time in prayer.

But the YFC World Congress had helped me build a bridge to the exciting world of believers from other cultures and to a lost world that needed to be reached with the Gospel. Those bridges would be very important in the years to come.

The local GARBC pastors and wives had an informal farewell party for me and Betty on September 9. These men had meant much to me as I'd tried to pastor my first church, and the wives had been a great help and encouragement to Betty. I wish every ministerial couple could have the same kind of love and support that we received from these godly friends as we started out in ministry. As a farewell gift, the men gave me a copy of Stuart Hackett's book *The Resurrection of Theism* and put their signatures on the flyleaf. I'm not sure I understand Professor Hackett's profound chapters, but I sure understand the love behind those signatures.

One pastor in our fellowship wasn't at the farewell party; but he had bid me good-bye at another meeting and had said, "I'm sorry you're leaving the ministry." He was one of the very few far-right separatists in our local fellowship and he had no place in his theology for a ministry like Youth for Christ. If you were going to serve the Lord, it had to be as a pastor, missionary, evangelist, or teacher, identified in some way with the local church. Parachurch ministries in general weren't of God, and Youth for Christ especially.

That wasn't the time or place for a debate, but I would like to have asked him if the Bible school he'd attended was a local church or a parachurch ministry; which local churches published the books in his library and the Bible from which he preached; whether the fellowship his church belonged to was a parachurch organization; what kind of church the summer camp was that his young people attended; and whether the mission boards his people supported were churches or parachurch organizations. Matthew Henry was right when he asked, "Who is so blind as he who will not see?"

During the years since that farewell party, I've worked closely with many parachurch ministries—Youth for Christ, Child Evangelism Fellowship, The Indiana Baptist Children's Home, Crystal Lake Youth Camp, Slavic Gospel Association, Back to the Bible, National Religious Broadcasters, Rural Home Missionary Association, Christian Booksellers Association, and a host of publishers and Christian publications—and though some of these organizations may occasionally have done things that I didn't approve of, I've seen nothing in any of them that leads me to believe that what they're doing is contrary to Scripture.

Granted, there are probably too many parachurch organizations today, but I believe the work of the local church would be severely hindered if we declared all these ministries unbiblical and abolished them. What would we do without publishers providing us with books and Bibles and educational tools? Or mission boards helping us get our volunteers to the fields and coordinating their work? Or schools training men and women for Christian service? Or camps giving our children and young people wholesome experiences in God's out-of-doors? One local church can't distribute New Testaments to school children or place Bibles in hotel rooms, but the Gideons can.

Perhaps I'm prejudiced because I was brought to Christ through a parachurch ministry and found my earliest Christian nurture there, but I can't see throwing the baby out with the bath water.

Back to our leaving East Chicago.

On September 5, the dear members of Central Baptist Church surprised me with a "This Is Your Life" program, with Bruce Love as emcee. He and one of the young ladies in the church, Joan DeBruler, had engineered the whole thing and brought together the people who had influenced my life: my parents, of course; my big brother Ed; my school chums John Kail and Bob Krajewski; Mrs. Beyda Lindbergh, one of my Sunday School teachers at the Mission Covenant Church; Bill Taylor, my boyhood pastor; Frances Ireland, who published my three magic books and was now Mrs. Jay Marshall; Mrs. Ed Bihl, in whose home we had prayed and studied Hebrews; Mrs. Dewey McFadden, whose husband had baptized me; John Cornwall, my first roommate at seminary, and his wife Barbara; our dear friends Joe and Dorothy Guthrie who sold me my library, book by book; and even the president of Youth for Christ International, Dr. Ted Engstrom, with his wife Dorothy. The climax of the program was Betty in her wedding dress followed by David pushing Carolyn in the stroller. David had just turned two and Carolyn was only six months old.

While there were a few inaccuracies in the script—nothing important—the cast was terrific!

Dr. Warren Filkin sent a lovely letter expressing his regrets that he couldn't attend because he was preaching in California and never missed a date. Bruce also read a telegram from the Bob Johnsons and letters from Everett Ostrom, the pastor who had confirmed me, and Owen Miller, pastor of First Baptist Church, Hammond, who had been such a good role model for me. Then everybody went to the assembly hall of the educational building to enjoy refreshments.

It's occasions like this that make a pastor feel very humble and unworthy of the very people he's serving. In the seven years I'd pastored the church, two of them as interim pastor, I know I didn't always do my best nor was I always filled with compassion as I preached to them or visited in their homes. Yet here they were, pouring out their love and asking God to bless us as we launched into our new ministry.

Betty and I were fortunate to start our ministry in the fellowship of such a caring and loving church. If I started naming people and what they did for us and meant to us, this chapter would get too long. As I look back, I can see that some of the members whom I considered weak were far better Christians than I thought. Central Baptist Church was composed of people who prayed, sacrificed, served, and loved, and who took in a young Christian and gave him an opportunity to serve the Lord. Over the years, they've prayed for us, and we're grateful.

# CHAPTER TEN

$$\boxed{1}$$

B ob Cook once described YFC workers as "nondescript individualistic . . . birds" and for the most part, he was right.

We were "nondescript." YFC people were ordinary men and women who weren't widely known (or known at all) in the Christian world before they identified with YFC. They were average people—pastors and missionaries, businessmen and businesswomen, laborers and professionals, teachers and Christian students from dozens of Bible schools and Bible colleges, retirees and young people—but they had one thing in common: a burden to reach lost teenagers around the world and the faith to believe that God would help them do it. God used YFC to give a platform of opportunity to a lot of people, myself included, who might otherwise have remained in the wings much longer.

Who ever heard of Al and Vidy Metsker before they started Kansas City YFC? But their faith built one of the longest-lasting and most effective youth ministries in America today. Al went to be with the Lord May 26, 1993, and his son Ronnie carries on the ministry with the zeal and devotion he learned from his godly parents.

Roy McKeown was known on the West Coast, but his association with YFCI gave him a worldwide ministry that eventually challenged him to found World Opportunities. And Roy mentored a number of men who made their mark in evangelism, such as singers Bill Carle and Greg Loren and leaders like Bob Kraning and Ken Phillips; and his influence on people in show business led to the transforming of many lives.

Along with Bill Carle and Greg Loren, the list of musicians who found an expanding and exciting platform in YFC would have to include Jack Conner, Joe Talley, Helen Barth, Phil and Louie Palermo, Merrill Dunlop, Kurt Kaiser, Jan Sanborn, Steve and Maria Gardner, Ralph Carmichael, Harold DeCou, Strat Shufelt, Gene Jordan, Theron and Thurlow Spurr, Gary Moore—and I could name a host of others.

Apart from his Western Springs, Illinois congregation and his "Songs in the Night" radio audience, how many people knew who Billy Graham was before God and Torrey Johnson laid hands on him to be YFCI's first staff evangelist? And look what happened!

Granted, when YFC really got moving, there were people who jumped on the bandwagon hoping to become famous, but they didn't last too long. The ones who got the job done just followed God's leading and did God's will and didn't worry too much about publicity. If their names ended up in the headlines, or were buried in an article in *YFC Magazine*, they neither complained nor bragged. They just went on doing their work because fame wasn't the test of success or God's blessing.

Just stop to think of some of the YFC "alumni" that God has dropped into places of leadership in the evangelical world, people like: Jay Kesler, president of Taylor University; Harold Myra, Paul Robbins, and Carol Thiessen at the *Christianity Today* publishing empire; Paul Cedar, president of The Evangelical Free Church of America; David Mains, host of "Chapel of the Air"; Mel Johnson, host of "Tips for Teens" radio and chairman of the board of Northwestern College; Dave Breese, president of Christian Destiny ministry; Bob Pierce, founder of World Vision; and on and on it goes.

This list of names is proof that God does indeed choose the "foolish things of the world to confound the wise . . . and . . .

the weak things of the world to confound the things which are mighty" (1 Cor. 1:27).

We were not only "nondescript," but we were also "individualists." At a staff meeting, I once heard Ted Engstrom say that the Wheaton headquarters staff was like a bunch of racehorses, full of energy, wanting to run in all directions at once; and his job was to face them in the right direction and try to keep them going that way without running him over in the process. The metaphor was an apt one.

When I started ministering on the YFCI staff, I was amazed to discover how versatile the men were. They could do almost anything and do it at a moment's notice! They could orchestrate a banquet, plan a club meeting or a rally, take over a church service, run a retreat, design a poster, promote an evangelistic crusade, plan a missionary trip, write a magazine article, tape a radio program, do an interview, meet a donor, think up a slogan, develop a long-range program for raising funds, and even ad lib a skit that sounded like they'd rehearsed it all week.

Individualists they were and absolutely honest in their dealings with one another. Anybody who was accustomed to avoiding accountability and doing a lot of waffling and excuse-making, or whose feelings were easily bruised, would never have made it at 109 N. Cross Street, because in that office, the work was planned and executed by means of candid no-holds-barred confrontations that we called "meetings." We had staff meetings, magazine meetings, club department meetings, overseas meetings, Winona Lake meetings, finance meetings, promotion meetings, and especially prayer meetings. Usually the same people attended whatever meeting was named on the memo, so everybody knew almost everything about what was going on. Sometimes Ted had a closed-door meeting, and then we'd have to wait until coffee break to find out what was going on.

In any meeting at any time, the atmosphere could change from the hilarity of a comedy to the somberness of a confessional. We'd be roaring with laughter one minute and praying the next minute and never feel as though we'd committed some kind of religious indiscretion in so doing. During our discussions, dumb ideas were quickly categorized as such, and woe unto the man who tried to impress you with his erudition. The people on the YFCI staff were all gifted with built-in "bunk detectors" and a phony didn't last long in their presence.

I didn't grasp it then, but later I understood what Ted Engstrom was doing in those meetings. He was the catalyst. He created the kind of atmosphere that gave each of us the freedom to be ourselves and say what we wanted to say. He kept the discussion on target (one joke could set us off on a detour) and made sure nobody was being unduly abused. Ted never tried to force any of us into some mold and he always encouraged us to grow and do better. If he made a stupid suggestion, he was the first one to admit it. (That was the safest thing to do.) By watching Ted in those meetings, I learned a lot about board chairmanship and have put what he taught me into practice many times since then.

Don't misunderstand me: Ted wasn't the ringmaster of a circus, trying to get all the acts to perform properly and on time. There were times when consensus determined what we'd do; other times, it was executive fiat. Ted was a leader—*our* leader—and we all loved him and would have died for him. And we knew he would have done the same for us. A few YFC people outside the office said that Ted was "rough," but those of us who worked under his leadership didn't think so. Down inside was a heart so tender that more than once it brought him to tears as he shared with us his burden for YFC around the world. Tough-minded and tenderhearted: that was our fearless leader.

Bob Cook was right: we were a bunch of "nondescript . . . individualistic birds." I never did ask Bob to explain what kind of birds he saw represented by the YFC leaders. Hawks? Eagles? Chickens? Doves? Peacocks? (We had a few of those in different parts of the country.) Parrots? But one thing was sure: if you were in YFC, you were *an owl* and were expected to function at night as well as in the day. If you complained about your schedule, somebody was bound to quote Bob Cook and say, "If anybody around here is getting any sleep, he's backslidden!" Our wives and children didn't always appreciate the unpredictable nocturnal habits of the YFC birds, especially at Winona

Lake when we'd attend all-night prayer meetings, but somehow we all survived.

At this stage in life, I'm no longer an owl; I go to bed with the chickens. As I look back, I wonder how I ever survived putting in eight hours at the office and then working at my typewriter at home until after midnight. Betty and David and Carolyn were very patient — and good sleepers!

# 2

When I started working in the YFCI headquarters office in Wheaton in September 1957, besides Ted Engstrom, the *dramatis personae* included:

*Evon Hedley,* Canadian businessman and YFC leader who replaced Ted as Executive Director. Later he followed Ted into the ministry of World Vision. Evon watched the budget very carefully but knew what it meant to walk by faith. He was a good balance to some of the "racehorses."

*Jack Hamilton* was the architect of the YFC Club program and talent contests and quizzes. Jack hailed from Kansas City where he was mentored by Dr. Walter L. Wilson, "the beloved physician," and the mentoring took. Jack could repair a typewriter, design a building, write a quiz manual, or speak to 5,000 teenagers, and do all of them well. He had the knack of discovering hidden talent and challenging young men and women to go to work for the Lord. In 1960, Jack moved his ministry to Los Angeles YFC and Bill Eakin became Club Director.

*Sam Wolgemuth* was Overseas Director, a Brethren in Christ bishop who in 1952 left his church in Pennsylvania to go to Japan to serve the Lord through YFC. He joined the headquarters staff in 1956 and became president of YFCI in 1965. Whenever in a staff meeting Sam quietly said, "Men, I have a check in my heart about this," we put on the brakes, looked at the road map and took time to pray for God's guidance. (During a YFCI financial crisis, the staff was discussing ways and means of raising funds, and Sam's response to one idea was, "I have a check in my heart about that." Somebody said, "Sam, a check in the hand is worth two in the heart." We were all a bunch of comedians, even when we were broke.)

**The Wheaton YFCI staff about 1960. Seated: Jack Hamilton, Carl "Kelly" Bihl, Ted Engstrom, Sam Wolgemuth, Evon Hedley. Standing: Carl Weir, myself, Jim Wright, Bob Collett, Harry Hosmer, Bill Eakin, "Wendy" Collins, Jack Daniel, Charles Hennix, and Peter Quist.**

*Jack Daniel* was Vice President for the Central States Area of YFC and had his office in the YFCI headquarters building. YFC had ten administrative areas in the United States and Canada, each managed by a vice president who was elected at the Winona Lake convention. Jack later was named Administrative Vice President for YFCI and became Ted's right-hand man. Jack has a wonderful sense of humor, but I must confess that it took me several weeks to understand him and accept him. He is a creative guy who has a way with words that is most effective, and he's gotten a lot of kidding about his name.

*Carl "Kelly" Bihl* is the son of Mr. and Mrs. Ed Bihl in whose home I learned to study the Bible and pray. (The nickname

"Kelly" is a corruption of the Swedish version of the name Carl.) "Kelly" could preach, sing, play the saxophone, and pray, and was one of YFC's staff evangelists. (As I recall, along with the Palermos, our staff evangelists were Cedric Sears, Jack Cochrane, Don Lonie, Ted Place, and Ed Midura.) Later "Kelly" became Organizing Director of YFCI, but I've forgotten what that title involved. (Sometimes we'd get new titles instead of raises.) "Kelly" won a lot of teenagers to Christ. In 1963, he succeeded Ted as president of YFCI.

*Peter Quist* was our Business Manager, a jolly Dutchman from Grand Rapids who sometimes got blamed for a lot of things that weren't his fault, but he took it graciously and kept on giving his best. Under the glass on his desk was a card on which Pete had written: "Faith is living without scheming." Peter practiced that as he kept the office working smoothly and managed the circulation and advertising for *YFC Magazine*.

*Jim Wright* directed the Follow-up and Counseling ministry. It was his job to help thousands of new Christians get an appetite for the Word of God and prayer, unite with local churches, and reproduce themselves in the lives of others. It wasn't easy. He developed a series of concise but adequate follow-up courses for children, teens, and adults, and he taught local staff people how to use them effectively.

*Wendell "Wendy" Collins* was the YFC Club Field Director when I joined the staff. Then he became YFCI's first full-time Lifeline Director, which meant managing YFC's ministry to juvenile delinquents. When Wendy later developed the Teen Team program, Bruce Love took his place in Lifeline. A Teen Team was a group of five to seven talented teenagers who ministered overseas for an extended period, traveling from city to city and seeking to win teens and establish YFC programs. Wendy was a great idea man who, with Bruce Love, served behind the scenes at our Winona Lake convention as producers for the evening rallies.

*Mel Larson* had been associated with *YFC Magazine* from its inception and was serving as managing editor when I came on staff. However, he had recently resigned to become editor of *The Evangelical Beacon*, official magazine of the Evangelical

Free Church of America. After leaving Wheaton, he continued to attend monthly magazine meetings until Vernon McClellan was selected to replace him and was introduced to the magazine family in the January 1958 issue. Mel was Swedish (a point in his favor), a gifted writer, a man whom Bob Cook called "the quiet prince." In the few short weeks I worked with Mel, I learned a lot about professional journalism. Mel wrote *Life with the Palermos,* the first book I edited and published after becoming Director of Literature. If anybody writes a book about the great Christian journalists of this century, Mel Larson must be in it.

*Ken Swanson* had served with YFC in Japan and was now YFCI Public Relations Director. Before the annual YFC convention, Ken and I would visit the greater Winona Lake area and distribute press releases, posters, and bulletin inserts to help promote the conference. Ken also ran the film showings at Winona Lake, a task for which I never envied him.

When you're young, you do crazy things, like work in an office 50 miles from home. Five days a week you drive 100 miles a day in peak traffic, and because you own only one car, you isolate your wife and two little children in an upstairs apartment from 7:30 A.M. to 5:30 P.M. Only by the grace of God did our family survive those first five months. David was two and Carolyn only six months old, and Betty had her hands full. God has a special crown for her when she gets to glory.

It pains me even to remember those days, because the only regret I have as I look back at my four years in YFCI is that I was away from home too much. During our years in Wheaton, Bob and Judy came into the family; so there were four children who deserved some affection and attention from their father. Our children needed a resident father and my wife deserved something more than a husband who showed up for bed and breakfast. I suppose other staff families faced similar demands, and maybe all of us thought we were really being spiritual by asking our wives and children to sacrifice for us. I can't change it now, and I'm grateful that the Lord brought us through unscathed.

Wheaton, Illinois is a suburb of Chicago that's known for being an expensive place to live. Because there are so many nonprofit religious organizations there, and because it's a good place to live, property taxes are high. The YFCI men already on location used to joke about living in houses with wall-to-wall carpeting and back-to-the-wall payments, or living in houses "completely surrounded by mortgages." Having lived in a parsonage/apartment for four years, Betty and I had no equity to work with, so we couldn't afford to buy a house, and there didn't seem to be much chance for building one. But the Lord answered prayer and solved the problem for us.

One day Jack Hamilton suggested I contact his friend Dick Whitmer, a local contractor who was also a devoted Christian and a supporter of Youth for Christ. I met Dick at the office and he presented us with a package we thought we could handle. He owned two lots on West Roosevelt Road and wanted to develop them. He could get the financing for us and build us a three-bedroom house with a full basement for only $1,000 down. I borrowed the $1,000 from my parents, we signed the papers, and Dick went to work. On February 18, 1958, my family and I moved into 1217 West Roosevelt Road and my commuting days ended.

But my traveling days didn't end. When I look at my datebooks for those years, I marvel that I was able to carry a full work load at the office and still go from Dan to Beersheba preaching the Word. Sometimes I was gone for two weeks at a time, and most weekends were tied up with Saturday night rallies and Sunday services in churches. Some of the Wheaton YFC wives jokingly referred to themselves as "the YFC widows," but they stood by their husbands and prayed for them.

Since I had been a pastor and had developed a small reputation as a Bible teacher, I received many invitations to conduct conferences in local churches, some of them in the greater Chicago area. I would put in a full day at the office, go home to eat and change clothes, and then drive to a church to preach, arriving back home too late to kiss the kids good night. God blessed His Word, I learned a lot about preaching, and the offerings helped me keep my account in the black; but if I had it to do over again, I'd say no to half of those meetings, and I think the Lord would have been pleased.

During our years in Wheaton, the Lord added two more arrows to our quiver. Robert Edward was born May 31, 1958, and Judy Lorraine on April 15, 1960. They probably thought they had a part-time father, and maybe they did; but Betty did a terrific job of caring for them while I was gone and while I was home. They couldn't have wanted a better mother and I couldn't have wanted a more encouraging wife.

During my first two years on staff, I was one busy fellow. When I was in the office, I was writing and editing; when I was out of the office, I was preaching. My writing consisted of everything from articles in *YFC Magazine* to copy for donor mailings and promotional folders. (We were always promoting some great YFC event.) I also wrote teen books that were distributed by "Miracle Books." *A Guidebook to Ephesians* was published in 1957 to be used by the YFC quizzers, and *A Guidebook to Galatians* followed the next year. These were the first Bible study books I ever published, never dreaming that more than a hundred titles would follow.

I confess that I also did some "ghostwriting" for some of the men whose schedules were full or whose idea account had gone temporarily bankrupt. The magazine had deadlines to meet and we couldn't wait for late copy. I've never investigated the ethics of ghostwriting, but I'm amazed to see how much of it is done in the evangelical publishing world. More than one well-known preacher or ministry leader depends on ghostwriters to produce the books and magazine articles that bear their names, and some of them even have "ghost preachers" to supply them with sermons.

More than once, I've been asked how many research assistants I've had to help me write sermons, radio messages, books, and articles, and when I say "none," people don't believe me. I've discovered that if I maintain my walk with the Lord, read widely, build a file of ideas, stay in contact with people, keep my eyes and ears open, and budget my time wisely, the Lord helps me write what I have to write when I need it. Nothing I've written will win a Pulitzer Prize, but at least what I've written has met somebody's need somewhere, and at least I've met my deadlines.

Sometimes instead of ghostwriting a piece, I'd write the article myself and use a pen name. Ken Anderson used to help me in this journalistic brinkmanship. Ken's pen name was "Norman E. King" and mine was "David Warren," my older son's given names. At that time, Ken was associated with Gospel Films in Grand Rapids. Later he started his own studio in Winona Lake, Indiana and became involved in training Christian cinematographers and journalists overseas. I picked up a lot of practical journalistic know-how from Ken whom I consider to be one of the most creative Christians I've ever met.

Our magazine readers, of course, didn't know what Ken and I were doing, and we'd receive letters from readers complaining about Norman E. King (or David Warren) and asking for more articles from Ken Anderson and Warren Wiersbe! Sometimes it was the other way around. It just shows that you can fool some of the people some of the time.

While on this theme, I must tell you about my ghosting for Ted Engstrom. A Christian publisher of Sunday School literature regularly requested him to write youth programs for a curriculum they produced for local churches. The publisher would assign the theme (dating, Christmas, Bible study, or what have you) and give you the format to follow; all you had to do was pour in the content and make it sound exciting. Ted was just too busy to write these programs, so I did it for him, and we split the honorarium. The same publisher occasionally asked me to write for them, which I was glad to do. More than once, "Ted's material" was accepted on the spot while mine was sent back to be reworked! Maybe that was my punishment for playing "Let's Fool the Editor."

Along with my own articles and the ghosted pieces, my writing for *YFC Magazine* included book reviews and the "devotional calendar" which I called "Prep Time." The word "Prep" was an acronym for the four "steps" to a healthy devotional time: Prepare yourself to meet with God; Read the Bible; Examine your life; Pray. When under the leadership of Harold Myra, *YFC Magazine* became *Campus Life*, this feature was wisely dropped.

Another one of my tasks was to scan the scores of publications that came to the office each month from organizations that were on our "exchange" list. Many of these were denominational publications that would print our YFC news releases and thereby prove that I was not laboring in vain. Ted would look at the publications first, mark important items, and then give the stack to me. While I was scanning the magazines for YFC news, I also noted other items of interest and clipped them out to be used in a newsletter I wrote called "Horizons" which was sent regularly to all YFC directors.

"Horizons" was a potpourri of YFCI news and promotion, plus facts and statistics I'd gleaned about teenagers, interspersed with ideas for promoting local rallies and clubs, plus anything else that might help a local YFC staff do their job better. Eventually, "Horizons" became a monthly magazine called *YFC Eye* (YFCI—clever, no?) which I ground out for nearly two years, with the help of Carol Thiessen, whom you'll meet later. Each department head had a column and Carol and I dropped in "Horizons" and whatever else would help give us sixteen pages of reading matter.

In October 1959 after about two years as editor, Vernon McLellan resigned to move to another ministry, and I was asked to take over as editor-in-chief. Vern had done a splendid job of bringing new ideas to both the design and content of the publication and he wasn't an easy man to follow. I'd had two years' experience in the "magazine meetings," so I knew pretty well what to expect, and I knew Ted would back me and give me all the help I needed. Furthermore, accepting the new post meant I wouldn't have to be on the road as much, a fringe benefit Betty and I welcomed with joy. I think the children did too.

I was moved to a different office, given a new title and new responsibilities, and was even granted a raise in salary, but I wasn't replaced in the Literature Division. It was assumed that I would keep editing and publishing books and writing copy for promotional pieces and whatever else needed to be printed. Fortunately, Ted had already recruited Carol Thiessen from the staff of Moody Church to be my Editorial Assistant, so between the two of us, we managed to keep the presses rolling.

Carol had been part of Detroit's "Voice of Christian Youth" for several years, so she came to YFCI with just the experience needed. She also came from an illustrious evangelical family. Her father, John C. Thiessen, was one of the esteemed instructors at Detroit Bible College, now Tyndale College, and her uncle, Henry C. Thiessen, chaired the Bible and Philosophy Department at Wheaton College and wrote a popular systematic theology text. (It was his book that carried me through my ordination examination.)

Carol was the best assistant any editor could want. She could do anything: write an article, issue a press release, edit a book, design a folder, proofread copy, run a mimeograph machine, and even build a display booth. One year at the Winona Lake convention, Carol built the *YFC Magazine* booth while I sat in our makeshift office grinding out press releases. Knowing my lack of manual dexterity, the staff took this in stride, but Ted thought it was very funny. (I doubt that he could have built the booth.) Carol is now on the editorial staff of *Christianity Today,* along with two other former YFC-ers, Harold Myra and Paul Robbins.

As I got more involved with the magazine ministry, I soon discovered that it was the "war department" of YFCI because not everybody was sure what the publication was supposed to be and do. For one thing, *YFC Magazine* was a "house organ" that promoted YFC functions, sold YFC books and trinkets, and reported on YFC doings around the world. At the same time, the magazine was supposed to minister to the teenage reader by sharing the Gospel, encouraging godly living, and teaching the Word. If we had too much YFC news and promotion, some of the teenagers complained. If we had too much "edifying content," some of the rally directors complained. It was a no-win situation.

But that wasn't my biggest problem. Some of the YFC people on the West Coast thought the magazine was too stodgy for teenagers and needed a complete face-lifting and a whole new direction. Under the leadership of Roy McKeown, YFC in California was doing some very creative things; and *YFC Magazine* just didn't excite their teenagers. Every year at the annual convention business meetings, somebody from the Western Area would do an autopsy on the magazine and call for change. Usually a few West Coast directors cornered me between convention meetings and threatened to stop buying and promoting the magazine if we didn't move it into the twentieth century.

Actually, there was more to this battle than disagreement over the magazine. Even back in the late '50s and early '60s, the West Coast in general and California in particular were a different world from New England and the Midwest, and YFC leaders on the West Coast were able to do things in their programs and publications that the rest of the rallies couldn't do without alienating churches and donors. Local and regional Christian standards determined what could be done in YFC rallies and clubs, but the magazine had to be designed for YFC people across the nation, and that wasn't easy.

I may be wrong, but I got the impression that more than one local YFC leader came to the annual Winona Lake Executive Council meetings with a "we/they" attitude, determined to challenge the views of the Wheaton staff and promote their own ideas. Some local rallies were big enough to go it alone and didn't really need the services of the Wheaton office. They owned their own camps and teen centers, and several rallies had their own publications. All of us on the Wheaton staff did what we could to help Ted keep the racehorses running together in the same direction, but it wasn't easy. Being president of Youth for Christ had to be one of the toughest assignments in the Christian world.

On workdays in Wheaton, Wendy Collins, Bruce Love, Bill Eakin, Jack Daniel, and I often went up the street to the drug store for our morning coffee break, during which we'd discuss YFCI policies and politics. We called ourselves "The Bonfire Boys," a name that we borrowed from the Walt Kelly "Pogo" comic strip that was then running in the Chicago *Daily News* and was avidly read by some of us. When Ted or Evon Hedley saw "The Bonfire Boys" assembling, they'd smile benignly at us but secretly wonder what we were up to. Actually, we were up to nothing, but we didn't make that known. We were wrongly identified as a "power bloc" in the office and we wanted it kept that way. Ted could have broken the thing up any time he wanted to, but he humored us along. He knew we were harmless.

That didn't mean he didn't watch the clock, because Ted didn't want us warming a drug store booth when we should have been working at 109 N. Cross Street. However, he knew that all of us were overworked and underpaid, so if we took an extra five minutes, he didn't complain. He also knew that the "upper echelon" of executives sometimes took "working lunch hours" that lasted a lot longer than our coffee breaks.

One morning, I had to get a haircut in order to be ready for a preaching engagement, and I wanted to get to my office without Ted seeing me. But as I walked in the front door of the building, there he was, chatting with the receptionist. Seeing my hair was trimmed, he said rather sternly, "Surely you didn't get a haircut on company time!"

"Why not?" I replied. "It grew on company time."

# CHAPTER ELEVEN

$$\boxed{1}$$

I've mentioned the annual YFC Winona Lake convention several times, so perhaps I'd better pause to tell you what it was like.

Winona Lake, Indiana is a little town on "beautiful Winona Lake," adjacent to Warsaw, Indiana. Warsaw is the county seat of Kosciusko County and has a population of about 8,000. The town of Winona Lake is much smaller, but during the summer, its population swelled as it became the temporary home for thousands of Christians who attended the summer Bible conferences. When you thought of Winona Lake, Indiana you thought of Grace College and Seminary, Winona Lake School of Theology, the Rodeheaver Music Publishing Company, the Westminster Hotel, the Winona Hotel, the Winona Lake Bible Conference, the Billy Sunday Home, and the Billy Sunday tabernacle. Many evangelical believers considered it a sacred place, their summer Mecca.

The Winona Lake Bible Conference was founded at the turn of the century by some of the best-known preachers of that day, including J. Wilbur Chapman, W.E. Biederwolf, and Billy Sunday, who was assisting Chapman at that time. It was an era when, following the example of D.L. Moody's "Northfield," Bible conferences were springing up across America, and Wino-

na Lake was one of the most famous. The British Bible exposi-
tor G. Campbell Morgan once lived there, and Homer
Rodeheaver, Billy Sunday's song leader, lived in a lovely home
on "Rainbow Point," right on the lake. I once had dinner in the
Rodeheaver home with his daughter Ruth Rodeheaver Thomas
as hostess. The only time I met her father was when he came to
Northern Baptist Seminary in 1952 to deliver the "Wilkinson
Lectures." He died in 1955.

The houses adjacent to the conference grounds were owned
by Christians who rented rooms to the summer guests who
couldn't get (or didn't want) reservations in the hotels. Many of
these houses had special names like "Saint's Rest," "Haven of
Rest," "Shiloh," and "Elim." During one YFC convention, it
was my responsibility to give a guided tour of Winona to a *Time*
magazine reporter and his photographer, and they couldn't believe the names on the houses. They kept saying to me, "Is this
for real, or do they do this just for the convention?" I assured
them it was real and that the owners would be greatly offended
if we laughed at the names they had chosen. However, the
rental accommodations didn't always live up to the names on
the houses; many were the jokes told about both the accommodations and the saints who collected the rent.

But God's people didn't mind discomfort as long as they got
to hear great preachers like Donald Grey Barnhouse, H.A. Ironside, Billy Graham, J. Sidlow Baxter, James McGinlay, William
Culbertson, and all the other pulpit giants that conference director J. Palmer Muntz brought to Winona Lake to minister.
Those were the days when the only preachers you could hear
on national radio were M.R. DeHaan, Theodore Epp, and
Charles Fuller, so you had to go to a conference to hear the
others.

For many years, YFCI leased the Winona Lake conference
facilities for two weeks every summer and packed it out with
thousands of teenagers and adults from all over the world. The
basic schedule for an average day looked like this:

7:00 A.M. — Prayer Meeting
9:00 A.M. — "Club House" for teens

10:45 A.M. — Morning Bible Hour in the Tabernacle
1:30 P.M. — Prayer Meeting
2:30 P.M. — Teen Training Seminars, choir rehearsal,
sports program
6:15 P.M. — Counselor Training sessions
6:30 P.M. — "Hillside" service
7:30 P.M. — Evening Rally in the Tabernacle
9:30 P.M. — Film showing

During the second week, dozens of "Teen Talent" and YFC Bible Quiz contests would be going on, and the conference grounds would be gripped by a spirit of excitement.

But don't let that schedule fool you; it was just the tip of the iceberg. All of us on the YFCI staff had our own work to do plus our convention work, so we were busy people. Once each week we'd gather at a local church for an all-night prayer meeting led by Peter Deyneka, Sr.; during the second week, we had to attend the official YFC convention meetings and cast our votes, and some of us were "officials" at the quizzes and contests. Carol Thiessen and I published the daily newspaper and announcement sheet, interviewed people, sent news releases to their home papers, and more than once, I was the speaker for the Morning Bible Hour. During the day, we had to do our share of evangelical politicking, which included greeting the donors and listening to the complaints of the YFC directors.

When did we eat? Usually after we'd finished counseling the people who came forward at the Tabernacle Rally, and there were usually dozens of them. Our work done, we'd drive five miles out of town and converge at the Steer Inn where we'd relax and enjoy a good meal without being interrupted by somebody looking for the solution to a problem or asking for our autograph in their Bible. For two weeks out of the year, all of us were famous. A teenager once asked Wendy Collins if he was famous, and he told her he was; so she asked him to autograph her Bible. He signed "Billy Graham."

The only meeting on that schedule that needs any explanation is "Club House," and I'm not sure anybody can really explain it. You simply had to be there and experience it. "Club House" was designed specifically for the teens—we didn't encourage adults to attend*—and was a combination of a YFC Club meeting, an amateur hour, and a sanctified free-for-all. But it drew hundreds of screaming teens to the Rodeheaver Music Center, an old wooden barn of a building that has since been torn down. Maybe "Club House" helped to hasten its demise.

The program at "Club House" was usually directed by Jack Hamilton, Bill Eakin, Jack Daniel, and Wendy Collins, who in turn drafted anybody they needed to help fill up the hour. One morning Dave Breese was recruited to recite "Casey at the Bat"; and in the middle of his recitation, we threw eggs at him. Like a bunch of clowns, we'd often throw water or confetti on the audience. The teenagers loved it; the adults thought we were crazy. Maybe we were, but the whole idea was to give the kids opportunity to expend their energy so they'd be ready to settle down for the Morning Bible Hour, and it worked.

I think it was Bill Eakin who came up with the idea of having a "teenage radio soap serial" throughout the week, and it fell my lot to write the script, assisted by Eakin and Hamilton and whoever happened to be walking past my office in the conference administration building. There were days when I finished the script just minutes before "Club House" was to start. Our two masterpieces—"Frontier Mortician" and "Crush, the Story of a Teenage Romance"—have since been published and pre-

---

*One day we announced that the teens had to prove they subscribed to *YFC Magazine* or they couldn't get in. Unfortunately, Dr. Theodore Epp, the Morning Bible Hour speaker, chose that day to attend and he couldn't get in. He told Ted and Ted gave us all a lecture on how to treat a visiting dignitary. A few days later, Dr. Epp got wet from water we'd thrown out on the audience. Years later, he must have forgotten (or forgiven) that I was part of that evangelical frivolity; otherwise, he probably wouldn't have invited me to succeed him at Back to the Bible.

sented in many places; fortunately, very few people ever associate the two skits with me!

Dave Foster told me he was at a youth conference in Britain where they presented "Frontier Mortician," and somebody asked Dave who wrote it. "I didn't have the heart to tell him it was one of America's best-known Bible teachers and authors," he told me; I was grateful.

I was the "announcer" for the mock broadcast and frequently interrupted the story with bizarre commercials. The kids loved it. It did them good to see their YFCI "heroes" acting like a bunch of kids themselves.

During one episode of "Frontier Mortician," Pete Quist brought down the house with a slip of the tongue that made him famous forever in YFC. Instead of reading "Why are you strapping me to this table?" he read "Why are you stripping me—" and the crowd exploded. Pete's frequent bloopers were sometimes funnier than the original script.

We did "soap serials" at "Club House" only two years, and then decided to quit while we were ahead—and still had jobs. Some of the adults didn't like "Frontier Mortician" because they thought we were joking about death, which I suppose we were; but as Walt Kelly's "Pogo" said, "Usually you joke about things you aren't afraid of." Anyway, we had a great time writing and producing the programs, and we didn't worry too much about the criticism. YFC staff people weren't hardhearted, but they were thick-skinned.

When you have thousands of people coming and going for two weeks, and you feature in your program some of the finest preachers and musicians in the land, you're bound to attract a few eccentrics, and we had our share. Bob Cook used to remind us, "Remember, boys, where the light shines the brightest, the bugs come flying in."

There was one man who showed up every year at the prayer meetings and prayed the same prayer: "Lord, make Youth for Christ International a national organization." I hope the Lord knew what he was praying about because we sure didn't.

And there was the fellow who came to every meeting wearing his long chain of Sunday School perfect attendance pins. He kept them in the pocket of his coat, but if anybody paid any attention to him, he'd whip them out as fast as the Lone Ranger drew a gun. The chain hung there like a venetian blind, bearing silent witness that the wearer had been out of mischief for many Sunday mornings.

Knowing that Ted Engstrom was involved in publishing, one retired man kept pursuing him with manuscripts in hand and telling him, "God has given me the pen of a ready writer." Gifted at delegating, Ted told him to see me because I was in charge of all the publishing in YFC, so the fellow began to pursue me. He knocked at my hotel room door one afternoon while I was taking a short but badly needed nap.

"The Lord has given me the pen of a ready writer!" he told me after I had opened the door. "I have a book manuscript here that I've written in which I prove that John 3:16 does not teach that God loves the whole world."

"Really?" I replied, with an obvious yawn which he ignored. "Then what does the word *world* mean in John 3:16?"

"The elect!" he almost shouted.

He was suddenly silent, and during the lull, I said: "You know, my brother, life has enough problems even when we believe that God loves the world. What would happen if we *didn't* believe it? Life would be unbearable! I don't suggest you publish that book."

At one of the all-night prayer meetings, some fellow was informing the Lord what had happened that day in various parts of the world, and how those events had fit into what was written in Scripture. I happened to glance up and see Phil and Louie Palermo stealthily moving in his direction. Just then, the man said, "O Lord! I need somebody to help me out!"

"We'll help you out!" said Phil and Louie, and gently taking him by the arm, they led him from the church auditorium and prayed with him privately outside. Somebody started singing a hymn and the meeting was back to normal again. YFC people were always ready, "in season and out of season."

While I'm on the subject of prayer meetings, I must relate the classic story about Peter Deyneka, Sr., who usually led our YFC prayer sessions. The staff had gathered late one evening in the Rainbow Room of the Westminster Hotel, and Peter was praying with great fervor, something he'd learned in his native Russia. The longer he prayed, the louder his voice became, until word came down from the hotel guests that he was keeping them awake.

Getting the message, one of the YFC men said, "Peter, the Lord's not deaf!"

Peter replied, "He's not nervous either!" and kept right on praying.

I first preached at Winona Lake on Tuesday, July 2, 1957, at the 6:30 P.M. Hillside service. This was the unpretentious beginning of a ministry at summer and winter Bible conferences that continued for thirty-five years and took Betty and me from Florida to Oregon and New York to Texas, with several stops in the Midwest on the way to Canada. It's been a full life.

The Hillside at Winona Lake is an area maybe 200 feet from the Billy Sunday Tabernacle where a couple of hundred people shared an informal outdoor service while sitting on park benches on the grassy slope, fighting mosquitoes and flies, and waving to friends passing by. On the raised concrete platform were ancient folding chairs for the participants, a piano that may have entertained Noah's three sons, and the radio engineer's controls. He saw to it that thirty minutes of the forty-five minute service were broadcast over WMBI.

If you were asked to preach on the Hillside, you had to be prepared to rough it. The acoustics were terrible, the insects intolerable, and some of the people unmanageable, especially those with little children. No matter how large the crowd or how enthusiastic their singing, their joyful sound was either swallowed up in the early evening air or drowned out by the musicians rehearsing in the Tabernacle and the motorboats racing on the lake. One evening we even had an airplane overhead pulling a banner inviting us to the auto races on the other side of the lake. On the Hillside, the preacher's only encouragement was the knowledge that the radio listeners could hear him loud and clear, provided the telephone wires were connected and the transmission equipment in working order.

Promptly at 6:25 P.M., the emcee of the meeting would greet the people and give them a pep talk, which included introducing the speaker and making him sound so important that everybody would want to stay there and not drift over to the Tabernacle and get seats for the evening rally. Then the emcee would lead the congregation in the singing of a familiar song, because the people at WMBI wanted the program to come on with "live" music. During the song, the light bulb attached to a nearby tree would suddenly come on, announcing that we were "on the air"; and after finishing leading the hymn, the emcee would say something like this:

"This is _____ welcoming our radio listeners from beautiful Winona Lake where we're gathered on the Hillside on the third day of the Youth for Christ International Thirteenth Annual Convention, and what a day this has been! I only wish you could have been here!" He'd then recapitulate the major events of the day, give the promotion for the next day, and invite everybody listening to drop everything and "drive to beautiful Winona Lake and get in on the blessing."

Then he'd pray briefly and introduce a special musical number, which might be anything from Jack Conners' skillful playing of the marimba to a Teen Talent contestant singing a solo, accompanied by a courageous pianist who not only knew how to push the keys down but also how to pull them up again without interrupting the flow of the music.

By 6:45 P.M., the speaker was supposed to be presented to the radio audience, and he had about thirty minutes to raise the dead. If a speaker actually held his crowd until 7:15 P.M., he was identified as exceptional and promoted from the Hillside to speaking at one of the more important indoor meetings. Fortunately, I'd done enough street preaching not to be distracted by friends calling to each other, children chasing squirrels, or musicians tuning up instruments and vocal cords just a short distance away.

They put me on the Hillside again the next year, and then I graduated to the Morning Bible Hour for the first week of the convention. One year I did a series on "the pictures of the Bible in the Bible" (light, food, water, etc.); and the next time, at the request of the Club Department, I surveyed the Epistle to the Romans, which was the quiz book for the following school year. After I left YFCI for pastoral ministry, Ted was gracious enough to invite me back; on that occasion I taught Philippians, which was also an assigned quiz book.

The Morning Bible Hour was broadcast over WMBI, which gave the speaker an opportunity to reach thousands of people in the WMBI listening audience as well as those in the Billy Sunday Tabernacle. It also meant you didn't waste valuable radio time talking about things that were trivial and irrelevant, nor did you discuss sectarian theology. (The Moody radio people on the grounds always gave the speakers a list of things not to do or say.) I've been involved in Christian radio ministry for over thirty years, and I thank God for what radio has taught me about preaching. I wish every preacher could have at least six months' experience as a radio preacher. It would probably result in the preacher preparing shorter introductions, going on fewer detours, developing clearer outlines, and giving greater emphasis to the essentials of the faith and the importance of personal commitment to Christ. A lot of time and energy are wasted in some pulpits.

However, broadcasting the meeting not only gave a wider audience for preaching, it also gave a wider audience for promoting, and YFC had something to talk about: Teen Talent contests, Teen Teams, *YFC Magazine,* the evening Tabernacle rally, the YFC red leather Bible, visiting dignitaries, overseas visitors, and even lost and found. The week I taught Romans, I got on so late one day that I had less than twenty-five minutes to survey several chapters. It was important that we close by noon or we'd mess up the WMBI afternoon program schedule. Important people like Bob Pierce could go overtime and get away with it, but I wasn't that important.

However, no sooner did I close my study that day when the radio department at Moody Bible Institute and the YFC office at Winona Lake began to get phone calls from angry listeners who insisted that they "cut out the foolishness" and give the preacher time to preach. Some of them even threatened to stop supporting YFC. During the rest of the week, I had all the time I needed for ministry.

# 5

Apart from a great deal of prayer and planning, one of the things that helped to make the annual Winona Lake convention go smoothly was the behind-the-scenes direction and control by the people whose job it was to make things work right and work on time.

Time was a key factor, especially in the evening Tabernacle rallies. If an announcement was too long, or a soloist talked too much before performing, or somebody showed up late, we got nervous because it meant trimming precious minutes from an already packed hour-and-a-half program. The important thing was to prepare the way for the preacher and give him enough time to sow the seed and reap the harvest. In spite of all our frivolity and promotion, the main burden on our hearts at Winona was getting kids to make decisions for Christ. That's what we prayed for and that's what we worked for. We wanted to see the prayer tent filled night after night, with Jim Wright and Ben Weiss and their counselors helping young people trust Christ and find the will of God for their lives.

Believe me, the evening rally was a production. It involved a teen choir of 400 or more voices, an orchestra, special sound effects, special lighting, microphones galore both on and over the huge platform, a big Baldwin organ, at least two concert grand pianos, and dozens of people who would participate in one way or another. And in the wings, calling the signals and watching the clock, were Wendy Collins and Bruce Love. Humanly speaking, these two men held the key to the meeting's success night after night.

It was an education to watch the evening rally from behind the scenes. Wendy and Bruce were a perfect team, keeping touch with the men who ran the lights and the sound system, helping the participants take their cues on time, calming the nervous, giving orders to the hesitant, and even sympathizing with the people who complained that they weren't getting enough time on the program. I once saw Wendy cancel a number by a well-known soloist because there just wasn't enough time for the song. That's when you found out who among the musicians was really a professional. The amateurs got angry and sat in the wings pouting, while the real pros took the cancellation in stride and rejoiced that somebody else had a chance to minister, even if there wasn't time for their own presentation.

During the 1958 Winona Lake convention, we opened each evening rally by launching a "rocket" from the platform, with the choir doing the countdown and then singing John Peterson's "It Took a Miracle." But even the launching of a rocket didn't upset Wendy and Bruce, whose record was better than that of NASA. I don't recall their having to abort a single launch.

## Chapter Eleven

Nineteen fifty-nine was a special year for YFC and a very full one. It was our fifteenth anniversary year and we called it our "Year of Miracles." It began in January with the Tenth World Congress on Evangelism in Madras, India, and climaxed December 28–30 with 10,000 teens and adults spending three days in Washington, D.C., at the first "Capital Teen Convention." Between those two events occurred our regular Winona Lake convention, two leadership training schools in Kansas City, the Eleventh World Congress in Mexico City, and a conference at Boca Raton, Florida.

I didn't attend the Madras Congress, but in preparing the copy for the promotional folder, I got a painful introduction to the delicate issues involved in international politics. Some of the staff thought we needed to say something about the need to evangelize India now because of increased Communist activity in the country, so I included that in the copy. The staff liked what I wrote, but the India Consulate in Washington didn't, and a week before the delegates were to leave for the congress, the forty visas Sam Wolgemuth had applied for were all refused.

Did we ever pray! The delegates had planned a brief visit to the Holy Land en route to India, and by faith they left for Beirut. Sam contacted missionary Cliff Robinson in New Delhi, and Cliff suggested that Sam send him a cable that he could present to Premier Nehru, stating that YFCI was a nonpolitical religious organization seeking to help young people. Sam sent the cable, by the grace of God Cliff got it to Nehru, and the decision was reversed. All the visas reached the delegates in Beirut in time for them to fly to the congress in Madras.

Not a bad series of miracles to start off our "Year of Miracles"! You can be sure that from then on, I was very careful what I wrote, no matter what the other staff men might suggest.

I did attend the World Congress in Mexico City, my first and last ministry visit to Mexico. A few weeks before we were sched-

167

uled to leave, I began waking up in the mornings with headaches and pains in my neck. Our doctor thought it might be from an infected tooth, so I went to my dentist, and sure enough, one of my lateral incisors was abscessed and had to come out. I lost my headaches and neck pains, but I gained a temporary partial plate with one tooth on it that was difficult to keep in place. "My plate is sort of a blessing," I wrote Betty from Mexico City, "because it forces me to slow down and enunciate more clearly—good when using an interpreter." If the thing had fallen out during a sermon, I was prepared to say, "Well, I'm telling you the tooth, the whole tooth, and nothing but the tooth." But I doubt that the interpreter would have known what to do with the statement. After I returned home, my dentist put in a beautiful permanent tooth that I'm still wearing.

We flew on Mexicana Airlines and I noticed that the stewards on the plane were wearing ordinary street clothes and not their official uniforms. Their explanation was simple but not too logical: *they were on strike.* I was glad to see that the cockpit crew were wearing their uniforms. At least they weren't thinking about walking off the job. "The Lord was with us on the flight," I wrote Betty, "no sickness or trouble; and I got a whole book read."

We arrived to discover that much of the expected preparation for the congress had not been made. Our dear Mexican brethren had arranged for an auditorium for Sunday afternoon's opening rally, but they hadn't provided any chairs to seat the expected 3,000 people! I admired Ted as he patiently (through an interpreter) questioned the local committee to find out what still needed to be done and then told one of the YFC staff to go do it along with one of the local committee members. It was important that we not give the impression that we were invading and taking over. Eventually, everything got straightened out and the rally was a success. Ted spoke and several hundred people responded to the invitation.

At 6 o'clock that evening, all of us were given our preaching assignments. "My gang had to taxi to the middle of nowhere," I wrote home. "Even the taxi driver got lost, and he didn't speak any English, so it's a miracle we got to the church at all. The meeting had actually started at 6:00, so when we arrived at 7:55 (late), the invitation was over. But we greeted the folks, the girls sang and played, and I gave a *short* message."

As usual, my job at the congress was press and public relations, as well as putting out a daily news sheet for the American delegates. I also assisted Dave Grant in the daily session for the college kids. YFC had rented space on the sixth floor of a downtown office building and furnished it with a telephone, an English typewriter (somebody rewrote my releases for the Spanish press), and a Gestetner mimeograph machine. Some company donated the furniture and halfway through the congress came and hauled it away!

When I wasn't in the office, I was attending a congress meeting or a planning session, speaking at a meeting, or resting in room 438 at the Regis Hotel, trying not to get sick. My doctor in Wheaton, Marvin DeHaan, son of radio preacher M.R. DeHaan, told me how to stay well: drink only bottled water or boiled water (coffee, tea); keep your mouth shut in the shower; eat no fresh fruit, vegetables, or salads, and use bottled water when you brush your teeth. He gave me some pills to take daily and they worked. I was one of the few American delegates who didn't spend several days during the congress either languishing in bed or wearing out the plumbing.

Not having an international stomach, I played it safe at meals. My breakfast every morning was coffee, two pieces of toast, and two hard-boiled eggs. After a few days, when the waitresses saw me walk into the hotel coffee shop, they knew exactly what to prepare. At the end of the two weeks, both the hen and I were bored, but I didn't care. I'd been born with a cellophane stomach that could make me throw up just by thinking about it, and I saw no reason to take any chances. Even at home, I had to be careful what I ate, and I wasn't about to experiment with bilingual regurgitation.

Wendy Collins was in charge of assigning where the preachers would speak each night, a task that he called "blessed organized confusion." I don't know how many evangelical Protestant churches there were in greater Mexico City, or how many of them even wanted YFC speakers, but the list and schedule Wendy was given was woefully inadequate, and he had to start from scratch and compile a new one. I don't know how he did it, but in a short time, he had the best, and perhaps the only, register of evangelical churches in Mexico City, and he practically had to guard it with his life.

With over eighty teams going out each evening, there were bound to be some mix-ups, but they shouldn't happen to the president. Ted Engstrom was sent to speak at one of the city's largest evangelical churches, and with him were three girls from Owasso, Michigan, known as "The Owasso Trio." (What else?) Their singing and playing in a YFC Teen Talent contest had earned them the privilege of going to the congress. I can't recall what instruments they played, but one of them carried a big bass fiddle.

Ted and the girls arrived at the assigned church while the service was in progress and had to walk down a long center aisle, instruments and all, to get to the platform. Once on the platform, Ted introduced himself to the presiding minister as the president of Youth for Christ and the speaker for the evening.

"No, señor," replied the pastor. "That's tomorrow evening."

It did no good to argue in public, so Ted said, "Well, since we're here, can't we do something?"

"No, señor. That's tomorrow evening."

Not wanting to parade again down that long center aisle, Ted asked if the platform door would take them outside, and being assured that it would, he and the girls opened the door and started walking down a long hall, Ted graciously carrying the bass fiddle. The farther they walked, the narrower the hall became, until they found themselves at a rather close-fitting dead end. (Remember, they're carrying large instruments, including a bass fiddle, and Ted Engstrom is six feet two inches tall.) There was nothing to do but turn around, walk down the hall, open the platform door, march down the stairs, and ignominiously exit down the center aisle.

I never did find out what happened the next night.

The concept of the Capital Teen Convention was born in the heart of Bill Carle, YFC's singing ambassador. Bill saw it as an opportunity for thousands of teens to get a good dose of religion and patriotism while at the same time telling the world that not every American teenager is a juvenile delinquent. The architect of the convention was Roy McKeown, YFC vice president for the Western Area and director of Los Angeles YFC. There were obstacles and problems galore, but God used Roy and his staff to get the job done, and before the convention ended, over 1,000 teens had trusted Christ and more than 2,000 had responded to a call for dedication to Christian service.

The promotional folder for the convention called the event "Our Greatest Venture of Faith," and it was. The office clowns had a lot of fun with that slogan. "This is something you can really get your teeth into — Our Greatest Denture of Faith." We all had tons of extra work to do during the busy Christmas season preceding the convention, but it was worth it.

I got to sit right up front at the Press Table and mingle with reporters from dozens of newspapers and periodicals. They couldn't understand how thousands of energetic young people could be together for three days and still be so well-behaved. One of the local papers printed an editorial commending the YFC teens for proving that young people didn't have to get in trouble in order to have a good time. The hotel managers were amazed that there had been no riots in the halls and that nothing had been damaged. Washington, D.C. welcomes thousands of high school seniors every year, but December 28–30, 1959 the city noticed that the Christian crowd was different.

Ted wrote in the February 1960 issue of *YFC Eye,* "Thanks to every one of you terrific rally and club men who made the Capital Teen Convention the tremendous success that it was! Here was YFC teamwork at its very best. To my mind, this

Convention was the finest event in YFC's history—and what a climax to our fifteen years and the ("Miracle Year") program. To God be the glory!"

In 1960, YFCI launched its "Decade of Destiny" ten-year program, but I was destined to be a part of it for less than two years. By September 1961, Betty and I would be back in the pastorate, this time in Kentucky.

# PART FOUR
# Calvary Baptist Church

# CHAPTER TWELVE

$$\boxed{1}$$

In 1956, YFC began holding an annual midwinter convention which usually met for four days in a Chicago area hotel. It was primarily a time of inspiration, fellowship, and instruction for YFC workers at a time of the year when we were prone to suffer post-holiday doldrums. It was also a good time to promote the YFC events for the coming year.

The 1961 midwinter convention convened at the beautiful Ambassador Hotel in Los Angeles. It wasn't a sacrifice at all for the Wheaton staff to bid farewell to a Chicago winter for a week and head for sunny California. As always, Roy McKeown and his staff treated us like royalty and made sure everything was done with the efficiency and polish that was their trademark.

"From the looks of this program," Ted wrote in the December 1960 *YFC Eye,* "this year's Midwinter Convention is going to be the greatest in YFC's history." The fact that there had been only five midwinter conventions in YFC's history didn't keep Ted from using superlatives. But he was right; it was a great convention.

The *Los Angeles Times* gave us some excellent publicity and even quoted from one of the seminars I gave on "The American Teenager." But the big news was Ted's announcement on Thursday evening that YFC would sponsor a "World Teen Convention" in Jerusalem sometime after Christmas in 1963. The success of the Capital Teen Convention had convinced all of us that YFC was ready to conquer the world. The *Times* article about the "parley in Jerusalem" was accompanied by a photo of Ted Engstrom, Roy McKeown, and me, all staring off into space as though we'd just heard the sound of the trumpet. Ted looks like he's whistling or had just sat down on an ice cube. How I got included in the picture is a mystery to me, except that I probably gave the reporter the Jerusalem congress press release.

"Where will you house that many people at prices they can afford?" somebody asked.

"We'll use tents if we have to," was the reply, and the Wheaton wits immediately began calling the event "The Capital Tent Convention."

"How will you handle practical everyday things like hygiene and meals?"

"If the Lord could take care of 2 million Jews for forty years in the desert, He can take care of us for a week. We'll work it out." To us, nothing was impossible.

Over the centuries, the Holy City has seen many invasions, but it was spared the experience of 25,000 teenagers from around the world converging on its sacred soil, because the World Teen Convention never took place. The sheer magnitude of the logistics, the size of the budget, and the situation in the Middle East combined to turn our dream into a nightmare, and the idea was abandoned.

Some YFCI staff members weren't too excited about the Jerusalem Convention to begin with, but we had a good time discussing it. Over our coffee cups, the Bonfire Boys suggested the following seminars: Walking on the Water; Cooking with Manna; Getting Water from a Rock; Considering the Lilies; and Rapid Reading from Right to Left. Given enough time, maybe Phil and Louie Palermo could have presented a session on conversational Hebrew.

2

But all during that convention in Los Angeles, I was fidgety and uncomfortable. More than once I said to myself, "What am I really doing here?" When the rest of the delegates went to Disneyland for the afternoon, I went to my room to think and pray and read my Bible. I would rather have gone to Disneyland, but something was wrong in my soul that had to be settled.

I knew what it was but I didn't want to face it. I'd experienced that same disquieting feeling during my last year at Central Baptist Church before the Lord moved me to YFCI. It was the Lord "detaching" me and preparing me to move to another ministry. Betty and I were happy in Wheaton, enjoying our home, friends, church, and ministry; a change wouldn't be easy for any of us in the family.

I was scheduled to fly home Friday and leave the next day for Covington, Kentucky, to speak for Dr. Eastep at the Sunday services of Calvary Baptist Church. Dr. Eastep had experienced a heart attack in 1959 and had invited me to fill the pulpit several times. I guess I was candidating and didn't know it. I'd spoken there two Sundays in 1959 and then conducted a week-long Bible conference the fall of 1960. But during the weekend of January 8, 1961, I was to discover that he wanted me someday to come to Covington to serve as his associate and then become pastor of the church. He had hinted at this during the Bible conference the previous autumn, but he didn't seem to be in a hurry, and neither was I. Apparently this had been in his mind and his prayers ever since he'd ministered at Central Baptist Church back in 1954. You never know when somebody's measuring you.

Betty and I prayed a lot and began to watch for indications of the Lord's leading. But the longer we prayed, the more convinced I was that we had to make our move quickly. (The Lord didn't explain why until a year later.) One day in May, I phoned

Dr. Eastep and told him I felt my work was winding up at YFCI and that we were prepared to come to Covington that fall if the church wanted us. This caught him by surprise because he wasn't planning for us to make this move for another two years, and he wasn't sure adequate housing would be available by September.

Dr. Eastep was scheduled to speak in Springfield, Illinois at the end of May, so on Friday, June 1, Betty and I drove to Springfield to confer with him and Mrs. Eastep about the details of the new ministry. Everything seemed to fall into place, and Betty and I felt good about accepting the call. We knew our leaving YFCI would be misunderstood by some and criticized by others, but that was even true when we left Central Baptist.

Dr. Eastep phoned me June 15 to tell me that the evening before, the church had enthusiastically voted to call us, so now I had to tell Ted. It hurt me to give Ted that letter of resignation, because I knew it would hurt him to receive it, but we both knew we had to obey the Lord's will and trust God to work out the problems. We didn't have anybody to handle *YFC Magazine,* so I agreed to edit it "at a distance" until God sent a replacement. Ron Wilson eventually followed me as editor, assisted by Harold Myra, one of our contributing writers whom I'd been "nurturing." Eventually Harold became editor, and that led to a new name — *Campus Life* — and a new and exciting ministry for both him and the magazine. Today Harold's directing the influential *Christianity Today* publishing enterprises, and it all started when he sent his first article to *YFC Magazine* and we bought it. I delight in telling people "I knew him when!"

The following letter appeared in the Calvary Baptist Church bulletin on Sunday, July 1:

June 19, 1961

Dear Dr. Eastep:

This is to confirm our recent conversation of June 15, 1961. I am thrilled with the call to become associate pastor of Calvary Baptist Church and feel that the Lord would have me accept the call.

I have given my resignation to Dr. Engstrom, effective September 1, 1961. My wife and I sense only too deeply the prayer we are going to need to minister effectively for His glory. We realize our weaknesses and certainly want to encourage the people of the church to pray for us. The assurance of their love and prayers would be the greatest encouragement we could have as we begin our ministry among them.

May the Lord grant Calvary Baptist Church many blessings as we work together in the days that remain before He comes again.

Sincerely in Christ,

Warren Wiersbe

I preached at Calvary on July 16, and the next weekend, Betty and David flew down with me so the church could get acquainted with them and they with the church. It was one of the worst plane rides I've ever experienced—there must have been deep holes in the air pockets—but David sat through it as though flying were always like that. I didn't tell him otherwise.

It was a demanding summer.

I was scheduled to be the Bible Hour speaker the first week of the Winona Lake convention and also to preach in August during the YFC week at Maranatha Bible Conference in Muskegon, Michigan. At the same time, Betty and I had to sell the house, pack our belongings, prepare four children for the move, and wind down our responsibilities in Wheaton. We also wanted to squeeze in a week's vacation with her parents in Clinton, Wisconsin. I had the magazine to edit and some other writing deadlines to meet, so it was a busy time. But we could tell that people were praying and God was lubricating the machinery for us.

Dr. Eastep phoned to see if we could delay our move a couple of weeks until the church got the housing cared for to his satisfaction. Knowing that they would have to build a new sanctuary someday, Calvary Baptist Church had purchased several houses on Tibbatts Street; and we were to live in one of them. Mr. and Mrs. George Evans lived next to the church and offered to move up the street and let the Wiersbes live in 3711 Tibbatts. George had been a deacon in the church for many years and Mrs. Evans was on the staff as church visitor, ministering primarily to the shut-ins and the older women. The Evanses turned out to be the best friends and helpers any pastor and his family could ever want.

Our real estate ad in the *Chicago Tribune* drew some inquiries but no buyers, and we had to leave the house unsold when we moved on September 13. Eventually a family moved in and rented it from us, and when they relocated, we sold the house at a loss to the first buyer who came along. In a wonderful gesture of generosity, Calvary Church made up the difference. That's the kind of people they were; they loved their pastors and couldn't do enough for them.

Let me tell you about the church.

Because of Dr. Eastep's unique ministry, Calvary Baptist Church in Covington, Kentucky was widely known in the '60s; but when the church was organized in 1920, its beginnings were anything but auspicious. The church grew out of a split in a church in the Latonia section of Covington, a split that had something to do with some church officers attending the Latonia Race Track, one of the most popular places in northern Kentucky. The new church floundered—three pastors in the first six years—but then called D.B. Eastep on March 6, 1927, and things began to change.

"I would never have accepted the call to be pastor had I known of the conditions that existed in the church," Dr. Eastep said later, but he was certainly God's man for that ministry. His compassionate pastoral work, his faithful exposition of the Bible, and the emphasis on prayer and pastoral leadership brought both conflict and blessing to the church, but eventually the work began to prosper. When the church started in 1920, there were eighty-nine people in the Bible (Sunday) School. When we arrived there in 1961, the average attendance was ten times that amount.

The Bible was central at Calvary. The annual Bible conference brought to the church such outstanding preachers as W.B. Riley, William Pettingill, James McGinlay, Vance Havner, Norman B. Harrison, Herbert Lockyer, Sr., and H.A. Ironside. In 1930, Dr. Eastep had set up his "Whole Bible Study Course" for the Sunday School (which he preferred to call Bible School), and he prepared the study outlines which were distributed to the classes. Everybody from the junior high department through the adult classes followed the schedule and studied the whole Bible in seven years, covering the key chapters in every book in the Old Testament and every chapter of every New Testament book except Mark and Luke. Dr. Eastep taught all the teachers each Wednesday evening before the midweek service, and this enabled the personnel in the younger departments to keep up with the course.

After we'd accepted the call to the church, Dr. Eastep asked me to start writing the study outlines, beginning with the minor prophets. (The church was then going through the Bible for the fifth time.) Once we'd moved to Covington, I also taught the teachers each week before the midweek service. During our ten years of ministry at the church, I wrote expository outlines for the entire "Whole Bible Study Course." Eventually these outlines were collected into two volumes and published by Calvary Book Room. I don't know how many thousands of sets of these simple outlines have been distributed, but I've received appreciative letters from people all over the world, especially missionaries and pastors, telling of the help the outlines have given them in their study of the Bible. Since then, I've revised and expanded the original outlines, and now the two volumes are available from Victor Books.

The organization of the church was simple. Along with a Sunday School staff, there was a board of deacons, elected by the church and chaired by the pastor, and that was it. (We had a trustee board too, but only to satisfy the laws of the Commonwealth of Kentucky.) The deacons and pastor met monthly, usually before the Sunday evening service, and church business was carried on by the congregation at the midweek service. The church staff, deacons, and Sunday School workers pretty much made the plans, and the congregation was happy to follow their leadership.

I must mention that we didn't take up collections at our public meetings, except for love offerings for visiting preachers or missionaries. There were collection boxes at each of the exits and the people were encouraged to put their tithes and offerings in the boxes as a part of their worship. One Sunday, a little boy who was visiting asked his friend what the boxes were for, and the lad said, "That's where we put our offerings for the Lord."

"How does the Lord get the money?" the visitor asked.

"I'm not sure," his friend replied. "I think Brother Eastep empties the boxes and then gives the money to God."

One other feature marked Calvary as unique among churches: the congregation practiced church discipline. I had tried to exercise church discipline in my first pastorate, but I failed miserably and only made enemies. However, at Calvary, the members respected the leadership of the pastors and deacons and sought to walk in the fear of the Lord. We didn't have to do it often, but there were a few times when repentant members were publicly forgiven and restored, and unrepentant members were publicly dismissed. Dr. Eastep did a good deal of pastoral work that involved behind-the-scenes discipline, and I learned to follow his example.

As I look back on our ministry at Calvary, I thank God that our family was there during those ten critical years when our children were growing up. When we moved to Covington, David was six years old, Carolyn was four, Bob, three, and Judy only one and a half, but they were privileged to grow up in a church where the Lord was honored, the Bible was taught systematically, God's people were loved and disciplined, and their father didn't have to attend a committee meeting every night of the week.

We usually had our evenings together as a family, and if I had to be out of town in ministry, I knew that the staff and the whole church family would keep an eye on Betty and the children and give them any help they needed in an emergency. Our annual summer vacation was a delightful time at Williams Bay, Wisconsin, not far from Betty's family in Clinton, and we were able to visit my family in Hammond, Indiana as we drove up and back. At "the Bay," the children were able to swim, fish, and be pampered by their grandparents, and I caught up on my reading and napping.

# 5

Vance Havner was conducting a Bible conference at Calvary the week we moved in next door to the church. I'd heard him preach many times from Winona Lake and Moody Founder's Week, but this was the first time I'd had the privilege of meeting him personally. I feel sorry for today's younger generation of believers who never got to hear Vance Havner in person. He was unique and nobody can replace him. When I read his books, I hear his voice speaking, and what he says does my heart good. I was privileged in later years to share conferences with him at Winona Lake and Moody Bible Institute, and he preached for us at Moody Church, and the fellowship we enjoyed was very special. I miss him.

There were nine of us on the church staff in 1961: Dr. Eastep, who was now in his thirty-fourth year as pastor; myself, associate pastor (but everybody knew who the "boss" was); Mrs. D.B. Eastep and her sister Mrs. Dorothy Kidd, who managed Calvary Book Room; Bob Montgomery, minister of music; Raymond Abbott, building superintendent, assisted by Loretta Carter; Mrs. Wilda Smith, church secretary and Dr. Eastep's secretary since 1942; and Mrs. George Evans, church visitor.

We called each other "brother" and "sister," and all of the staff lived in church-owned houses adjacent to the church buildings. (The Easteps and Mrs. Kidd lived in a lovely apartment on the second floor of the new beginner building.) I've enjoyed all the staff people I've worked with over the years, but there was something very special about the Calvary staff, and they will always have a cherished place in our hearts.

My ministry was to help Dr. Eastep in the preaching and pastoral work, write the material for his "Whole Bible Study Course," and oversee the youth ministry. When Dr. Eastep was out of town in meetings, which was frequently, I'd do the Sunday preaching, teach his men's Bible School class, and lead the Wednesday evening service, which usually drew 400–500 people. I know there's nothing magical about the midweek service, but I'm sorry to see it dying across our country. At Calvary, we found it to be an oasis in the middle of the week, a time when we could encourage each other, pray, and learn from the Word.

On January 4, 1962 we inaugurated "The City-Wide Bible Class" which met on Thursday evenings in our chapel, and I was the teacher. It was an opportunity for people from the area to get systematic Bible teaching without abandoning their own churches. The newspaper advertisement said: "An informal, informative, and inspiring hour with the Bible that will enrich your life and help solve your problems." It also assured people that I had "a unique way of making the Bible come alive [using] blackboard charts and outlines. . . ." The chapel was packed the first several weeks of the class, which meant at least 200 people, and I taught Ephesians each week until spring. The next year I taught "Christ in the Old Testament," and then the Book of Revelation.

There was a lot of work for me to do, and there were a lot of people to care for, but Calvary Baptist Church was a pastor's paradise, and I felt privileged to be there.

# 6

On Monday morning, March 19, 1962, our phone rang at about 6 o'clock. It was Mrs. Kidd.

"Brother Wiersbe, please come to the apartment right away," she said. "Mr. Eastep passed away during the night."

I hurriedly dressed and quickly walked to the apartment where Mrs. Kidd met me at the door. Mrs. Eastep was in the living room weeping quietly. Dr. Eastep was lying in his bed, but his soul was home with the Lord. He had preached the day before at Norwood Baptist Church in Cincinnati and had come home feeling quite well. In fact, a few weeks before, he had gone to the Cleveland Clinic for his annual checkup, and the reports had been very encouraging. On March 4, the congregation had celebrated his thirty-fifth year as pastor of the church, and I was looking forward to working at his side for many years and learning from him. But he was taken from us, and now we all knew why the Lord wanted me and my family in Covington so soon.

Their son Dan, an aeronautical engineer at General Electric in Cincinnati, soon arrived at the apartment, and difficult as it was, we had to start making plans for the funeral and the ministry transition that had to come. The news of Dr. Eastep's death spread rapidly, not only in northern Kentucky but across the country, and soon the church office was receiving phone calls from people asking, "Is it really true?" The Monday evening *Kentucky Post* published an article that was more a tribute than an obituary, and even the local radio stations announced his homegoing.

His body lay in state in the church auditorium from Tuesday afternoon through Wednesday afternoon, and at 2 o'clock, the funeral took place. Working in shifts, some of the men of his Bible class served as an honor guard all Tuesday night. D.B. Eastep had been the unofficial "bishop" of northern Kentucky, the friend of pastors who needed encouragement and counsel, and the shepherd of a devoted flock, and now he was in heaven. The church family was in a state of shock, and outsiders were predicting that, with Dr. Eastep off the scene, the church would start to die.

Wednesday, March 21, was a difficult day for all of us. The church auditorium was packed with mourners, but as I conducted the funeral service, assisted by Bob Montgomery, I felt buoyed up by the love and prayers of the Calvary church family. There was a long funeral procession to the cemetery where we laid the body to rest. That evening at the midweek service, Don Suttles, one of the deacons, read Joshua 1, made several practical comments, and then announced that the deacons recommended that the church call me as pastor, and they did. God buries His workers but His work goes right on.

Thursday morning I was at the church assisting Mrs. Smith in cleaning out Dr. Eastep's desk and answering his mail when George Evans walked in and said he wanted to see me. Betty and I had learned to love George Evans and his wife; they had practically adopted our two boys, especially Bob, who became a substitute grandson to them. But what did George want?

When we were alone, he looked at me with tears in his eyes and said:

"Brother Eastep was my pastor for many years, and now he's gone. I want you to know that now you're my pastor and I'll do anything that has to be done to help you carry the load and get the job done. I'll wash your car, polish your shoes, drive you to meetings. I'm here to serve the Lord and you just as I did when

Brother Eastep was here."

I was speechless; I wanted to cry. Even now, as I relive the scene in my imagination, I can't keep the tears from coming. I never asked George to polish my shoes or wash my car, but I did lean on him for counsel and prayer support, and he was one of the finest deacons any pastor could ever want. In fact, the way all the deacons and church family rallied around their new young pastor—I was only thirty-two years old—brought me and Betty the strength and encouragement we needed. In her thank-you letter to the church family in the April 1 bulletin, Mrs. Eastep wrote, "As we have followed Eastep for the past thirty-five years, we shall follow Pastor Wiersbe as he follows the Lord and leads us in serving Him."

Dr. Eastep had been preaching a series from Hebrews 11 at the midweek service, so I just picked it up the next Wednesday and kept it going. I also continued the Sunday morning series I'd been giving on the seven words of Jesus from the cross. I don't recall that I had to cancel any of the Bible conferences that were on my schedule, but I did have to write a lot of pastors who thought I was going to fulfill Dr. Eastep's schedule! Some of them just couldn't understand why his schedule didn't go right along with the job!

As the weeks progressed, it became evident that I would need an assistant to help carry the load, particularly the work among the young people of the church. Providentially, I was scheduled to speak in May at YFC in Charleston, West Virginia, and there I renewed my acquaintance with Cedric and Jean Whitcomb, whom I'd first met when I was in Wheaton and Cedric was directing YFC in Racine, Wisconsin. In fact, it had been my privilege to marry Cedric and Jean at Calvary Memorial Church in Racine where Cedric had grown up. During that weekend, as I watched them work with the teenagers, I began to get the impression that this was just the couple I was looking for to assist me at Calvary.

Cedric and Jean spent Thanksgiving week with us in Covington that year and Cedric preached at the evening service on November 25. It was no secret that they were getting acquainted with the church and the church with them. It wasn't until a year later, January 16, 1963, that we were able to issue a call and they were free to respond. They moved to Covington in June 1963, and we had five and a half wonderful years serving together. Cedric and Jean built one of the finest church youth ministries I've seen anywhere. They also gained valuable pastoral experience that helped them prepare to serve effectively when they left Calvary for First Baptist Church, Northville, Michigan.

On Anniversary Sunday, March 24, 1963 — my first anniversary as pastor of the church — we hit a new high in Bible School with 1,565 people attending! It was an exciting day that proved to the pessimists in Covington that D.B. Eastep had done his work well and Calvary Baptist Church was not in danger of dying.

# CHAPTER THIRTEEN

Twice in my ministry I've been called to follow great men of God to whom the Lord had given long and successful ministries: D.B. Eastep at Calvary Baptist Church and Theodore Epp at Back to the Bible broadcast. The second was the more difficult of the two because it involved a worldwide ministry, but I think in both situations, the transitions went smoothly.

One thing that made the transitions easier was the fact that I was handpicked by my predecessors to follow them and was already on the job. Another factor was that I agreed for the most part with the principles of ministry that my predecessors had followed and had no desire to make a lot of immediate changes and start doing things "my way." That some changes had to be made, there was no question, but I had to be patient, prayerful, and wise. Bridge-builders can't afford to rock the boat or they'll end up sinking it.

Over the years, I've seen leaders almost wreck ministries by making too many changes too fast. Instead of getting to know the people, the ministry of the church, and the nature of the "field," they immediately tried to prove themselves "leaders" by moving Sunday School classes, asking people to resign, re-writing the church constitution (to suit their style of leadership), restructuring the services, and appointing a committee to purchase new hymnals. The result was chaos instead of change, and reaction instead of action, and, leaving the wreckage behind, the new pastor then departs for another ministry, leaving it to the next shepherd to find the flock and straighten out the mess.

Another element in my own "bridge-building" that made things easier was the sincere cooperation of the people I had to work with in those ministries. Each time the Lord has put us into a new ministry, we've been given dear dedicated people who helped us find our way and avoid the pitfalls that might have brought embarrassment and damage.

This was certainly true at Calvary. A week after Dr. Eastep's funeral, Mrs. Eastep asked me to visit her at the apartment so we could talk about my future plans for the church. Perhaps some pastors have found it a problem to have their predecessor's family in the congregation, but my experience was just the opposite. During my ten years at Calvary Baptist Church, nobody was more encouraging and helpful than Mrs. Eastep and Dan. In fact, after the funeral, Dan said to me, "I just want you to know that we're behind you 100 percent. If you find any 'Eastepites' causing trouble in the congregation, send them to me!"

During our conversation, Mrs. Eastep assured me of her wholehearted support. "I know that Durward wanted you to succeed him," she said, "so the church didn't look for anybody else. If you hadn't already been here, we'd have had to send to Wheaton to get you. I also know that changes are inevitable in the years to come, but I'm convinced you'll maintain the strong ministry of the Word of God that has built the church."

I told her I wanted her to continue as manager of the Book Room and teacher of her ladies' Bible School class. I also admitted that at the age of thirty-three, I felt totally inadequate to pastor a noted church like Calvary and follow a great and godly man like D.B. Eastep.

"Never mind," she said. "The people love you, God has called you here, and He will help you."

Once again I found myself a bridge-builder, this time helping a great church define its identity as it ministered in new ways to a new generation.

2

It must have been difficult for ten experienced and seasoned deacons to accept the leadership of a young man who had pastored for only seven years, but they did it, and God blessed our work together. Some of them had served with Dr. Eastep for decades, and yet they gave me the same love and respect that they had given him. This doesn't mean that they were robots who automatically rubber-stamped my ideas, because we had our share of honest disagreements. However, there was a unity of heart and spirit that kept disagreements from becoming divisions, and once a decision was made, we all got behind it and maintained a united ministry.

During our six months together, Dr. Eastep had generously opened his heart and shared his thinking with me, and this was a tremendous help to me as I planned the church's course for the future.

"I'm afraid I overreacted to some things early in my ministry," he said one day as we were out making pastoral visits. "Now I see that I was wrong."

"What kind of things?" I asked.

"Well, I used to brag that we had *preaching* services instead of cantatas at Christmas and Easter, but the Lord can speak to people through good music as well as through a sermon. And I didn't want a kitchen or dining room in our church building because the churches in this area were always having banquets and dinners. But you find a lot of eating going on in the Bible."

In the years that followed, Bob Montgomery and the church musicians presented some wonderful concerts, and after we built the new church sanctuary, we put a kitchen in the old auditorium when we remodeled it. Some of the "old guard" were unhappy with these innovations, but most of the people breathed a sigh of relief that their church was updating its ministry and facilities.

God blessed His people and the work continued to grow. We had over 1,600 people in Bible School on my second anniversary and our average Bible School attendance was starting to get near 1,000. Several guest speakers and musicians ministered at the church, including my YFC buddies Bill Eakin, Bruce Love, and Pete Quist, as well as people like Lehman Strauss, David Allen, Strat Shufelt, Fred Brown, Howard Sugden, Jacob Gartenhaus, Bob Cook, Pat Zondervan, Jack Wyrtzen, and a host of others. Over the years, the Calvary family was privileged to hear some of the finest preachers and musicians in the world.

The church was gracious to let me have a "wider ministry" to speak at schools, churches, and conferences throughout the United States and Canada. Dr. Eastep used to remind the people that it was right to share their pastor with others because the pastor is a gift to the whole church and not just to one local assembly. I was careful not to be gone too much, but some of the folks thought that being gone even one Sunday was too much.

I think it was Dr. R.G. Lee, long-time pastor of Bellevue Baptist Church, Memphis, who said to a church member who complained of his being gone, "Well, look at it this way. If the substitute preacher preaches better than I do, you should be thankful I was gone. If he preaches worse than I do, you should be thankful I came back. Either way, you're thankful!"

In April 1963, I ministered for the first time at the great Highland Park Baptist Church in Chattanooga, Tennessee, pastored at that time by Dr. Lee Roberson. It was a delight to teach the Word to that large congregation and to the many students attending Tennessee Temple University. The school had given Dr. Eastep his honorary Doctor of Divinity degree and would give me one in 1965.

Dr. Lee Roberson is a Christian gentleman. I've known him for over thirty years, and only once do I recall hearing him say a critical word about a brother preacher, and what he said was right and needed to be said. I've seen him walk away from a group of preachers when their conversation was starting to descend to the level of gossip and criticism. His associate J.R. Faulkner is a man who can do anything from preach a sermon to lead a choir or paint a banner for a missions conference. He was Dr. Roberson's right arm at the church, the finest "second man" I've ever seen in any ministry.

In August 1963, Betty and I made the first of many trips to the Canadian Keswick Bible Conference, located north of Toronto on beautiful Lake Rousseau. One of the blessed by-products of that visit was meeting Dr. and Mrs. Howard Sugden who became dear friends and with whom we've often traveled and ministered. Howard was a mighty preacher of the Word and a man who loved good books and good preaching. He had over 20,000 volumes in his library at South Baptist Church in Lansing, Michigan, where he served faithfully for forty years. Lucile is an excellent Bible teacher in her own right, and we had great times together. In 1971, we four went to Great Britain and spent several weeks visiting famous churches and the many historic places with which that land is so greatly blessed. (We also visited bookstores.) We went back again in 1976, and in the years that followed, Betty and I would make fourteen more visits to Great Britain for both ministry and holidays; it's one of our favorite places on Planet Earth.

If ever there was "a pastor's pastor," it was Howard Sugden. Wise in the ways of the Lord and the secrets of the human heart, his counsel was sought by pastors who phoned him, wrote him, and even stopped at his office unannounced, all seeking encouragement and help in solving church or personal problems. It was always a delight to share a pastors' conference with Howard and hear him answer questions. His keen sense of humor kept us amused and his spiritual insights kept us amazed. He and I wrote *Confident Pastoral Leadership* together, a book that pastors tell me has helped them immensely.

Howard and I would chat over the phone perhaps once a week, and occasionally I would go to Lansing to preach at

South Baptist Church. Howard went home to be with the Lord on October 14, 1993, and I miss him. It was my privilege to preach at the funeral service, although it wasn't an easy thing to do. Betty and I have many happy memories of our times with the Sugdens and their friendship has enriched our lives.

# 3

So many things happened during our ten years at Calvary Baptist Church that I can't share them all, but four events stand out: my nearly being killed in an auto accident; my meeting a blind man named George Hipshire; our building a new church sanctuary; and our meeting Dr. and Mrs. D. Martyn Lloyd-Jones.

In 1965, our family moved from Tibbatts Street to a house five miles from the church in the neighboring town of Taylor Mill. The houses next to the church building on Tibbatts Street were destined to come down to make way for the new sanctuary, so the church found a lovely house for us in Taylor Mill that offered the children lots of fresh air and open space. Ray Abbott, our building superintendent, told me he hated to see us leave the neighborhood, but it was probably a good thing because he was running out of glass to repair the church windows that faced our house! Apparently David and Bob, while playing in the backyard, had broken more than one pane with baseballs, arrows, or other unguided missiles, but Ray had never said one word to me about it until the week we moved. Evangelist Fred Brown once told me that if he were a pastor, he'd rather have Calvary's building superintendent on his staff than any staff member from any other church.

On Friday evening, June 10, 1966, Betty and I attended a farewell party for one of our church families who was moving to Hawaii, and we arrived back home about 10 o'clock. After taking Barbara Abbott, the baby-sitter, home, I was driving up

Taylor Mill hill when a car came around the curve going at least eighty miles an hour and hit me head-on. I didn't see the car coming but even if I had, there was no way to avoid the collision. The driver was a young sailor, home on leave, and out enjoying his new car. He and a friend had visited several taverns along Taylor Mill Road and were speeding to their next appointment, which, for the driver, happened to be death.

My seat belt saved my life. I was knocked unconscious, but I stayed in the car instead of being thrown through a couple of windshields. However, the broken glass hit me in the head and face. When I woke up and saw blood and glass all over my body, I actually thought I was having a dream. Then I heard a voice say, "Can you open your seatbelt and get out?" It was one of the men from the emergency squad. Somebody along the road had seen the crash and phoned the police.

Have you ever heard the wail of a siren from *inside* an ambulance as you lie on a stretcher wondering if the end has come? It's an eerie feeling, believe me. I'd lost a lot of blood, but the paramedics took good care of me and got me to the St. Elizabeth Hospital emergency room. Before I went unconscious again, I was able to give the nurse my doctor's name and my home phone number, and that's all I remember until I woke up the next day in the intensive care ward, plugged into all kinds of medical machinery.

Most doctors aren't in their offices at that hour of the night, but our doctor was. In fact, one of the faithful members of Calvary Baptist Church was Dr. Bob Smith's appointment for that hour, and when she got the news about her pastor, she immediately began to phone our church people to get them to start praying and spreading the word. A nurse at the hospital phoned Betty and she phoned our neighbors Harold and Evelyn Frakes. Evelyn stayed with the children and Harold drove Betty to the hospital. They had to drive past the site of the accident on Taylor Mill hill, but there were so many emergency vehicles there that Betty couldn't see what our Pontiac looked like.

Our church family began to arrive at the hospital to stand with Betty, to pray, and do whatever they could to help. John and Ruby Heisler stayed with Betty the whole night and even took my glass- and blood-saturated clothes home and cleaned them. In the days that followed, they were a great help to Betty. Ray Abbott drove Barbara back to our house to stay with the children and relieve Evelyn Frakes. Betty phoned them the next morning and gave David, now almost eleven years old, the news that their father was in critical condition in the hospital. The hospital personnel were wonderful to Betty and gave her a room near the Intensive Care ward where she could get some rest. They even gave her a private telephone! So many people, both in and out of our church family, did so much that I couldn't begin to name them all.

**Our family Christmas picture, 1964. Left to right: Carolyn, Bob, Warren, David, Judy, Betty.**

Saturday evening, at least 400 people assembled at the church to pray for me as well as the family of the dead sailor, and the other boy who had survived the crash. "Thousands Pray for Minister Hurt in Crash!" announced a long article in Monday evening's *Kentucky Post*. The reporter had interviewed Cedric Whitcomb who was now the "acting pastor" of the church, a temporary promotion he hadn't expected.

Thanks to the goodness of the Lord and the skill of Dr. Bob Smith and his medical team, in a few days I got off the "critical" list and was listed as "fair." There had been no internal injuries, but I had multiple fractures in my left rib cage and over fifty stitches in my head and face. Eventually they wheeled me out of intensive care into my own private room. Betty had to put a sign on the door to keep people out, and the volunteers at the visitors' desk were warned not to let anybody see me unless they were on the "approved list" that Betty prepared. Cedric Whitcomb and Bob Montgomery visited me daily and kept me abreast of the work at the church. My brother Tat drove down from Hammond to see me, and people who couldn't get in phoned to get the latest reports.

Since visitation was severely restricted, people sent cards; from thirty to fifty a day arrived either at home or at the hospital. The volunteer who delivered the mail to my room handed me a stack of cards one day and said, "Mister, what kind of business are you running up here?" I also received letters and telegrams from all over the country from friends and total strangers assuring us of their prayer support. We counted over a thousand pieces of mail, and I still have every card and letter in a big box.

People also sent flowers and other gifts, and Betty seemed to have all the helping hands she needed for whatever had to be done. It was one of the greatest outpourings of love and concern we'd ever experienced, and it made us glad we were a part of God's family. What wonderful friends and neighbors the Lord had given us!

I was in the hospital twelve days, including Father's Day and our thirteenth wedding anniversary. (On Father's Day, Betty brought the kids downstairs on the sidewalk and I waved to them from the window.) Dr. Smith permitted me to go home provided I would rest for several weeks. Betty and David and Cedric came to get me and David felt very grown up as he helped push the wheelchair and open the doors. In a few days, he'd turn eleven, and he was glad he was anticipating a birthday party and not a funeral.

The most difficult thing about my convalescence wasn't the

pain or the difficulty of getting in and out of bed. That eventually went away. It was feeling so absolutely helpless as Betty ran
the household with her usual efficiency and as the staff and
leaders at Calvary kept the ministry moving smoothly. Cedric's
preaching was blessing the congregation, people were being
saved, and the work experienced no setback whatsoever. Mrs.
Evans and her crew had conducted Vacation Bible School in my
absence, with an average attendance of 886!

After nine Sundays out of the pulpit, I was at last permitted
to preach on Sunday morning August 14. The *Kentucky Post*
wanted to announce my return on their Saturday church page
and I practically wrote the article for them. "I Could Have Bled
to Death . . . but Rescue Squad Was There!" was the garish
headline they wrote, but it attracted a lot of attention, and we
had a great crowd that morning. Week by week, little by little, I
worked my way back into my regular pastoral work, grateful to
be alive and grateful to be privileged to serve such a wonderful
church.

It was during my convalescence that I got acquainted with
George Hipshire, one of the most remarkable Christians I've
ever known. Hearing about my accident, he wrote me a most
encouraging letter, neatly typed, and when I investigated, it
turned out he was blind! He lived with his mother in nearby
Newport, Kentucky, but because of his blindness, he had been
retired from Union Central Life Insurance Company in Cincinnati where he'd worked for thirty-one years. We corresponded,
then chatted over the phone, and then we met in person.

Before I tell you why George was so remarkable, let me give
you a bit of background. When he was seven, he lost his left
eye. As an adult, he got diabetes and his gangrenous right leg

had to be amputated. When I first met George, he was wearing an artificial limb. As the diabetes got worse, he lost the sight of his right eye, and six months after Betty and I had left the area for Chicago, his left leg had to be amputated. But in spite of these handicaps, George was a happy person and a radiant Christian who lived each day to the full and kept amazingly active. A local newspaper article about George, published at the time of his second amputation, was titled "Blind and Legless, He Finds Blessings in His Handicaps!"

After my recuperation, George and I got better acquainted by occasionally having lunch together. Anybody who knows me well knows that I have no sense of direction and could get lost a mile from home. Betty has always been my navigator because she has the built-in radar of a homing pigeon or a guided missile. I knew how to find George's house in Newport, and he could always recognize the sound of my car as he waited on the front porch.

"Where are we eating today?" I'd ask after he was safely buckled into the front seat. He'd name a restaurant and then add, "I'll show you the way." And he would! It was literally a case of the blind leading the blind. I would be lost two blocks from his home, but George always knew where we were and where we should be. He'd call off the landmarks as we passed them and then jokingly caution me not to get lost.

Once at the table, George would amaze everybody by eating as though he could see everything on the table and on his plate. I'd tell him that his vegetables were at 10 o'clock, his meat at 2 o'clock, and his potatoes at 6 o'clock, with his salad by the vegetables and his coffee by the meat, and he'd never miss a bite. I'd usually cut his meat for him and see to it that anything added to the table was identified and located.

George had a unique witness in northern Kentucky. While he still had one good leg, he'd go to the "Y" once a week and swim. He wrote me in one of his letters:

Yesterday was my day at Central Y. The Lord gave me many opportunities to witness for Him. These came so effortlessly, and it was a real blessing to me to have several occasions to tell what God has done for me . . . I am there for more than an hour and fellows come and go. They talk and make some comment regarding my being able to maneuver so well. This is all the opening I need. . . .

He was an excellent amateur poet and usually sent his friends an annual Christmas poem. His 1966 Christmas poem was called "These Are My People":

These are my people—the halt, the blind,
The favored ones who daily find
A path through immobility,
And light that just the sightless see.

These are my people—the sorely tried,
Whose innate fears have been defied,
Whose hindrances and times of stress
Become their ladders to success.

These are my people, who so abound—
The friends adversity has found,
Who take my arm and lead the way,
And turn my darkness into day.

These are my people—the ones in need.
To these I owe a debt indeed—
To live, to love, to lift, to pray;
And with God's help, my debt I'll pay!

For my fortieth birthday in 1969, George sent me a special "birthday poem" entitled "At Forty: To my friend, Warren W. Wiersbe."

The thirty-inch waist is a thing of the past;
The once-narrow hips are exceedingly vast;
The muscles have slipped, and the fat is amassed
      At forty.
The hair in perplexity cannot decide

To leave you completely or sparsely abide,
While gray pokes a hole in your masculine pride
    At forty.
The sight is okay, but that print sure is small;
You go to the phone, give the eye man a call;
His bifocals bring you the nastiest fall
    At forty.
The teeth start to worsen, then drop out of sight;
You cover your mouth as you gum every bite,
And hope that your dentures will fit good and tight
    At forty.
Your mind is forgetful and nerves show the wear;
You go to the mirror and sullenly glare
At a middle-aged goat with a few wisps of hair
    At forty.
You're apt to be giddy; you're apt to be bored;
You're apt to buy things that you cannot afford,
UNLESS you are Wiersbe and trust in the Lord
    At forty.

George included "At Forty" in a book of his selected poems that was published in 1970 by his former employer, Union Central Life Insurance Company of Cincinnati. I treasure my copy of *A Singing Heart* by George Hipshire, "the Blind Bard of Kentucky." I treasure even more the encouragement George gave me through his letters, our times together, and the glowing example of a life of faith that knew how to trust God and overcome obstacles. George said it best in the title poem of the book, "A Singing Heart."

A singing heart, a heart of song,
    A gift from heav'n above.
To whom do joyful hearts belong?
    To those who know God's love.
Who, undeterred by circumstance,
    And unperturbed by loss,
Have let adversity enhance
    The value of their cross.

And faith evokes the will to fight
  Discouragement and fear,
As songs break forth in grand delight,
  Because the Lord is near!
A loyal friend in times of stress,
  Of noble life, a part,
Ingredient of true success —
  A happy, singing heart.

I must add that George played the piano and sang and often gave concerts at retirement homes, hospitals, and churches, and more than once he presented a complete assembly program at local schools. Because of his courageous victory over his handicaps, he could carry his testimony to some places where most of us ministers weren't permitted to preach. George Hipshire was unique and I count myself fortunate to have known him.

As the Lord continued to bless the ministry of the church, we began to run out of space for both Bible School and the Sunday morning services, and once again, the pastor who couldn't read a blueprint was confronted with a building program. Our church auditorium seated about 800 people, but no matter how much we encouraged people to squeeze in and be friendly, there just wasn't enough room. The ushers put folding chairs in the aisles and in the narthex—something that the firemen across the street frowned on—but that didn't solve the problem. Then we installed closed-circuit TV in the chapel and encouraged our own members to worship in the chapel and leave room in the main auditorium for the visitors.

We arranged to have deacons in the chapel to oversee the

service and counsel with people who made spiritual decisions during the invitation. During the sermon one Sunday morning, I noticed that a couple of little girls sitting right in front of me in the front pew were fooling around and making a disturbance. At Calvary, the ushers usually dealt with such matters quickly, but the men didn't want to walk down the aisle and make an even greater disturbance while I was preaching. I took it as long as I could and finally said rather sternly, "Now I want you two girls in the front pew to behave." They immediately obeyed.

Unknown to me, there were two girls *in the front pew of the chapel* doing the same thing! When they heard the preacher on the TV monitor say, "Now I want you two girls in the front pew to behave," they were frightened because they couldn't figure out how I saw them misbehaving! I think I got a reputation for second sight that I didn't deserve, but the incident did encourage the children and young people to behave during services.

The church appointed the deacons as a Building Committee and engaged the professional services of Harley Fisk, the architect who had designed the church auditorium and the beginner building. I don't know how many meetings we had or how many alterations we made, but we finally ended up with a design that the church approved. The new auditorium would seat about 1,800 people and provide educational space for the youth department. We planned to remodel the old auditorium for adult Bible School classes, the church library, and a much-needed kitchenette. The new sanctuary would cost nearly a million dollars, which was a lot of money in the '60s, but Calvary is a generous church and we had a third of the amount already in the building fund.

After three years of praying, planning, and giving, we broke ground on March 19, 1967, my fifth anniversary at the church. There were over 1,700 people in Bible School and the people gave over $9,000 toward the new building. On my sixth anniversary, March 17, 1968, the Bible School attendance was 1,846, and the building fund offering totaled $13,658.27! What a privilege it was to pastor a church like Calvary!

But it wasn't easy carrying on the ministry right next to a

construction site. Our people were very patient, far more than was their pastor. One day during the early stages of the building program, I asked Harley Fisk, "When are we going to get out of this hole?" His reply was the greatest sentence sermon I've ever heard: "Preacher, if you don't go down deep, you can't go up high."

October 6, 1968, was our first Sunday in the new building, and Lehman Strauss was with us for a week of Bible conference ministry. In the September 15th church bulletin, I wrote:

When we move into the new auditorium, let's keep some things in mind:

1. *It will not be perfect.* Nothing man does is perfect. We will correct every mistake that can be corrected, and we will learn to live with what cannot be changed. It is a mark of maturity to be thankful for the best and patient with the rest!

2. *It will not please everybody.* Even the good things aren't perfect! We all have different likes and dislikes, and in all of us there is a prejudice against anything new or different. But I believe all of us will *rejoice* to have more space to fill for the glory of God. We will not complain or criticize; rather, we will thank God for His goodness and then go to work to win souls. A murmuring, fault-finding spirit will grieve the Lord.

3. *It will not fill itself!* It's our job to fill it up! If we refuse to fill the auditorium, then we have greatly sinned against the Lord in even building it.

4. *It will be a blessing!* Once we have adjusted all the controls, taken out the kinks, located our places in the pews, and seen God work in hearts, we will be blessed with our new auditorium and look forward to meeting in it week by week.

On November 24, we combined our annual Thanksgiving Service with the Dedication Service for the new building. It was a great and glorious day, climaxing many years of faith and sacrifice.

The only sorrow the church family experienced that week was when I told them the following Wednesday evening that

## Chapter Thirteen

Cedric and Jean Whitcomb would be leaving us at the end of the year to take up the ministry at First Baptist Church, Northville, Michigan. During those weeks that Cedric had served as "acting pastor," he discovered how much he enjoyed ministering to the whole church, and he and Jean concluded that it was time to move out of youth ministry. God confirmed that decision and gave them fruitful ministries in Northville and Marysville, Michigan. They have been dear friends for many years and it was a special privilege to have them on our staff.

# CHAPTER FOURTEEN

$$\boxed{1}$$

W hen I was on the staff of Youth for Christ International-
al, one of my tasks was to review books, and not all
the books that came to my desk were written for
teens. Ted got first choice of the books, I was second in line,
and after that, the books were up for grabs.

One day I received the first volume of *Studies in the Sermon
on the Mount* by D. Martyn Lloyd-Jones, published by W.B.
Eerdmans. I was flying to Michigan that weekend, so I dropped
the book into my briefcase, planning to read it when not occupied with ministry. I confess that I wasn't prepared for what I
found in that book. The way Dr. Lloyd-Jones expounded the
Scriptures, and the truths he brought out and applied, totally
devastated me. I found myself reading the book *while on my
knees* and alternately confessing my sins and praising the Lord
for His blessings. I knew who Dr. Lloyd-Jones was, but I had
never been exposed to his preaching ministry, and I certainly
never expected to meet him personally. But I did.

It was on Wednesday, June 18, 1969, in the Calvary Baptist
Church bookroom.* At that time, Dr. and Mrs. Lloyd-Jones

---

*I also tell this story in chapter 14 of *Martyn Lloyd-Jones: Chosen by God,* edited by his
grandson, Christopher Catherwood (Crowborough, East Sussex: Highland Books,
1986).

were temporarily living in Cincinnati as the guests of Mr. and Mrs. A.M. Kinney, well-known Christian leaders in our area and friends of ours. "The Doctor" was editing his messages on Romans for publication and was also having a limited itinerant ministry in the States, and Cincinnati was a good central location for him.

Mr. Kinney asked me if I wanted "the Doctor" to preach for me some Sunday morning, and we selected June 22. Dr. Lloyd-Jones had come over from Cincinnati that Wednesday to see the new auditorium and get acquainted with the "preaching situation," and that's when I met him in the bookroom.

I took him on a tour of our new building. "Most churches are not built for preaching," he commented. "They are designed to be monuments to some architect or committee. I can see that your people have built this one for preaching." When he stood in the pulpit, he discovered that he wasn't facing an empty center aisle. "Good, good!" he exclaimed. "You can look right at them!"

He wanted to see all the building, including the large baptistery just above the choir loft. We kept the tank filled and the water in circulation through filters, so when I opened the door, you couldn't even tell that there was water in the tank—and Dr. Lloyd-Jones stepped right into the pool. To say that I was embarrassed would be an understatement, but he put me at ease. "Don't fret about it, not at all," he said with a chuckle. The next week, I received a lovely thank-you note from him, to which he added, "Sometime I'll come back and you can baptize the rest of me!"

When "the Doctor" arrived in my office (the British would call it "the vestry") the next Sunday morning, the following conversation took place.

"Is there a pulpit Bible?" he asked. "I didn't bring my Bible."

I ruefully admitted that there wasn't, and I offered to go to my library upstairs and get him any translation he wanted.

"Why, here's a Bible right here on your desk," he exclaimed. "I'll use it."

"Doctor," I said with some hesitancy, "that's a *Scofield Bible.*" I knew that he wasn't too sympathetic with dispensationalism in general and *The Scofield Bible* notes in particular.

"Oh, it can't hurt my sermon too much!" he said with a smile, and it didn't! That morning, he gave a masterful exposition of the first chapter of 1 Thessalonians (that's "*One* Thessalonians" in the Queen's English), and when I gave the invitation, several people stepped out to trust Jesus Christ. I knew that "the Doctor" didn't endorse altar calls, but I really believe he was thrilled to see this immediate response to his sermon.

After the service, the Kinneys took Betty and me and the Lloyd-Joneses to dinner, and I had a delightful time chatting with "the Doctor" about his predecessor Campbell Morgan as well as about preaching and ministry in general. What a privilege it was to have that intimate conversation with him!

A few Sundays later, I stepped into the pulpit to preach and saw Dr. Martyn Lloyd-Jones sitting in the congregation, desperately trying to hide himself behind the people sitting in front of him. I wouldn't have been so unnerved had I not been preaching from Romans that morning! But he was a gracious listener and after the service said some very kind things to me about the sermon. Then he added, "When you visit England, be sure to let us know!" And he gave me his phone number.

# 2

Howard Sugden and I had often talked about visiting Great Britain to see the historic churches where our preaching heroes had ministered, and our plans came to fruition the spring of 1971. Betty's folks came to stay with the children, and on May 16 — my forty-second birthday — Betty and I flew to Boston where we met Howard and Lucile, boarded a BOAC jet, and took off for three weeks of "holiday" in the land I'd wanted to visit ever since I'd met Sherlock Holmes.

My travel agent had notified TWA that it was my birthday, so

during the meal, the flight attendants sang for me and presented me with a birthday cake. One of the ladies in Howard's
church had given him a box of over a hundred homemade
chocolate chip cookies, so we were well-supplied with snacks
we really didn't need and didn't want to carry. Howard was
constantly asking Betty and me if we wanted a cookie and I'd
retaliate by offering him a piece of birthday cake. People must
have thought we were crazy.

Once we were settled in our rooms in the Mount Royal Hotel
on Oxford Street, I phoned Dr. Lloyd-Jones to tell him that we
had arrived in London.

"Welcome to England!" he exclaimed. "By all means, we
must get together!"

One evening, he and Mrs. Lloyd-Jones came to our hotel for
dinner, and then we all gathered in the Wiersbes' room to chat.
"The Doctor" was in an especially buoyant mood and dis-
coursed on places we should visit, the use of the Welsh language in preaching, faith healing, and revival. When he heard
we were planning to drive to Wales, he tried to teach us how to
read the Welsh language! Believe me, that was a lost cause.

The Sugdens and Wiersbes made a second visit to Britain in
the summer of 1976, and we met the Lloyd-Joneses at the Cambridge Arms Hotel in Cambridge. It was a warm summer day,
very warm for Britain, but "the Doctor" drove up wearing a
black suit, black tie, and black hat, looking very much like he'd
been trapped in a seventeenth-century Puritan time warp. After
a delightful lunch, he offered to give us a guided tour of the
"sacred places" in the city, which included King's College, Holy
Trinity Church where Charles Simeon had ministered, and the
"very room" where Henry Martyn had dedicated his life for
foreign missionary service. Henry Martyn happens to be one of
Lucile Sugden's heroes, so she was especially fascinated by that
aspect of the tour.

Then "the Doctor" said he would take us to Heffers, "one of
the greatest bookstores in the world." Howard and I thought
we had died and gone to heaven as we found ourselves surrounded by what appeared to be miles and miles of shelving,
all crammed with books about every subject we could name.

"Ask for any book and they'll have it," said Dr. Lloyd-Jones. To prove his point, he gave one of the clerks the title of a book. They didn't have it.

It was during this tour that Mrs. Lloyd-Jones said to Betty, "My dear, you must not let your husband work too hard."

"And how do I do that?" my wife asked innocently.

"My dear," Mrs. Lloyd-Jones replied, "I really don't know!"

We stayed in touch with Dr. and Mrs. Lloyd-Jones, writing to them occasionally and phoning when we were in the U.K., but we didn't see them again in person until June 1980. We were in Britain with our younger daughter Judy and our friend Beverly Johnson from Moody Church. We met the Lloyd-Joneses at the dining room of the Paddington Station, which was near our lodgings on Baker Street. This would be the last time Dr. Lloyd-Jones would dine out. When we were back in London a few weeks later, he was in the hospital at Shepherd's Bush, battling the disease that eventually took his life on March 1, 1981.

That evening, "the Doctor" ordered steak-and-kidney pie, then methodically proceeded to remove all the pieces of kidney and eat what remained.

"Why didn't you just order a steak?" I asked.

"Because I wanted steak-and-kidney pie!" he replied, which I guess is a logical answer.

He happened to see the bill when the waiter put it on the table. "My!" he said. "We ought to take up an offering!" But we were more than happy to pay the bill and would have done it again and again just to have the privilege of being with Dr. and Mrs. Lloyd-Jones and learning from them. As I reflect on these events, I'm amazed that I was so bold to phone such a famous man and ask him and his wife to dine with us. They were always gracious and treated us and our friends as if we were royalty and *they* were the ones privileged to be with us.

When I became senior pastor of the Moody Church in Chicago, Dr. Lloyd-Jones wrote a beautiful letter of encouragement. Among other things, he wrote: "I am overjoyed to hear of your call to this most important church. You will have a great sphere of influence there and I know God will bless you and honour you and use you to His glory."

Betty and I fully expected to devote the rest of our lives to the ministry at Calvary Baptist Church, just as Dr. and Mrs. Eastep had done. Humanly speaking, everything about Calvary Baptist Church encouraged us to stay right where we were. We had a fine staff; the congregation was simply wonderful; the work was growing (we had nearly 2,000 people in Bible School for my ninth anniversary); we had a new sanctuary; I was expanding my writing and conference ministries; our children were all believers and growing in the Lord (I baptized all four of them Sunday evening, June 14, 1967); and the Lord was blessing in every way. What more could we want? But I was starting to feel restless again, wondering if the Lord had a change in store for us.

In January 1971, my friend George Sweeting accepted the invitation of the Moody Bible Institute trustees to succeed Dr. William Culbertson as president, and that meant the Moody Church would be seeking a senior minister. During his five years at Moody Church, George had done an outstanding piece of work breathing new life into a historic ministry that had been without a shepherd for four years prior to his coming. Several times during his ministry there, George had invited me to come to Chicago and speak at one church function or another, but for some reason, the schedule had always prevented me from accepting. I gave the Bible studies at Moody Church's annual Home Missions Conference in February 1967, the week of the "big snow" that closed O'Hare Field and paralyzed the city, but as far as I was concerned, it was just another conference like many I'd already addressed. I came, I spoke and, when the airport opened, I went home. However, I think that during that week, a few people were taking my measure.

After his resignation had been announced, George phoned me to see if I could fill the pulpit at least one Sunday in July or August. I was scheduled to speak at the YFC Winona Lake convention July 5–9, so I told George I'd preach on the worst possible Sunday for a downtown church—July 4! I figured that the crowd would be small, and if I "bombed" in that important pulpit, it wouldn't do too much damage either to the church or to my reputation.

From the moment I walked into the vast auditorium of the historic Moody Memorial Church,* I felt right at home, and that frightened me just a bit. I preached on John 13 in the morning (it was Communion Sunday) and Psalm 1 in the evening and had a great time. "A wonderful day at Moody Church," I wrote in my devotional diary that evening. "Good crowds (in spite of the holiday) and joy and liberty in preaching." I wasn't an official candidate, but the Pulpit Committee asked if they could chat with me before the evening service, and I agreed to do so. I felt as though I'd known the committee members all my life, and that was really frightening!

Betty and I did a lot of praying and discussing when I got home. On July 14, I phoned Byrl Vaughan, chairman of the elders, and told him I was willing to be considered a candidate, and on Sunday evening, July 18, before the evening service, I broke the news gently to the deacons at Calvary Baptist. The following Friday, I flew to Chicago to meet with the Moody Church elders and other church officers, and on Wednesday evening, August 4, Moody Church called me to be their pastor and I accepted. It all happened in a month's time, but the Lord was in it.

The next day, we packed up and drove to Chicago to find a place to live. Carol Thiessen, a stalwart member of Moody Church, opened her home to us, so we didn't have to stay in a hotel or motel. Since Moody Church was located in Chicago, I wanted to live in the city rather than in the suburbs, but we had to consider the schools the children would be attending. God answered prayer in a wonderful way and led us to a house in the Edgebrook section of Chicago, a block from an excellent elementary school and a short drive from one of the city's bet-

---

*The building is "The Moody Memorial Church"; the congregation is "The Moody Church."

**Portrait taken while at Calvary Baptist Church.**

ter high schools. When we went to the building and loan association to arrange for the mortgage, we discovered we knew the president, Stanley M. Berntson, a fine Christian who had been active in Chicagoland Youth for Christ. Our loan was approved without delay! All I had to do was fly back a couple of weeks later to sign the papers.

We drove back to Covington on Saturday and I read my resignation at the close of the Sunday morning service. It was one of the most difficult things I've ever done, and I thought I would faint while I was doing it.

> Last Wednesday evening, August 4, The Moody Church in Chicago, extended me a call to become their pastor. I have accepted the call and will begin my ministry there September 1, the Lord willing.
>
> This was not an easy decision to make. I have accepted the call for one reason only: *I believe it is the will of God for my life.* I trust you will receive this resignation in that spirit and that we will pray for each other as we face the future.
>
> Thank you for ten wonderful years — for your encouragement, your generosity, your faithfulness, and your love. You will always be in our hearts and in our prayers.

Our people were stunned and left the sanctuary talking in subdued tones. Fortunately, we had a missionary scheduled to speak at the evening service. I doubt that I could have made it through the meeting if I'd been preaching.

Mrs. Eastep was very understanding. "You know that years ago, Dr. Ironside used to come here to preach," she said, "and he was a great help to my husband. If you were going to any other church than The Moody Church, I'd be disappointed, but we're just paying back the debt we owe to them."

The church held a beautiful "farewell evening" for us on Friday, August 20, and on Sunday, August 29, I preached my last sermon as pastor of what I still think is one of the finest churches I've ever encountered in all my ministry.

As I reflect on our ten years of ministry in Covington, I can see how God not only blessed us richly but also prepared us for the work He had planned for us in the years to come.

For one thing, writing the lesson outlines week by week for "The Whole Bible Study Course" enabled me to study the entire Bible in a fresh way and make original outlines of each Bible book and most of the chapters. Those outlines later became the basis for the *BE* series of Bible expositions that I've written for Victor Books.

I also gained considerable radio experience at Calvary, and this was important when I took up the "Songs in the Night" radio ministry at Moody Church, and later the responsibilities at "Back to the Bible." We started broadcasting our evening service live on December 3, 1967 over a local rock station, and I also produced a weekly Bible study program called "What's the Good Word?" and a question-and-answer program called "The Bible Speaks." For a short time, we also had a program called "The Radio School of the Bible." All of this experience was invaluable when I found myself involved in international radio ministries.

During my Calvary years, I wrote two books for Fleming H. Revell, *Be a Real Teenager* (now *Be Challenged,* published by Moody Press) and *Creative Christian Living,* as well as a youth column for *Moody Monthly* magazine, and this helped to prepare me for the writing ministry that the Lord would open up when I got to Chicago. *Creative Christian Living* is now out-of-print, but I "recycled" much of the material and included it in *The Strategy of Satan,* published by Tyndale House.

The Bible conference ministry expanded my network so that I knew many of the leading Bible teachers and preachers on a first-name basis and had preached in many of the leading conferences and churches in the United States and Canada. In my earlier years at Calvary, my circle of fellowship was limited to people of an "independent separatist" position, most of whom are still my friends, but my attitude gradually changed as I discovered that God was blessing people I disagreed with. As far as I know, in all my ministry, I have never shared the conference platform with anyone who denied the deity of Jesus Christ or His atoning work on the cross, but gradually I had learned to apply what St. Augustine wrote: "In essentials, unity; in nonessentials, liberty; in all things, charity."

This widening of my outlook upset some of the "saint watchers" in the fundamentalist camp, some of whom began to shoot at me in their publications. When I accepted the call to Moody Church, to them that was a giant step toward apostasy; for the church was interdenominational and I would have to "compromise" my Baptist convictions.* But I was a Christian first, a pastor second, and a Baptist third, and I didn't feel I was compromising at all. I see my convictions, not as walls to isolate me from others, but as bridges to help me reach out to others. It's not the strong but the weak who draw back in fear and refuse to love people with whom they disagree.

The years at Calvary gave me opportunity to learn how to direct a large staff as well as how to plan my schedule and use my time wisely. Those weekly radio and writing deadlines, along with sermon preparation and pastoral demands, kept me from going on too many detours. Yet I was able to take a day off each week, and each summer we enjoyed wonderful vacations with the children. Betty and I even found time for short excursions to favorite places like Berea, Kentucky, and Gatlinburg, Tennessee, to enjoy the autumn colors and the savory southern food. Berea is still pretty much as it was in the '60s, but, alas, Gatlinburg has, in my opinion, lost its rustic charm and become just another place for tourists to buy trinkets.

Finally, during my Calvary years, my reading interests en-

---

*During my seven years at Moody Church, I baptized only believers and did it by immersion. If anybody wanted to be baptized any other way, we arranged for it. When he was five years old, Mr. Moody had been baptized by Rev. Everett, a moderate Unitarian, and was not baptized again even after his conversion. Whenever the subject of baptism came up in his pastors' meetings, Moody would say, "Next question!"

larged and I discovered how much there was to learn from writers I had deliberately avoided for one reason (or excuse) or another. I fell in love with biography and autobiography, both secular and sacred, and began to build up that part of my library. I also began to collect books of sermons by the great pulpit masters and study them for my own soul's good. All of this proved to be a boon when I moved to Chicago and Wayne Christianson, editor of *Moody Monthly,* asked me to write the "Insight for Pastors" column, and the result was the "giant" trilogy—*Walking with the Giants, Listening to the Giants,* and *Giant Steps*—all published by Baker Book House.*

The saying may be a cliché, but it's true: God prepares us for what He's preparing for us. Our ten years at Calvary had brought us bountiful blessings and given us opportunities for all kinds of growth. During the next seven years at Moody Church, the Lord would test that growth and make us stretch even more!

---

*The biographies from *Walking* and *Listening* are now found in *Living with the Giants,* also published by Baker Book House.

# PART FIVE
# Moody Memorial Church

# CHAPTER FIFTEEN

$$\boxed{1}$$

W e moved into 6400 N. Tahoma on Tuesday, August 31, on what Chicago Cubs sportscaster Jack Brickhouse would have called "a beautiful day in Chicago." Mayor Richard J. Daley had been presiding over the city since his election in 1955 and would continue to do so until his unexpected death December 20, 1976.

When some of our friends heard we were moving to Chicago, their response was, "Chicago?" as though we were leaving for Siberia or the Sahara. I knew about the city's infamous politicians, notorious criminals, noisy streets, irritating traffic jams, and shabby neighborhoods, but in those days, I had a nostalgic love for Chicago and was happy to be back. After all, I'd spent three fourths of my life in the Chicago area and had fond memories of reading the Sunday comics in the *Chicago Tribune*, seeing the Christmas decorations in the Loop, meeting Harry Blackstone ("the world's greatest magician") backstage at the Chicago Theater, finding bargains in the used-book stores and riding the Lake Street "el." It felt good to be back, and if you had told me I couldn't "go home again," I wouldn't have believed you.

Now, two decades later, when I return to the Windy City, the noise upsets me, the traffic frightens me, and I can hardly wait to escape. I guess I've changed, and maybe the city has too.

Dwight Lyman Moody came to Chicago 115 years before we got there, on September 18, 1856, but even then it was a bustling city with nearly 100,000 people, a city known for its booming business as well as its dirt and crime. Only nineteen years old when he arrived, Moody had come from Boston to the Midwest to sell shoes and make money. He ended up winning souls, building Sunday Schools, founding a church, promoting the YMCA, and establishing a Bible school that has been serving God faithfully for over a century. Untrained and unordained, before he died in 1899, Moody had preached the Gospel to over 100 million people in America and the British Isles and had personally dealt with 750,000 souls. It was into this great tradition that Betty and the children and I were now stepping. We didn't feel up to it, but God had called us.

General Sherman was completing his "march to the sea" on December 20, 1864 when D.L. Moody founded the Illinois Street Independent Church in a mission hall he'd erected between Wells Street and LaSalle Street. He invited pastors from different denominations to form a council to approve the church and make it "official," but they wanted nothing to do with an independent ministry. All Moody wanted to do was provide a haven for his converts who felt out of place in most of the mainline churches, and he didn't want petty doctrinal and denominational barriers to get in the way of winning souls. I can't prove it, but I suspect that D.L. Moody was the father of the nondenominational independent church movement in America. Today, interdenominational churches are a familiar part of the religious landscape, but in Moody's day, they were considered novel if not heretical.

The church building was destroyed in the great Chicago fire of 1871, but Moody rebuilt and enlarged it and named it the North Side Tabernacle. Five years later, he moved the ministry to the corner of LaSalle and Chicago Avenue and called it the Chicago Avenue Church. In 1901, when the name was changed to The Moody Memorial Church, Dr. Reuben Archer Torrey was the pastor and also president of the Moody Bible Institute, now on that location. If Mr. Moody had been alive in 1901, I have a feeling he would have protested the putting of his name on the church.

When Paul Rader became pastor in 1915, he moved the ministry a mile north to a somewhat makeshift building on the triangular lot where North Avenue intersects Clark Street and LaSalle, and they called it "the Moody Tabernacle." It seated about 5,000 people and was filled night after night with people wanting to hear Paul Rader preach. While the ministry of Dr. Ironside at Moody Church was exceptional and greatly blessed, my reading of Moody Church history leads me to believe that the greatest days were under Paul Rader in that old tabernacle. He preached to great crowds night after night, and thousands came to Christ. The building was nothing to brag about, but the ministry brought great glory to the Lord.

The present Moody Memorial Church stands on that "tabernacle" property, along with two gas stations and a savings and loan association. At one time, the church owned the entire corner, but they sold it to pay off the mortgage on the new building. This left them without any parking, a tragedy for a city church, but in "the good old days" of street cars and five-cent fares, who worried about parking cars? Patterned after St. Sophia in Constantinople, and seating 4,000 people, it was built during the pastorate of P.W. Philpott and dedicated in 1925.

If my count is correct, I was the sixteenth pastor of the church. From 1864 to 1971, Moody Church was without a pastor for eleven years and had "acting" pastors for ten years, leaving eighty-six years of ministry under fifteen different men. Dr. Ironside stayed the longest—eighteen years—and his successor, Dr. Franklin Logsdon, about eighteen months. It wasn't easy to follow a sacred institution like H.A. Ironside whose name came to be identified with the church almost as much as was Mr. Moody's.

Dr. Ironside died in 1951, but in memory, he still roamed the halls of The Moody Memorial Church and occasionally showed up in the prayers of some of the faithful old-timers. The first official task I had as pastor was to lead the midweek service on September 1, and one of the first prayers I heard was offered by one of the long-time members who prayed: "Lord, we're thankful for our new pastor. Help him to preach verse by verse like Dr. Ironside!" Seven years later, when I resigned from the church, nobody was quite sure whether God had answered his prayer. Probably not. But that night when we got home after the service, I wrote in my devotional diary, "Had a wonderful meeting this evening! Real liberty and power. God is good."

$$2$$

I spent the next day at the church, unpacking my library and moving into the study, a room that E. Schuyler English called "a delightful hideout" and Harry Ironside described as "one of the coziest nooks for a student that I have ever seen." I wasn't able to do much hiding there, and I soon learned that I could get more studying done at home than at the church. But the study was indeed a "cozy nook" far above the noisy traffic of Chicago's near northside.

As a new citizen of Chicago, I had to go through all the annoying initiation rites that confront new arrivals: registering the car, getting license plates and a city sticker, registering the children at their schools, and passing a driver's test. I was the first one in the family to take the driver's test, and the examining officer asked, "What do you do for a living, Mr. Wiersbe?"

"I'm the new pastor of The Moody Church," I replied.

"The Moody Church!" he exclaimed. "Why, I knew Harry Ironside and heard him preach many times!"

That settled everything. The officer put me through a minimum of the required tests, and within less than thirty minutes, I had my driver's license. I hurried home and told Betty to get down to the license bureau right away and ask for the examiner who had "tested" me. She wasn't able to go just then, but with the help of Dr. Ironside, at least I was able to overcome what I thought would be the biggest challenge of moving to Chicago—

getting a driver's license.

However, moving to Chicago wasn't an easy experience for the children. David turned sixteen that summer, and had we stayed in Kentucky, it's likely he would have been president of his class and perhaps even class valedictorian. At an age when friends are especially important, he left his friends behind, and he wrote a lot of letters and made many phone calls during the first few months we were in Chicago. We enrolled him in a driver's training course right away so he could get his license, and once he was mobile, he felt more at home. Eventually, all the children found their niches and their friends at church and at school, and life in the Wiersbe household settled down to normal, or as normal as life can be when father is pastor of a city church.

Whether it was moving from East Chicago to Wheaton, Wheaton to Covington, or Covington to Chicago, our moves were beautifully orchestrated by my efficient wife who in a few days transforms a house into a home and makes her family feel like they've never lived anyplace else. When we moved from Chicago to Lincoln, Nebraska, she performed the same miracle again.

My first Sunday sermon as pastor was "Christ the Carpenter," based on Mark 6:1-3, and we had an excellent congregation in spite of the fact that it was Labor Day weekend. Many people came from other churches just to see what the new pastor looked like and so they could tell their friends that they'd attended Moody Church my first Sunday in the pulpit. We always had a large number of students attending from Moody Bible Institute and other Chicago schools, and people came in from all over the Chicago area. If we had awarded a weekly travel trophy, it would have gone to Russ and Raye Jeanne Ingraham who, Sunday after Sunday, faithfully brought their family from Elgin, Illinois, a distance of about fifty miles. Moody Church was a famous historic place, so each Lord's Day we would meet scores of visitors from all over the nation and the world. My congregation was a United Nations, quite different from what I'd been accustomed to for ten years at Calvary Baptist.

The Sunday bulletin for September 5, 1971, included the following notice:

Today we welcome Dr. Warren Wiersbe and his family to Moody Church. We have been praying for the Wiersbes as they have made the transition from Covington, Kentucky, to the Chicago area. Now let us continue to support them with our loyalty, love, and prayers, and get to know each them. Be sure to greet his wife Betty, David (16), Carolyn (14), Robert (13), and Judy (11). Please pray for the Lord's direction on behalf of the Calvary Baptist Church in Covington as they seek a man to assume the position of pastor.*

The following week, the bulletin contained this message from me:

Thank you for the warm welcome you have given to me and my family. We feel very much at home. Of course, it's going to take time to learn all the names and to understand the functioning of this great church, so please be patient with us.

So many of you have said, "We're praying for you!" This encourages us greatly, because it is only in the power of the Spirit that any spiritual work can be accomplished.

Thank you for your love and loyalty! With that great missionary William Carey, let's "Expect great things from God and attempt great things for God."

We never did learn the names of all the people. Like most downtown ministries, Moody Church was a "parade" as people came and went. However, there was a core group of several hundred believers who were devoted to the work, and we did get to know these leaders quite well. Without them, the church couldn't have ministered as it did.

As for understanding "the functioning" of the church, that was a challenge. It wasn't difficult to understand the church's constitutional structure, but it took me a year to learn how that structure actually worked. We had twenty-two committees and

---

*The answer to that prayer was my assistant, Galen Call, who succeeded me in 1972. He had a long and fruitful ministry at the church.

a Committee on Committees, plus a Board of Elders and a seventy-member Executive Committee composed of the pastoral staff, deacons, elders, and the major officers of the church. All these elected officers were assigned to the various committees, and each committee had the privilege of adding members, both men and women, from the congregation. All the committees and boards were advisory; it was the Executive Committee that carried the clout.

I decided that it would be impossible to attend every meeting of every committee, so I narrowed it down to Home Missions, Foreign Missions, Board of Elders, and Executive Committee. (Since I was chairman of the Executive Committee, I had to be there.) Only twice did I meet with the Trustees, so capably led by Carl Johnson, and that was to go over some ideas for remodeling Sankey Auditorium, and once I met with the Finance Committee to help solve some budget problems related to the music ministry of the church. Some people joked about our many committees and called the Executive Committee "the Moody Sanhedrin"; but over the years, I learned to appreciate the church officers and was grateful for the time and energy they invested in helping me carry on the ministry of this historic church in a difficult place. Perhaps some pastors would get more done if they'd trust the "lay" leadership of the church and quit trying to do everything themselves.

3

The official installation took place on Sunday evening, November 7, with my predecessor George Sweeting giving the charge to the church and my beloved preaching professor Lloyd Perry giving the charge to the pastor and bringing the main message. Many of our dear friends in ministry were kind enough to send encouraging letters when they got the news that I'd accepted the call to Moody Church, and some of these were excerpted for the installation folder.

Ted Engstrom wrote from his World Vision office: "I have just learned via the very active grapevine that you have accepted the call to Moody Church. That's really terrific! I am delighted both for the church and you. I am proud to be able to say, 'I knew him when'!"

Dr. William Culbertson, soon to become Chancellor of Moody Bible Institute, wrote: "Mrs. Culbertson and I were so happy to hear the news of your acceptance of the call to the pastorate of Moody Church. We are grateful to the Lord that the church will have the benefit and blessing of your Spirit-filled ministry, and that many of us will have the privilege of closer fellowship with you than we have been able to have in the past." Dr. Culbertson proved to be a great encouragement, but he didn't stay with us as long as we had hoped. God called him home November 16 and I lost a friend and a most grateful listener.

Jack Wyrtzen, founder of Word of Life Fellowship, wrote: "There is no one I would rather see become the pastor of The Moody Church than Warren Wiersbe. I have prayed for this man every Sunday for years. We greatly value his ministry." (It was very gracious of Jack to write, because at the last minute I had to cancel my week of ministry at Word of Life in order to go to Chicago and find a place to live!)

Publisher Pat Zondervan wrote: "Heartiest congratulations on your having been called to and your having accepted the pastorate of The Moody Church. You will be a great successor to George Sweeting. You will carry on in his train. May the Lord wonderfully and graciously bless you."

I gladly accepted George Sweeting's program, priorities, and pastoral staff. He did his work well and there was no need for radical change. Don Smith directed our "Songs in the Night" radio ministry and occasionally assisted at the piano. Jim Rands was in charge of Christian education and Tom Streeter shepherded the youth of the church. Tom later moved to Indianapolis where he planted a very successful church, and the youth ministry was taken over by Fred McCormick. Richard Dinwiddie was pastor in charge of music and Ed Shufelt was building superintendent.

If you recognize the name "Shufelt," perhaps it's because you heard his brother J. Stratton Shufelt sing in a meeting somewhere. "Strat" was minister of music under Dr. Ironside for several years and traveled widely in conference ministry. He was one of the finest worship leaders and soloists I've ever known and it was always a delight to minister with him in conferences here and there.

We were fortunate to have John Innes and Bill Fasig as our accompanists at the grand piano and the mighty Moody pipe organ. Following his retirement, Dr. Warren Filkin, my former professor at seminary, came to the staff to pastor the senior adults and was a great help to me. Paul Craig, a former missionary to Nigeria, was our business manager and saved me hours of time as he supervised the business affairs of the church. We had a large staff at the Day Care Center and the usual array of office secretaries, chief among them Evelyn Rankin, our church secretary, who was the office oracle and could tell you anything you wanted to know about the church and its people. Evelyn helped me get acquainted with the members of the church, especially the "old-timers," some of whom were shut-ins. I guess they didn't expect their new pastor to visit them, but I did and learned from them a great deal of important information about the church and its ministry.

One of the mistakes some pastors make when they go to a new field is to get so obsessed with the future that they ignore the past. While it's important to bring in new people, it's also important to appreciate the people who have "stayed by the stuff" and kept the ministry going year after year. I've often said that the past isn't an anchor to hold us back; it's a rudder to guide us. Blessed is that pastor who appreciates the rich heritage that sacrificing people have given to him.

I was looking forward to celebrating Christmas in Chicago. The members of the Wiersbe family were near enough to each other to get together, and our children would enjoy the lights and decorations and crowded stores. But our second Christmas in the Windy City was a difficult one. Ma had a massive stroke

December 17 and died four days later. The funeral was December 23. Maintaining the Swedish traditions she'd taught us, the family got together and exchanged Christmas gifts, but to us, it wasn't the season to be jolly. We were glad that Tat was still at home with Pa to help him in the lonely hours that were sure to come.

A city church is like a city hospital: it must welcome everybody, help everybody, and be directed by people who are experts in their fields. I was the "generalist" on the team, but without the "specialists," I couldn't have made it. The danger was that I'd become the CEO of a religious organization and stop being the shepherd of a flock, and I had to fight that danger constantly. There are many images of the church in the Bible, but the "corporation" isn't one of them. Churches need shepherds, not CEOs.

For one thing, I made visits. I had to be with our people or my own soul would dry up. I've heard the pastors of some large churches almost brag that they never visit in the hospitals to pray with the sick or in the funeral parlors to comfort the sorrowing, but I couldn't take that approach. God gave me a pastor's heart and I had to be with the people. It was impossible to go to all of them in every need, but I did my best to go to some of them, and it helped to keep my sermons from becoming cold and academic.

It wasn't always easy to make time for visiting because each week I had to prepare two sermons for Sunday, a Bible study for the midweek service, a Sunday School lesson (I taught the auditorium class, made up mostly of students), and a radio script for "Songs in the Night." When you add to these responsibilities other pastoral duties like weddings and funerals, counseling, meeting with staff members collectively and individually, and trying to function as an adequate husband and father, you can see that my days were full. I was certainly grateful for the staff people who were always ready to help and never complained.

I learned that the simple secret of getting my work done was to start each day with the Lord, plan each day wisely, and work ahead whenever I could. I had to plan my sermon series in advance so Don Smith could prepare the newspaper ads and other promotion, Carol Thiessen could design the Sunday worship folder, and Richard Dinwiddie could plan the music and select the hymns. I know all the arguments pro and con about sermon series and I'm willing for my ministerial brethren to "work out their own salvation," but I found it helpful to know where I was going. If the Lord burdened me to interrupt a series with a special message He'd laid on my heart, no great harm was done. In fact, the message probably had greater impact because it was an interruption.

At Moody Church, I continued the practice I'd begun at Calvary Baptist of walking throughout the auditorium before services and chatting informally with the people. It's amazing how much pastoral work I got done during those twenty or thirty minutes of friendly conversation. I also got to meet many visitors who were somewhat shocked that the "esteemed" pastor of Moody Church would descend from Mount Olympus and mix with the commoners! I never felt that way about it; I just enjoyed being with people and getting my heart warmed so I could preach with love.

There was another plus to this practice: having already shaken hands with most of the people, I didn't have to meet people at the door after the service but could stay at the front of the church and be available to anybody with a spiritual need who wanted to talk. Several of the elders and counselors would be nearby, and on more than one occasion, lost people came to know Christ and troubled saints were helped because God's people cared enough to tarry and listen.

I should add that this practice of "pastoral perambulation" is one I follow in my conference ministry as well, and the people seem to appreciate it. However, in more than one well-known church, this personal touch has somewhat intimidated the pastors, some of whom prefer to keep their distance. Like a jack-in-the-box, they pop out in time for the invocation and then vanish during the benediction. One famous minister said, "If you keep this up, Wiersbe, I'm going to have to change my ways!"

## 5

I must confess that, for many years, I disliked the administrative responsibilities of the pastorate until I realized that official church gatherings, like the Moody Church Executive Committee meetings, were actually opportunities for pastoral work on a broader scale. I could learn more about my people if I listened to their speeches in committee meetings than if I listened to their supplications in prayer meetings, because disagreements bring out either the best in us or the worst in us. During my first year at Moody Church, I carefully noted who spoke up in the various committee meetings *and to whom they addressed their words.* It didn't take long to discover who the "movers and shakers" were in the church and to see that *authority* didn't always go with *office.*

I don't want to give you the idea that these meetings were brutal, because they weren't, but they were very open and honest. One of the long-time elders told me that Dr. Ironside left the Executive Committee meeting one evening because he felt the discussion wasn't at all spiritual. "I'm going to go off and pray," he said, "and the Holy Spirit will be in my chair. When I come back, I want this matter settled." How it was settled without a chairman is a puzzle to me, but God works in mysterious ways. George Sweeting once came to the Monday night Executive Committee meeting carrying a machete which one of our church missionaries had given him. As he laid it on the table, he said with a smile, "Now, men, there'll be no trouble tonight!"

Only once in the seven years I was pastor did anyone verbally attack me in an Executive Committee meeting, and this was by a man who had been critical of my ministry since the beginning because I wasn't "separated" enough for him. One of his friends, a deacon, had physically attacked me a few Sundays before and had left the church after refusing to meet with me and the elders. I later found out that he had been undercutting Moody Church pastors for years. But he still had one accomplice serving on the Executive Committee, and that's the man who verbally assaulted me after I'd been at the church about five years.

"You are a liberal!" the man said. "You have driven away from this church one of its most spiritual members!"

Immediately dear Gil Andrews, one of our saintly elders, with tears in his eyes, got up and shuffled across the room and begged the man to apologize, but to no avail. There was nothing left to do but to ask the deacon to resign from the Executive Committee, and with him and his friend gone, the atmosphere in the meetings changed remarkably. Instead of meeting twice a month and devoting two or three hours to discussions, we started meeting once a month for an hour or so, and got just as much work done if not more. "Cast out the scoffer, and contention will leave; yes, strife and reproach will cease" (Prov. 22:10, NKJV).

One of the challenges I had to face was the relationship between Moody Church and LaSalle Street Church, located just up the street between The Moody Church and Moody Bible Institute and pastored by my friend Bill Leslie whom I'd known from my YFC days. Moody Church owned the LaSalle Street building, which had once been a branch church, but there were people in Moody Church who didn't like the "drift" of Bill Leslie's ministry. They felt he was getting too involved in social action and wasn't maintaining a conservative stance. A few ultraconservatives even suggested that we throw them out and start a new church.

Early in 1973, I asked George Cady, clerk of the church, to

give me a summary of all the discussions and official action relating to LaSalle Street Church, and when I read the report, I was amazed to discover how much time the Executive Committee had devoted to this one matter over the years without coming to any decision. I may be wrong, but I think that the real problem wasn't the LaSalle Street Church property or Bill Leslie's ministry. It was what the church and Bill's ministry symbolized: change. Without agreeing with everything Bill did, he was a courageous man who was trying to lead his church in applying the Gospel to the needs of the people living in difficult situations, and there were people in Moody Church who wanted nothing to do with change.

"Why don't we sell the building to LaSalle Street Church and let them run their own affairs their own way?" I asked at an Executive Committee meeting one spring evening. "Just because we own the building doesn't mean we can tell them what to do in their ministry."

The answer was quick in coming: LaSalle Street Church couldn't afford to buy the building. They just didn't have that kind of money in their budget.

"How much money are we talking about?" I asked.

After some discussion, the amount of $75,000 seemed to be accepted by consensus. I gave them a daring proposition:

"Suppose we ask LaSalle Street Church to raise $25,000 and Moody Church to raise $25,000, and we got another $25,000 from a foundation. If Moody Church gets the whole $75,000, would we let LaSalle Street Church have their building?"

The men spent a good deal of time discussing the sticky question of why Moody Church should raise money to help somebody buy a building from them. I told them I thought it was the Christian thing to do. After all, Jesus said, "It is more blessed to give than to receive" (Acts 20:35). Finally, when it came to a vote, the resolution passed. Now all I had to do was find somebody to give us that matching $25,000.

Because I knew of his concern for the inner city, I contacted Ken Taylor, founder and president of Tyndale House Publishers, and he agreed to match Moody Church's $25,000 with a grant from their foundation. I was sure LaSalle Street Church would have no problem raising their amount since numbers of believers in the Chicago area were concerned that the ministry at LaSalle Street Church prosper.

I told the Executive Committee that I would send out only one letter to the church family about this gift, that there would be no promotion from the pulpit, and that we would devote the entire month of July to asking God to send in the funds. If they didn't come in by the end of July (the worst possible month for raising funds), the whole proposition was off.

Did you know that on July 30, 1956, President Dwight D. Eisenhower signed the act of Congress that made "In God We Trust" the official motto of the United States of America? What happened on July 30, 1973, proved to me that our God indeed can be trusted! During the month, only $15,000 had come in for the LaSalle Street Church project, and I was prepared to concede defeat. But the evening of July 30, Bernie Elafros, our church treasurer, phoned to give me some news.

"Pastor, you won't believe what's happened. I just received a check for $10,000! We've made our goal for the LaSalle Street Church project!"

Betty and I wept and shouted and prayed and got so excited we acted like little kids. Not only had God answered prayer and helped us solve an irritating long-standing church problem, but He had silenced the critics in the church who were determined to resist change. It was as though God had leaned down and stuck a star on my forehead and said, "Keep going, son; your Father's with you. Just keep on building the bridge."

In God we trust!

Tuesday morning May 15, 1974, my brother Ed phoned me. It was his birthday and I was planning to phone him, but he beat me to it. His first sentence was to the point: "Pa died this morning at 7 o'clock."

My father had been struggling with cancer and emphysema for a long time and had been in a medical facility for five months, consuming oxygen and morphine. Now his long and courageous battle was over, and he and Ma were together again.

As I stood at my study window, staring at nothing and thinking about my deceased parents, it suddenly struck me that Ed and Tat and Doris and I were now the older generation in our family.

But that wasn't all. Ed's wife Janet was also suffering from cancer, and less than a month later, on June 11, the Father called her home. The service was June 14 and Ed asked me to bring the message. It was one of the hardest things I ever had to do.

# CHAPTER SIXTEEN

$$\boxed{1}$$

In his book *The Story of Moody Church: A Light in the City* (Moody Press, 1985), my friend Bob Flood calls the seven years of my ministry there "the Songs-in-the-Night-years." Perhaps "the radio years" might have been a better description, because in 1974 we began to air "The Moody Church Hour," a delayed broadcast of our Sunday morning service. It was carried by a number of Christian radio stations as well as by WEFM, one of Chicago's leading culture stations, and the mail we received indicated that the Lord used it to reach and help a great many people.

When we started "The Moody Church Hour," I told the staff, "We're not producing a radio program; we're taping a worship service. Let's keep that in mind." Not everybody agreed with my philosophy, and the pastoral staff had a rather warm discussion about it, but in the end, my approach proved to be the right one. If a baby cried or somebody sneezed or a police car raced past the church with its siren screaming, those noises only helped to create for our listeners the atmosphere of an actual local church service. Of course, our engineers edited the tapes and deleted announcements (they were a week old anyway), long pauses, and gross errors, but for the most part, listening to "The Moody Church Hour" was the closest thing to actually being in the auditorium and participating in our morning worship service.

But back to "Songs in the Night." The idea for this program was born in the creative mind and heart of Torrey Johnson when he was pastoring the Midwest Bible Church in Chicago. The first broadcast was aired by WCFL from the church auditorium on Sunday evening, June 6, 1943. Torrey patterned the format after Paul Rader's "Back Home Hour" and made it a conversational program with a devotional message backed up by quiet music. The fact that "Songs in the Night" has been broadcasting successfully for over fifty years is evidence that Torrey mixed the right ingredients in the right proportions.

The next year, the program moved to the Village Church of Western Springs, a suburb of Chicago, where Billy Graham was pastoring. As a teenager living in the greater Chicago area, I remember our family listening to "Songs in the Night" on Sunday evenings and hearing Billy Graham speak and George Beverly Shea sing. When Billy left the church to become a YFC evangelist, Lloyd Fesmire became pastor at the Village Church and was the voice of "Songs in the Night" for twenty-two years.*

In 1965, Lloyd Fesmire moved to a new ministry in New Jersey and the program continued only because stations were able to replay old recordings. In 1966, George Sweeting came to Moody Church and began praying for an international radio ministry, and "Songs in the Night" was the answer to that prayer. In 1968, "Songs in the Night" moved to Moody Church and has been there ever since. When I became pastor in 1971, the transition of speakers took place painlessly, and I remained the speaker on "Songs in the Night" for almost eight years. When Erwin Lutzer accepted the pastorate of Moody Church in January 1980, he became host of the program, and today the program is heard on 350 stations around the world.

Moody Church celebrated the thirtieth anniversary of the broadcast in 1973 by bringing back all the former speakers, including Billy Graham, for a special rally. On May 16, 1993, my

---

*For the sake of accuracy, I should mention that Peter Stam III was the radio speaker for a short time before Lloyd Fesmire arrived on the scene.

sixty-fourth birthday, the church commemorated the program's fiftieth anniversary, and all the speakers were there except Billy Graham. The church had a birthday cake for the program and a birthday cake for me!

Few listeners to Christian radio realize the hard work that's involved in turning out a quality radio program week after week. When I was at Moody Church, producing and distributing "Songs in the Night" involved the work of at least a dozen people, with Executive Producer Don Smith supervising the whole ministry.

The original scripts started with me, and I had to write four at a time because that's the number of programs we recorded at one taping session. I turned the scripts over to Don who circulated them among the musicians; they in turn suggested the music they wanted to use. Don's secretary typed the final scripts, complete with production instructions and the names of the songs, and these were distributed to the participants. Organist John Innes would arrange the music and Don would make sure all the musicians had their scripts and music arrangements.

We did our recording on the platform of Moody Church and usually had two engineers in the sound room. Bob Neff, a member of the Moody Bible Institute radio staff, was our producer, a man with an unerring sense of balance and timing. He and I each had a stopwatch. I had to make sure my narration stayed within the time limit, and he had to make sure the whole program didn't exceed its allotted time. Before each taping session, I'd read my script aloud to myself and time the reading. I'd write the numbers down and hand them to Bob, usually quipping, "My times are in your hands."

Even though it was hard work, I looked forward to those Saturday morning taping sessions. Tedd Seelye, to me the "dean" of Christian radio announcers, had been with "Songs in the Night" so long that he was already a legend. During our coffee break, Tedd and I used to get into some lively debates about everything from communications to theology, and it was a real experience of "iron sharpening iron." The entire staff was fun to work with and I confess that I miss them.

Don Smith dealt with the nitty-gritty of the "Songs in the Night" ministry, like contacting radio stations, maintaining the mailing list, sending out gift booklets to people who wrote in, and dealing with critical letters and phone calls. One day an angry lady phoned him and insisted that he take her name off the mailing list. Don promised that he would and asked for her name and address, both of which she refused to tell him! Don was killed in a tragic traffic accident in the summer of 1978. He was a gifted musician and radio producer; it was a great loss to the "Songs in the Night" ministry.

# 2

Accepting the pastorate of Moody Church opened for me the opportunities for ministry that usually accompany being associated with a "great church." People asked me to speak at their Bible conferences, publishers requested me to write books and magazine articles, and more than one Christian organization sent me invitations to become a member of a board. When I was pastor of Calvary Baptist Church in Covington, Kentucky, most of these people didn't know I existed, but when I became pastor of Moody Church, they suddenly got interested in me. It happened again when I joined the staff of Back to the Bible, and when I left, I slowly faded into oblivion. I'm not complaining; that's the way the system works.

Before we left Kentucky, I had begun to write the "Insight for Pastors" column for *Moody Monthly,* and I happily continued writing it during my Moody Church years. Editor Wayne Christianson was a dear friend of mine and a delight to work with, and we had many happy hours together. I wrote the column from 1971 to 1977, when it became obvious that it was time for a change, and the result was a trilogy that God has greatly used to help preachers around the world, *Walking with the Giants, Listening to the Giants,* and *Giant Steps,* all published by Baker Book House. *Giant Steps* is a daily devotional book composed of excerpts from the preaching and writing of fifty-two of the "greats." The biographies of the great preachers found in *Walking* and *Listening* are now combined in one new volume, *Living with the Giants.*

I've often been asked, "Other than recounting the lives of the great evangelical preachers of the past, what were you trying to accomplish in that series of articles?" Along with *information,* I suppose the main thing was *inspiration.* I wanted my readers, especially those in Christian ministry, to see how God prepared each of these men and used them in a variety of ways in the building of His church.

One of the perils of ministry today is *imitation.* Pastors go from seminar to seminar, learning new and "successful" methods for building the church, and sometimes forget that what works in suburban Chicago or downtown Denver may not work successfully in Casper, Wyoming or Wilton, Connecticut. If my study of Christian biography has taught me anything, it's that God uses different kinds of people in many different ways to get His work done, and it's a sin to imitate somebody else and expect to be a success. If we will just give ourselves totally to the Lord *and dare to be ourselves,* He will prepare us and use us in the way that best suits our gifts and personalities.

I should add that my articles contained numerous bibliographical references so that the reader could start building his or her own library of books written by my subjects. More than one loyal reader told me that they were "going broke" buying all the books I mentioned, but that it was a wonderful way to go!

Like Samuel Johnson, I enjoy the biographical part of literature most of all. I have about a thousand biographies and autobiographies in my library, and it was a delight during those nearly seven years to read the lives of the great Christians, digest the material, and then write the "Insight" columns to introduce these people to today's reading public. Just as Isaac had to dig again the wells that his father had dug (Gen. 26), so we today need to dig again the deep wells of Christian biography and church history to learn again the lessons that God wants to teach us. Many Christians are so busy trying to keep up with the books of the hour that they never catch up with the past to meet the people who belong to the ages, and this is giving them a warped view of the Christian ministry and the work of the church.

When I was an adjunct instructor in the homiletics department of Trinity Evangelical Divinity School in Deerfield, Illinois, a Chicago suburb, one term I taught a course on the history of preaching. There were perhaps twelve to fifteen people in the class, all of them keen students, but I was amazed to discover that they'd never heard of Harry Ironside or Paul Rader! Even some of the "greats" like Robert Murray McCheyne and George W. Truett were strangers to them. I had an exciting time introducing them to the "giants," and I think they benefited from meeting them.

I've been accused of being obsessed with the preachers who ministered in the Victorian era, and perhaps I am. Apart from the Apostolic Age, I doubt that any age in the church can match the galaxy of preachers who ministered in Great Britain from 1837 to World War I. (To be fair all around, I have to admit that we had a galaxy of great preachers in America during that same period.) Just as artists study the lives and painting of great artists, and musicians the lives and works of great musicians, so preachers must study the lives and sermons of the "preaching giants" in order to get a broader perspective on the work of the ministry.

# 3

I'd been ministering at Moody Church less than three months when Henry Jacobsen phoned me from Wheaton where he was serving as Adult Editor at Scripture Press. Other publishers had contacted me about potential books, but nothing they suggested seemed to catch fire in my heart. But Henry's idea was right up my alley: he wanted me to write a popular commentary on the First Epistle of John to carry Scripture Press's new "Victor Books" logo. (The name "Victor" comes from Victor Cory who, with his wife Bernice, founded Scripture Press.) The book would become a part of the new "elective series" that Scripture Press was introducing into their curriculum.

John's First Epistle has always been a favorite of mine. I'd taught it at various YFC conferences and preached it at Calvary Baptist Church, and I was excited about pulling all that material together and writing a book. I gave them the manuscript in the spring of 1972 and it was titled *On Being a Real Christian*. But that title had two strikes against it: Harry Emerson Fosdick, the famous liberal preacher, had published a book called *On Being a Real Person,* and G. Christian Weiss had written a book called *On Being a Real Christian*. While you can't copyright a title, it isn't a wise practice to give readers the impression that you can't think up a good title of your own. They wonder if you took time to write your own book!

Some anonymous hero at Scripture Press came up with the bright idea of simply calling the book *Be Real,* and that was the beginning of the *BE* series. I expected to write only the one book, but the editors at Scripture Press asked for more. They saw the potential for providing study material for the growing Sunday School elective program, as well as the home Bible studies that were springing up across the country. So I wrote *Be Joyful* (Philippians), then *Be Free* (Galatians) and *Be Rich* (Ephesians), and continued through the whole New Testament, climaxing in 1989 with *Be Courageous* (Luke 14–24), the twenty-third book in the series. Because the *BE* series got started at just the right time, with just the right format and promotion, it took hold and became a success. Now, over twenty years later, I'm writing commentaries on selected Old Testament books. More than 3 million copies of the *BE* books have been distributed around the world, in English and other languages; and the entire New Testament series is available in two clothbound volumes, *The Bible Exposition Commentary*. Nobody is more surprised at what happened than I am!

The *BE* series started out as part of the Scripture Press Sunday School curriculum, but it's also had a wide ministry as resource material for pastors and missionaries. On more than one occasion, pastors have told me that they've preached their way through my books and been grateful for them. I was once introduced at a seminary pastors' conference as "a man who needs no introduction because we've all read his books and preached his outlines." More than once, my wife and I have sat in a congregation, listening to the minister preach a chapter from one of the *BE* books.

Well, that's fine with me! If I didn't want to share what God's given me from the Word, I wouldn't have written the books to begin with. "Freely you have received, freely give" (Matt. 10:8, NKJV). However, since many people sitting in the pews read Christian books, a pastor is wise to give his sources, lest somebody accuse him of plagiarism and thus weaken his ministry. As the old saying goes, "Plagiarism is the highest form of compliment and the lowest form of larceny."

It's only when my material shows up in print, without permission and without documentation, that we have to draw the line. One pastor preached my outlines on Philippians without giving proper credit, and his church, not knowing where the sermons originated (according to the pastor), published and distributed them! I have copies in my library. The pastor apologized to me for what the church did, and I appreciated it.

It's unfortunate when a pastor has to "borrow" another man's messages in order to have something to say. One January, I was out of the pulpit for three weeks while ministering in Africa, and a frantic pastor in the Bible Belt phoned Moody Church to see when he'd get the cassettes of my messages. He was receiving them week by week and preaching every message to his own people!

To me, one of the great joys of ministry is living in God's Word and hearing His voice speak to me with the message my people need. As day by day I've studied, prayed, meditated, ministered to God's people, and waited before Him, I've always had a message to deliver. My sermons haven't always been noteworthy, but I've tried to make them spiritually nourishing and practical. At least I've been a voice and not an echo.

I was fortunate to have Jim Adair as my editor when Scripture Press launched the *BE* series. Jim and I have worked together for many years prior to his retirement, and there has never been a misunderstanding or even a critical word come between us. When it comes to editorial direction and spiritual discernment, Jim is one of the pros.

My task at Moody Church was again that of a bridge-builder. George Sweeting had done a masterful job of giving new life to the congregation and a new look to the building and the ministry, but when he moved up the street to become president of Moody Bible Institute, "there remained yet much land to possess." Church members long accustomed to Moody Church organization, Moody Church outlook, and Moody Church policies didn't always realize that changes needed to be made. They were like people who had been sitting in the same room for hours, not realizing how stuffy the air had become. Somebody coming in from the outside had to alert them.

In Sunday School, we began to concentrate on single young adults, our largest constituency in the high-rises that had been built near the church. Jim Rands, our minister of Christian education, started with about 20 singles, and before long, we had over 100. Within a few years, some of the singles became "doubles"; then the nursery started to run out of space. The couples ministry attracted other couples, and this meant more children attending Sunday School.

I recall the Sunday morning when Ed Shufelt told me there wasn't enough room for the Primary Department. When I asked him what he thought we should do, he replied, "Let's take the ladies' lounge and use it for a classroom." The ladies' lounge was a lovely room that provided comfortable chairs for elderly ladies who came to church early and needed a cozy place to rest. It wasn't used much during Sunday School, so Ed's suggestion seemed a good one.

**Portrait taken while at Moody Memorial Church.**

Until the ladies got wind of it! I admit that Ed and I could have been more diplomatic in our takeover, but when you have a roomful of active primary children, you can't wait for a referendum or a change in the constitution. You'd think those ladies would have been happy to see more little children in the Sunday School, learning about Jesus, but most of them weren't. Ed took most of the flak on that one, although I got my share, but eventually the Christian Ed Committee got official authorization, and the matter died down. Ed's only comment was, "At Moody Church, it's easier to get forgiveness than permission."

Another change we had to make was the integrating of the Moody Bible Institute students into the ministry of the church. Many of the students wanted to serve at the church to fulfill their Practical Christian Work assignments, but this meant that they wouldn't really be a part of the church structure and would often be out of town for school holidays. If they belonged to a campus ministry, such as the Moody Chorale, they'd often be away giving concerts.

We decided that the only way to build a strong church ministry was to use our own faithful people in Sunday School ministry and let the students serve as assistants. If students wanted to sing in the Moody Church choir, they couldn't sing in a campus group as well. We had a small tempest in a teapot for a few weeks, but the wind finally subsided and no damage was done.

On Sunday morning, April 3, 1977, as I was teaching the Auditorium Bible Class, I became very ill and knew I wouldn't be able to preach. Between the Sunday School hour and the morning worship service, I got the pastoral staff together and told them to take the service and do their best. I was going home.

While walking through the front lobby of the church, I ran into Erwin Lutzer, one of the instructors at Moody Bible Institute. Erwin and I, along with Mark Bubeck and Doug Steimers, two area pastors, had been meeting regularly for prayer, and I counted him as a good friend. I discovered that he had brought his family to the morning service and had found a parking place *on LaSalle right across from the church!* At that hour on a Sunday morning, finding a parking place across the street from the church was something like opening the Red Sea. The Lord's timing was perfect and I drafted Erwin to preach for me that morning. Little did either of us realize the consequences of that "chance" meeting.

In January 1978, Betty and I went to Africa to minister, accompanied by John and Virginia Elsen, long-time members of the church. John was a medical doctor and chairman of our foreign missions committee. If Paul could take Dr. Luke on his missionary journeys, I had every right to travel with "Dr. John." I asked Erwin Lutzer to preach the three Sundays I was away, and during those three weeks, he endeared himself to the congregation. Neither of us knew it, but he was actually candidating even before I had resigned!

Nobody but Betty knew that I was starting to get that "old feeling" again that my work at the church would soon be completed and we would be directed into another ministry. I was getting more and more invitations to write and to preach at various conferences, and I knew I couldn't possibly accept them and faithfully pastor the church. Things were going well in the ministry, people were coming to Christ, the budget was in the black year after year, and there was every evidence that God was blessing. But I was becoming more and more discontented.

Unless you've experienced it, you have no idea what a pastor goes through when he seeks the mind of God concerning his future ministry. How do you go about measuring your ministry? You can examine the tangibles, of course, like increased church attendance, membership growth, the number of conversions and baptisms, increased giving, and new opportunities for outreach. There are also the intangibles, like church unity, people excited about the ministry, personal growth in the people, new problems because of new challenges, and an "anointing" of the church organization so that things move fairly smoothly. We enjoyed many of these blessings at the church, but still I had a restlessness in my heart.

Our three weeks in Africa were exciting and rewarding and really a turning point for me. I ministered to hundreds of national pastors in Nairobi and then to scores of Africa Inland Mission missionaries at their annual field conference at Rathy in Zaire. We had a great time with some of our Moody Church missionaries, including Don and Alene Dix, Don and Merle Lindquist, and Paul and Kathy Buyse. When the time came for us to leave, I was glad to return home, but I didn't want to go back to Moody Church. I wasn't facing any special problems, and many pastors would gladly have changed places with me, but I had to face the fact that the Lord was turning my heart more to conference ministry and writing.

On Saturday, February 25, I wrote in my devotional diary, "Today I asked the Lord to give me some small indication of His will concerning my remaining at Moody Church." On Sunday, April 16, I wrote, "Today was a difficult day for me. Difficult to preach." I recall one Sunday in April when I said to Betty as we drove home from church, "I don't think I can take another Sunday. If I stay here, it will kill me." She wanted me to stay on at Moody Church, and she kept quoting Dr. V. Raymond Edman's counsel to his students at Wheaton College, "It's always too soon to quit." But I wasn't quitting. I knew that my work was done. I had built the bridge and everything was ready for the next man to come.

On Sunday, May 7, I gave my letter of resignation to Byrl Vaughan, chairman of the elders, and then I met with the elders before the service to discuss the logistics of my move. That was a difficult meeting for me, but it was even more difficult the next morning to tell the other pastors at our weekly staff meeting. By the time the Executive Committee gathered that evening, the word was out, so my announcement was not a surprise. The committee accepted my resignation with regrets.

July 2, 1978 was my last Sunday to minister as pastor of Moody Church. After that, Betty and I would be stepping out by faith like Abraham and Sarah, with no guaranteed income, to minister as the Lord would direct. Moody Church asked Erwin Lutzer to become their "stated pulpit supply"; and in January 1980, he became pastor of the church. At this writing, Erwin is still faithfully serving at Moody Church, having stayed longer than any other Moody Church pastor except H.A. Ironside. One day Erwin jokingly said to me, "You know, Warren, you fought the battles and I came in and claimed the spoils."

But that was my job, to be a bridge-builder.

# PART SIX

# Back to the Bible and Beyond

# CHAPTER SEVENTEEN

$$\boxed{1}$$

In the weeks that followed, it felt strange not to be pastoring a church. Since leaving YFC seventeen years earlier, that's all I'd been doing. Now I had no board meetings or staff meetings to attend, no visits to make, no counseling to do, no sermons and Sunday School lessons to prepare, and no meetings to lead. I still had radio scripts to write because I'd agreed to stay with "Songs in the Night" until the church called a new pastor. Quite honestly, I was glad for this one continued connection with my friends at Moody Church.

Technically, I was "unemployed"; but my calendar was full, and Betty and I had a busy summer. After my last Sunday at the church, we took a week's vacation and then flew to California where I ministered at the Mt. Hermon Bible Conference. I had a week's conference near Cleveland, Ohio, where my good friend Ken McQuere was pastoring the Riverview Church, and I also spoke at the Winona Lake and Gull Lake conferences. Between meetings, I wrote *Be Ready,* prepared "Songs in the Night" scripts, answered mail (how I missed the ministry of Claudia Gerwin, my Moody Church secretary!), and packed and unpacked my luggage. With all the traveling I did, at times I felt like I was back in YFC, except that Betty was often able to travel with me.

By the goodness of the Lord, invitations to write and preach continued to come in. I also received invitations to become a part of other ministries. The first week I was away from Moody Church, Richard DeHaan and I met at O'Hare Field in Chicago to explore a possible association with Radio Bible Class, but I didn't feel this was the route the Lord wanted me to take. A couple of Bible colleges furtively contacted me to see if I was presidential material and soon discovered I wasn't. A West Coast publisher offered to pay me a year's salary if I'd revise and expand the outlines I'd prepared at Calvary Baptist Church so he could publish them, a task I later accomplished for Victor Books.

I don't know how many church pulpit committees contacted me to see if I wanted to return to the pastorate, which I didn't. I'd preached for seven years from one of the nation's best-known pulpits and no other church interested me at the time. The committee from one large well-known church told me that, if I became their pastor, all I'd have to do was preach on Sundays—no committee meetings, no counseling, no visiting. I couldn't convince them that it wouldn't be possible for me to preach effectively if I were divorced from the people I was trying to help.

Gradually, life took on a predictable pattern. When I was home, I'd study, write books, and get ready for the next conference. While I was traveling, I'd do as much reading and studying as I could, always trying to stay ahead of those inevitable deadlines. Except for those days when I was so weary from traveling that I had to sleep in, I was still an early riser and spent the first hour of the day in my devotional time. Betty and I enjoyed meals together and didn't experience any of the frustration of the wife who said to her newly retired husband, "I married you for better or for worse but not for lunch!"

# Chapter Seventeen

Before I continue with the ministry story, however, I must pull together the threads of the years I've just described and update you on what happened to our four children, all of whom were — and still are — very important to our lives and our work.

David graduated from Taft High School in 1973 and spent the summer working on the staff of Moody Church's camp, Camp Moyoca, located on Loon Lake near Antioch, Illinois. Contrary to what the ex-campers may tell you, "Moyoca" is not an old Indian name that means "the beds are hard and the showers don't work." It's simply an acronym for MOody YOuth CAmp. As you already know, I'm not a camper myself, but by some freak occurrence of providential genetic engineering, I fathered two sons who love the out-of-doors and, for some bizarre reason, find great delight in camping.

All four of our children attended Moyoca during the summer months, and one summer at camp, David surrendered his life for full-time Christian service. He enrolled in the Pastors Course at Moody Bible Institute and graduated in 1976. Since I was preaching in "the church up the street" which many of the Moody students attended, it wasn't easy for David to be just another student on campus. The instant a new friend discovered that his last name was Wiersbe, a fact David carefully guarded, the next statement was usually, "Is your father pastor at Moody Church? I read his books!"

Let me digress and recall the first time I met the well-known Christian musician Don Wyrtzen. It was back in the '60s and I was speaking on The Island at Word of Life, Schroon Lake. Don showed up one afternoon while I was taking a walk. He introduced himself and I was careful *not* to say, "Oh, you belong to Jack Wyrtzen, the famous youth evangelist!" We sat and chatted for perhaps an hour about the will of God, Christian music, and what it means to walk with the Lord. Years later, Don told me how much he appreciated the conversation and especially the fact that I let him be himself—Don Wyrtzen—and not the son of his famous father. Of course, now Don is famous in his own right, but back then, his identity was a sensitive matter to him.

It can be tough to be the son or daughter of a parent who's prominent in any field. People expect you to be somebody special and they won't let you be yourself. The first time I discovered this was when I interviewed Gigi Graham for a YFC magazine article. I opened the interview by telling her that I had been converted to Christ through her father's ministry, but the statement didn't seem to impress her. She gave me a look that said, "Is this interview about *me* or my famous father?" From that point on, I concentrated on her—Gigi Graham, teenager—and not on the fact that she belonged to a famous family.

Interestingly enough, the two boys in our family have usually played down the Wiersbe name, but the two girls have made the most of it. When Carolyn attends a church music conference, she'll approach almost any well-known Christian musician with, "Hi! I think you know my father!" That usually breaks the ice, and from then on, Carolyn learns as much as she can from her new acquaintance. Judy is a bit more reserved in her approach, but she manages to drop her maiden name into the conversation when doing so might prove helpful.

After graduating from MBI, David enrolled at North Park College in Chicago. This is one of the official schools of the Mission Covenant Church of America, and David's getting his degree there in 1978 brought great joy to all our Swedish relatives. But before that, in January 1977, he became pastor of Grace Evangelical Free Church in the Chicago suburb of Schiller Park. In June 1977, he married Susan Vaughan, whom he had met at Moyoca. Susan was the older daughter of Byrl and Vivian Vaughan, and Byrl was chairman of the elders at Moody Church. David was ordained October 5, 1980, and he and Susan ministered at Grace Church until 1982, when they moved to Hope Evangelical Free Church in Roscoe, Illinois, near Rockford.

It's an interesting fact, though certainly not a unique one, that all of our children found their mates because of the ministry the Lord gave us. David and Bob both found their wives in the Moody Church family. Bob and Karen were married in 1985. Carolyn met her husband at Grace Evangelical Free Church when she assisted her big brother with the music ministry. She and David Jacobsen were married in 1979.

Judy's husband came from Highland Park Baptist Church, Southfield, Michigan, near Detroit, where I preached many times when the church was without a pastor. I usually stayed in the home of Harvey and Ann Johnson and couldn't help but notice and appreciate their son David. One day I suggested that he meet our Judy, which he did—over the telephone. Then he started to drive to Chicago to see her, and the rest is history. David and Judy were married in 1982.

Carolyn wanted to be a nurse, so she attended the school of nursing at West Suburban Hospital in nearby Oak Park, the Midwest mecca for Christian nurses. (More than one Wheaton College or Northern Baptist Seminary student found his wife at West Sub.)

We'd known for years that Bob was the scientist in our family. As a child, before playing with a new toy, he'd try to take it apart to see what made it work. So, after graduation from high school in 1976, he enrolled at DeVry Institute in Chicago and got his degree in electronics. He now works for AT&T in Naperville, Illinois. One day, he told me what he did, but I didn't understand it, so I won't try to repeat it.

Judy told us she wanted to be a teacher, and I told her she was wasting her time because God made her to be an executive secretary. After suffering through less than a year at Northeastern University in Chicago, she changed campuses and enrolled in the Metropolitan School of Business, and my prediction proved to be right. If a church publication needs to be written and distributed, or an event organized and promoted, Judy's the one to do it. She's ministered full time as a pastor's secretary and occasionally serves her local church a couple of days a week on her computer at home.

At this writing, Betty and I have five grandsons and two granddaughters, and we're praying that God will keep His hand on all of them and, if it's His will, call them into His service. After all, my great-grandfather John Carlson prayed me into the ministry years before I was even on the scene! If we're going to have a preacher of the Gospel in every generation of our family, we've got to follow his example.

┌─────┐
│  3  │
└─────┘

Shortly after I'd arrived at Moody Church in 1971, my good friend Peter Deyneka, Sr., phoned to tell me he was coming over to my study to pray with me. Peter and I had often prayed together in YFC prayer meetings, and being with him was like experiencing a personal revival. I can still hear him say, "Much prayer, much power! No prayer, no power!" He was a man of great faith and always challenged me to trust God and do exploits for Him.

After we'd prayed, Peter told me he wanted me to serve on the board of the Slavic Gospel Association, a ministry he and his wife had founded in Chicago in 1934. SGA was a ministry that operated by faith and depended on prayer, and I already knew some of the board members. I accepted Peter's invitation and served until 1983. Ten of those years I was chairman of the board and during that time once again found myself a bridge-builder.

The first bridge we had to build was from the old generation to the new. It was time for Peter, Sr., to step aside and hand over the reins of the ministry to his gifted son Peter, Jr. This decision was easy to make officially in the board meeting, but it was difficult to implement realistically in the daily work of the mission. Like many founders of ministries, Peter Deyneka the elder had a tough time letting go.

Shortly after the transition, Peter, Sr., phoned me at the Moody Church.

"Brother Wiersbe!" he exclaimed. "My heart is broken! Peter is changing things! Mission going to fall apart!"

I assured him that the Lord wasn't going to let the mission fall apart, and that what we needed was a good time of prayer. So he came to the church and we spent thirty minutes on our knees; after that, he felt better. This happened two or three times in the ensuing months, but gradually the tensions subsided as Peter, Sr. realized that his son was doing a splendid job directing the work of the mission.

Our next task was to relocate the mission offices from Kedzie Avenue in Chicago to Wheaton, Illinois, the "evangelical Vatican" where dozens of other parachurch ministries are located. The neighborhood at Kedzie and California was decaying and the expanding program of the mission was screaming out for more space. The Lord provided us with facilities near Wheaton College, complete with a boardroom and small warehouse. (The board used to meet for lunch at the Montgomery Ward cafeteria in the Chicago Loop.) We relocated, computerized the office, and found ourselves in the twentieth century.

But there was another bridge to build, this time with the board. The SGA board was composed of godly pastors and businessmen, some of whom had been with Peter Deyneka, Sr., for many years. God had used their experience and spiritual wisdom to guide and protect the ministry for four decades, and not a one of them would you want to replace. But there comes a time in every organization when you need new blood on the board, so Peter, Jr., and I worked together in recruiting younger men to serve. I think the changes we made were nonthreatening and the board meetings moved along smoothly, at least from my point of view as chairman. Sometimes it was painful for me to be the catalyst who had to process the words and feelings of the board members and come up with suggestions that would satisfy everybody. I knew the men were of one heart and mind even if they disagreed on the details of how to get things done.

At an SGA board meeting, prayer was the most important activity of the evening, and it wasn't just a religious routine that was listed on the agenda. Prayer was the powerhouse of the ministry. Often in the midst of a board discussion on a critical issue, we'd stop to pray and ask God for the wisdom we needed to make the right decisions. An organization has to have a constitution and by-laws or it will generate chaos, but rules and regulations don't guarantee that the ministry will work. They're only the rails the train runs on; the power in the engine's boiler comes from prayer. I thank God for all that I learned about prayer because I was associated with SGA all those years.

When Betty and I moved to Lincoln, Nebraska, in 1982, it became difficult for me to keep close touch with the SGA ministry in Wheaton or attend board meetings regularly, so I resigned from the board and turned the job over to my long-time YFC friend, Evon Hedley, who was working with Ted Engstrom at World Vision. He proved to be the right man for the job.

But before leaving my SGA years, I must tell you about my aborted ministry trip to Australia. I was invited by a group of believers in Australia to go there for two weeks of itinerant ministry, including a Holy Week "Keswick" conference. Although I didn't relish that long flight from the United States to Australia, I felt it was a good opportunity both for SGA and the ministry of the Word; so I accepted. Then the committee asked me to send them a few tapes of my preaching, which I did, and they canceled the invitation! No explanation was given. I'm still wondering what they heard on those cassettes that made them change their minds.

Someone has described an itinerant preacher as a man who is free to choose whatever city he wants to starve in. During my "itinerant years," from July 1978 to September 1982, I certainly didn't starve, nor did I lack for places to minister. The Lord was gracious to open doors for me and provided more opportunities than I could handle.

Ken Meyer and Warren Benson asked me to teach some

courses in practical theology at Trinity Evangelical Divinity School in nearby Deerfield, Illinois. I guess they felt the students needed to hear somebody fresh from the trenches. I protested to both of them that I had no academic credentials and no training in education, but they wouldn't listen. So, I ended up teaching courses in doctrinal preaching, evangelistic preaching, the history of preaching, the spiritual life of the minister, conference ministry, and "ministry in the contemporary church." The last course turned out to be a study of the images of the church in the New Testament and what each image taught about pastoral ministry. In subsequent years, several of the students who took this course told me it was one of the most helpful studies they had taken during their seminary years.

Being in the halls of academia was a new experience for me and I'm not sure I really fit. I was surrounded by brainy people with earned doctorates from famous schools, and here I was stumbling along with a lowly bachelor's degree. Each year at commencement, I'd admire the beautiful academic regalia that was displayed as the faculty marched in. But it was exciting to rub shoulders with the evangelical scholars on campus, and I certainly learned a lot from the students. Walt Kaiser, our dean, took a big chance when he hired me. He had more faith than I did.

The instructors were expected to devote a certain number of hours each week to counseling the students. Some students feel more comfortable chatting with a pastor than with a professor, and I guess I became the unofficial pastor on campus. Sometimes the sign-up list on the door of my office was full and other times it was empty, and occasionally a fellow instructor would come with a personal burden. I enjoyed discussing the theological topics of the day with other faculty members as we drank coffee between classes, and I was careful not to expose my ignorance too much. They were all very kind to me and treated me as if I knew something.

You never know what surprises a counseling session may bring. The wife of one of my students came to see me one day to express her grief at not being able to have a child. She was a nurse, and every time she assisted at a birth, it broke her heart that she wasn't a mother. I gave her the phone number of a fertility doctor who had been recommended to a couple I knew and forgot about the matter. Like Jacob, was I God that I could grant them a child?

A few months later, during coffee and conversation with a couple of the homiletics professors, my counselee came rushing into my office exclaiming, "I'm pregnant! I'm pregnant! And I owe it all to you!" It took some explaining to my associates, believe me, but I was glad she was going to be a mother.

Teaching the course on the images of the church in the New Testament got me interested in biblical symbolism and the use of imagination in preaching, so I began to study the subject seriously. I now have nearly 300 books in my library devoted primarily to imagination, metaphor, creativity, and allied themes, and out of this study came a Doctor of Ministries course I've taught for both Trinity and Dallas Seminary entitled "Imagination and the Quest for Biblical Preaching." I've also written a book on the subject for Victor Books. I'm convinced that too many preachers analyze the Bible to death and end up doing pulpit autopsies instead of declaring the Living Word. An outline is not a message any more than a menu is a meal or a map is a journey.

From August 17, 1979 to March 5, 1982, I was "Eutychus X" and wrote a column each fortnight for *Christianity Today*. (That meant over fifty fortnights.) I think it was Carol Thiessen who convinced her boss, *CT* editor Kenneth Kantzer, that I was a safe risk for what could be a dangerous assignment. Not every Christian has a sense of humor, and satire can sometimes cut deeper than the writer intends. Some believers don't seem to know the difference between being *serious* and being *solemn,* so I dedicated myself to the task of trying to get God's people to laugh at themselves, hoping it would make all of us easier to live with.

There was certainly no lack of material for the column because some of the things that go on in the Christian world are really quite laughable. Like Will Rogers, I didn't have to make anything up; all I had to do was report the news. If I only read the advertisements in some religious publications, I'd have enough material to keep me going for months, and if I kept my eyes and ears open at a Christian "trade show," I was set for years. Carol Thiessen occasionally sent me bizarre advertising pieces that came across her desk (I wasn't the only one getting mail from the religious weirdos), so my "idea file" was usually overflowing.

In case you missed them, here is one of my favorites.

### The Trumpet Shall Sound When?

We are pleased to announce the first annual "Eutychus Pan-Prophetic Conference," which will meet for the first time. (Please note the hyphen.) There will be four conferences, each one devoted to a different view of prophecy. At no time will the delegates meet together since there is enough trouble in the world already without adding more. Also, we sell more books this way.

The Amillennial Conference will meet in Rotterdam. Highlight of the conference will be a tour of the tulip fields, directed by a noted Calvinist scholar, yet to be chosen. Dr. Herrmann von Ritterhavenhorst will give a series of lectures on the real reasons why Calvin never wrote commentaries on Daniel and Revelation.

The Pretribulation Conference will assemble in Dallas and last only one day, although it may seem like a thousand years. We are not revealing the day or the hour, so be prepared. There will be a special display of old prophetic charts, as well as a series of lectures on why pretribs write commentaries only on Daniel and Revelation and ignore the other 64 books of the Bible. All delegates who register early will receive a free pocket calculator for figuring out prophetic dates.

The Midtribulation Conference will last exactly three-and-a-half days, Greenwich time. Several locations are under consideration, including Mt. Saint Helen's, Rome, and Chicago. Music will be provided by "The Uncertain Sound," a trumpet trio composed of students from three confused seminaries. There will also be a lecture on olive trees and candlesticks, plus a panel discussion on why midtribs write commentaries on only half of Daniel and Revelation.

Finally, the Posttribulation Conference will be held on the Mount of Olives and will last for seven days. White robes are included in the convention fee. We are anticipating a numberless multitude, so get your reservation in early. No lectures are planned, but there will be a great deal of singing — and maybe some tears and much sighing.

The management reserves the right to cancel all conferences should the Rapture take place. If it does, we'll all get together and enjoy a panel discussion on "What difference did it make who was right anyway?"

It was gratifying to receive mail from people whose opinions really carried weight. When I finished my stint as Eutychus and editor Ken Kantzer told the world who I was, I received the following letter from the late Joe Bayly, then vice president of David C. Cook Publishing Company:

Dear Warren:

Now that your cover has been blown, I can let you know that in my opinion and perhaps more importantly in the opinion of my sons, you are the best Eutychus to have struggled with those deadlines in our memory.

I am sorry that you are now finishing your stint, but know what a sigh of relief you must be breathing. The balance you maintained when you wrote, the subtle humor, the relevance to present situations — all these made it

a most valuable part of *Christianity Today.*
Thank you and best wishes in your future writing.

To me, receiving that letter from Joe was like winning a Pulitzer Prize in literature. But not all the mail was complimentary. The wife of a well-known Christian author chastised me for having fun with the titles of her husband's books, and one of my Trinity students, not knowing to whom he was writing, took me to task for a column he disagreed with. (*Never* attack an anonymous adversary. It might turn out to be your professor.) Any column that alluded to dispensationalism was bound to elicit some negative mail, and if I jested about something in the local church, at least one pastor was sure to react. Some of the critical letters were actually funnier than the columns they were attacking!

Having published more than a hundred books and ministered as speaker over two international radio programs, I've received more than my share of criticism. When the critics are right, I thank them and learn from the experience. When they're wrong, I gently try to help them, but I don't always succeed. In all my years of public ministry, I can remember receiving only three letters of apology from people who had sent me nasty letters. Some believers are as slow to apologize as they are to laugh.

Ken Kantzer had this to say in his "Editor's Note" when my last "Eutychus" column was published in *CT* March 5, 1982:

> For nearly three years, Eutychus X has entertained and enraged readers of *Christianity Today.* In spite of ourselves, he has also instructed us. To me it was special fun, because he always directed his sharpest thrusts against those causes with which he himself identifies. My friends would complain that he was picking on them. He was — and on me too. But especially on himself. And we all grew bigger because of it. Now Eutychus X moves into "retirement," and we can all finally learn who this tormenter of Israel really is: Pastor Warren Wiersbe. Once editor of *Youth for Christ* (now *Campus Life*) magazine, he was for

several years pastor of the well-known Moody Church in Chicago. Author of many books, he has more recently been engaged in radio and Bible teaching ministries in addition to his writing. We are grateful for his ministry to us through this column.

Here's my farewell column.

### Swan Song

I think it was Charles Dickens who said, "It is always difficult to do something for the last time." Or was it Richard Nixon? At any rate, whoever said it obviously never served on a church committee, purchased anything on the installment plan, or spent much time at the dentist.

This is the last column to be signed Eutychus X. In a fortnight, Eutychus XI will take over. To him or her, I hand the torch: May your fingers not be burned and may the smoke not get in your eyes. It's difficult to type while holding a burning torch, but you'll get used to it.

I want to thank the eight people who wrote me complimentary letters. I also want to thank the people who sent hate mail. My, what a collection I have! I realize that you have had a difficult time writing nasty letters to an anonymous enemy, but now the veil is drawn, and your target is here for all to see. I plan to use your letters in a future book, which will be a study of humor in evangelical ministry. I hope to get access to the Youth for Christ International files, and several seminaries have invited me to sit in on their faculty meetings.

"But has this Eutychus X experience done anything for you?" asks my inner man. Of course it has! For one thing, I have learned that too many Christian people and organizations can't laugh at themselves. They take themselves too seriously, and this makes them stuffy. I have also learned that some people are not serious enough about humor, and this makes them shallow. Schiller was right: "Nothing serves better to illustrate a man's character than the things which he finds ridiculous." That means I've been telling on myself all these months—but so have you!

Nobody said it better than Swift: "Satire is a sort of glass, wherein beholders do generally discover everybody's face but their own."

No tears, now! Let's not fog up the mirror!

A happy spring to you all, and to all—good-bye.

I talked with some of my publishers about doing a book of the "Eutychus" columns, but they weren't enthusiastic. If I'd written my columns about marriage enrichment, demonism, or how to increase church attendance, the publishers would be fighting for the material. It just proves that evangelical Christians can't afford the risk of laughing at themselves.

# CHAPTER EIGHTEEN

$$\boxed{1}$$

Wednesday October 4, 1978, I was scheduled to fly to Detroit to speak at four sessions of the Christian Businessmen's Committee annual convention in Dearborn, but before I left, I had a conference in the Red Carpet Room at O'Hare Field that changed the direction of my ministry. I met with Dr. Theodore Epp, founder and General Director of Back to the Bible, and his brother-in-law, Melvin Jones, Executive Director of the organization, and we discussed my possible involvement with the broadcast.

Since "Back to the Bible" and "Theodore Epp" were household words in the Christian world, I was somewhat familiar with the ministry, but Mr. Epp and I had met only in passing at the 1960 YFC Winona Lake convention when he had been the Bible Hour speaker. That's the time he got upset by the crazy things we did at Club House, like not letting him in because he didn't have a subscription to *Youth for Christ Magazine,* but he seemed to have forgotten all about the incident, much to my relief. If he'd known he was interviewing the author of "Frontier Mortician" and "Crush" to be his possible successor, he might have flown back to Lincoln and started looking elsewhere, and I wouldn't have blamed him.

During our conversation, I was surprised to hear these two

men—brothers-in-law for thirty-eight years—call each other
"Mr. Epp" and "Mr. Jones." In YFC, we addressed each other
by our given names, and at Moody Church, the pastoral staff
and I had been on a first-name basis, except in the public
services. During the seven years that Theodore Epp and I
worked together, we always called each other "Mr. Epp" and
"Mr. Wiersbe," or sometimes we'd get chummy and say
"Brother." Once I called him "Dr. Epp," and the look on his
face let me know that he didn't enjoy being "doctored," even
though one of his three honorary degrees had come from prestigious Wheaton College.

I learned that three different Christian leaders had phoned
Mr. Epp the same week to suggest that he consider me as a
possible successor. Because he didn't think it was right to
"steal" a pastor, Mr. Epp hadn't approached me while I was
pastoring Moody Church, but after I resigned, the way was
clear for him to contact me. Over the years, Mr. Epp had quietly
observed several younger preachers and had even invited some
of them to be guests on the broadcast, but he hadn't found
what he was looking for. I wasn't sure that I was what he was
looking for, but I was willing to see how the Lord might lead
us.

The conversation was purely exploratory and I asked my
share of questions. How much administration would be
involved? Would I have opportunity for Bible conference ministry? How long did Mr. Epp plan to remain as general director,
and what office would he have after resigning? What would be
my relationship to the board and to the eight other offices
around the world? What was the composition of the listening
audience? Was the ministry open to change? I asked Mr. Epp,
"What changes would you make in the broadcast if you were
younger and making plans for the next ten years?" I don't recall
his reply; I think my question caught him by surprise. I made it
clear that I wasn't interested in a "custodial" ministry that
would only monitor conformity and promote the status quo,
and Mr. Jones said that the broadcast was open to changes.

The upshot of the meeting was that they suggested I visit the
headquarters office in Lincoln, Nebraska, and tape some pro-

grams as a guest speaker. The programs would be released three months later, and then the office could determine how the listeners responded to my ministry. Since Mr. Epp occasionally had guest speakers on the program, the men didn't think we'd be sending out any signals. (Actually, we *did* send out a clear signal and a lot of people caught it.) If the response was good from the broadcast family, I could then become an associate teacher and fly to Lincoln regularly to produce programs. If listener response continued to be enthusiastic, then Betty (excuse me, "Mrs. Wiersbe") and I could move to Lincoln, and eventually I would become General Director.

At that time, I was still speaking on "Songs in the Night" for Moody Church, but the men assured me that my occasional guest appearances on "Back to the Bible" wouldn't create any problems. So, I made my first visit to Lincoln and Back to the Bible December 6–8, 1978, and I liked what I saw. The facilities were modest, the people were very devoted to the Lord and to their work, and the ministry had a good reputation among other Christian broadcasters. (In the months that followed, every Christian leader I talked to said the same thing: "When you think of Back to the Bible, you think of *integrity.*") The staff people I met in Lincoln seemed like old friends. It was like my Moody Church experience on Fourth of July weekend in 1971: I felt like I'd been there all my life. But we still had to find out what the radio family thought of me, and that would take time. Obviously, nobody was in a hurry.

# 2

From 1978 to 1982, conference ministry and writing kept me very busy, and I was also teaching at Trinity Evangelical Divinity School and flying to and from Lincoln, Nebraska, to produce radio programs. Betty was having an effective ministry to the wives of my ministerial students at Trinity, and we were enjoying getting to know some of the people on campus. The winter of 1979 found me at Bethel College "Founder's Week" in St. Paul, Minnesota; the annual Baptist Seminary Conference in Grand Rapids, Michigan; Moody Keswick in St. Petersburg, Florida; the Boca Raton, Florida, Bible conference; and services at a number of churches, including three successive Sundays at the People's Church in Toronto, Canada. I did a number of guest appearances on "Back to the Bible"; and the experts there continued to monitor the mail to see how well I was being received by the people who had listened to Theodore Epp for years.

As I review my datebooks for those years, I get the impression I was in the air more than I was on the ground. This was especially true as opportunities increased for overseas ministries. In October 1980, Betty and I had three weeks of itinerant ministry in Great Britain under the sponsorship of Slavic Gospel Association. In January of 1981, we ministered for The Evangelical Alliance Mission (TEAM) at the field conference at the Christiansen Academy in Rubio, Venezuela; and in June of that year, we flew to Belgium to minister at the European Child Evangelism Fellowship conference. We fell in love with Sam and Sadie Doherty and their staff of dedicated missionaries in Europe, many of them from Northern Ireland, and they were kind enough to invite us back for CEF conferences in Holland (1983), Denmark (1986), and England (1989). When I look at the ministry of CEF in Europe, I have to say (paraphrasing Sir Winston Churchill), "Never have so few done so much with so little, to the glory of God!" It's a miracle ministry and it's been an honor to have a small part in it.

The "Back to the Bible" listening audience responded positively to my Bible-teaching ministry, so in January 1980, Mr. Epp named me "assistant teacher," and this announcement told everybody that I was the heir apparent. From then on, I would take one week of broadcasts each month, which meant spending more time in Lincoln, and that meant more trips to O'Hare Field. In 1981, I was named "associate teacher" at the broadcast and given more work to do. Once again I found myself facing the task of building a bridge from the founder to the future, but I had the feeling that this bridge wouldn't be easy to construct.

In our annual Christmas letter to our family and friends, Betty and I called 1982 "The Year of the Changes." On April 24, Judy became Mrs. David Johnson and moved to Farmington, Michigan, leaving Bob and Betty and me at 6400 N. Tahoma. In June, when Betty and I were in Lincoln, she found just the right house for us, with plenty of room for my library, so we began to prepare for a move, which took place September 18. We bought the Lincoln house before selling our house in Chicago, but the Lord sold it for us in a short time. Bob stayed in the Tahoma house until October, when he moved to his own apartment in nearby Skokie, Illinois. We welcomed our first granddaughter August 20 when Rebecca Joy Jacobsen was born to David and Carolyn. David and Susan resigned from the ministry at Grace Free Church in Schiller Park and moved to Roscoe, Illinois, to pastor the Hope Free Church. We were all playing family fruit-basket upset!

The May 21 issue of *Christianity Today* contained the following article which was my personal assessment at this stage in my life. When our son David read it, all he said was, "Dad, you sure must have been in a mellow mood when you wrote that!" I guess I was.

### Mid-Life Crisis? Bah, Humbug!

When I was getting started in my profession, I used to wonder what happened to preachers when they got old. (In those days, "old" meant somewhere in the 40s. I have since recalculated.) I supposed that old preachers, like old soldiers, did not die; they just faded away. Now that I have reached middle age, I am getting my answers.

Not that I am old. (As I mentioned before, I have recalculated.) True, I can no longer sign John 8:57 after my name ("Thou art not yet fifty years old"), but there are plenty of other verses to choose from. My friends who own pocket calculators tell me that nobody can know when he is at middle age until he knows how long he will live. But even if the Lord graciously grants me fourscore years, I am still past that midpoint, and that makes me a middle-aged minister.

Dante found himself "in a dark wood" when he arrived at "the middle of the road of life," but it was his own fault. He admitted that he "strayed from the straight path." Byron had nothing good to say about the middle years: "That horrid equinox, that hateful section / Of human years, that half-way house, that rude / Hut. . . . " His experienced estimate was that our middle years are the time "when we hover between fool and sage." I think Byron must have followed Dante off the straight path.

Not that middle age doesn't have its special problems. Bob Hope once defined middle age as that time of life "when your age starts to show around your middle." My wife told me that swimming was good for my figure, and I asked her if she had ever looked at a duck's figure. Many golfers I know are tediously overweight, and I don't golf anyway. I still get my exercise by carrying books up and down the stairs and occasionally strolling about the neighborhood.

But I sometimes have a problem understanding what is going on in the high councils of Christendom. A whole new vocabulary has developed while I was out of the room parsing a Greek verb. The church renewal movement has occasionally given me slight headaches, and I have to pray extra hard before reviewing books by some authors. The new "tell-it-like-it-is" school of biography and autobiography upsets me. I sometimes feel like taking a shower after reading such stuff, and I suppose that dates me.

All sorts of new winds are blowing. Fences are coming down that used to seem sturdy. The fellow who used to draw the boundary lines was run over by a gang of protest marchers and we don't see him any more. Perhaps that's the biggest problem of the middle-aged minister: he is not always sure where he belongs. He is too wise to follow every flag that marches by, and yet he has no desire merely to be a spectator.

# Be Myself

Some ministers solve this problem by jumping on a noisy bandwagon and hitching their future to an evangelical superstar, a "man with a cause." Their own light is dim, so they live on a borrowed glow. "There is safety in numbers" they argue; but, as a witty British minister once remarked, "There is more safety in exodus."

I have never felt happy on a bandwagon. Like Thoreau, I tend to listen to a different drummer. I have never asked my friends to follow my flag; all I have asked is that they give me the privilege of following it myself, and I will do the same for them. Jehovah is a God of infinite variety and there is no need for us to be carbon copies or clones. Too many middle-aged ministers huddle together for warmth and safety when they ought to be out cutting new trails for the gospel.

All the books tell me that my middle years are a time for evaluation. I am embarrassed to confess that I never had an identity crisis. My parents always reminded me who I was, and when they forgot, my two brothers and sister took up the quarrel with the foe. I don't recall that any of my professors ever lectured on the subject, although more than once I did have a crisis trying to identify what they were lecturing about.

The books also tell me that the middle years bring threats of fear of failure. Perhaps they do. My own feeling is that God and his people have treated me far better than I deserved, and that God has balanced the blessings and burdens in a beautiful way. My early optimism has become realism; I trust there is no pessimism. I am not as critical as I used to be, not because my standards are lower, but because my sight is clearer. What I thought were blemishes in others have turned out to be scars. In my earlier years, I was one of the six blind men describing the elephant. Today I can see the elephant clearer and also the other five men.

A friend once said to me, "I want to get mellow, but not rotten." A good point. I recall that one of the great saints prayed, "Lord, don't let me become a mean old man." I suppose this has special relevance when we see others achieving goals that, to us today, are either dreams or memories. When I read the news columns of religious periodicals, I am amazed at the number of "immature young men" who are filling important places of leadership. Why, I knew some of those fellows way back in Youth for Christ days! They were just kids!

It is easy to look at the future in a rearview mirror, but that kind of driving always leads to a collision. God is building his temple, and I would rather stand shouting with the youths than sit weeping with the aged. True, some things are changing; but they have always been changing. I am reminded of the reader who complained to William Randolph Hearst that his newspaper was not as good as it used to be. He replied: "It never has been." I believe that God still saved the best wine until the last, and that the path of the just still gets brighter and brighter, even if we sometimes find ourselves looking at the glory through our tears.

Yes, there are many compensations to the minister who reaches middle age. I have lived long enough to be thankful for unanswered prayer. Here and there, I meet people who were helped along the way by something I said or wrote. I admit that it makes me feel old when I dedicate the children of parents who were little imps in churches I have pastored, but it makes me feel happy to know I helped to give them a good start. I have fathers and mothers, brothers and sisters in the Lord all over the world, and that gives me a good feeling—especially when I travel and need someplace to hang my hat.

I like to think I have matured a little. I don't know as much about prophecy as I used to, and I have stopped hunting for obscure texts that will stun congregations. I have learned the hard way that there is a difference between an outline and a message, and I wince when I remember some of the sermons I have preached. How patient were those congregations that listened and loved and encouraged! They came for bread, but too often I gave them a stone—but they were kind enough not to throw it at me.

God has taught me that he blesses people I disagree with and does not ask my permission. No, I have not abandoned my theology. The foundation is still the same, but I must confess that I have rearranged the furniture and even tossed out a few pieces that don't seem so important anymore. I have learned to love my neighbor, even if he wears a different label from mine. And I have learned not to be afraid of truth, because all truth is God's truth, no matter what the channel. When I meet a new Christian friend, I major on what we agree on and let the disagreements take care of themselves.

Regrets? Just a few, but nothing major. God has ruled and overruled, and I have no room for complaint. I am not running around quite as much—not because there are no opportunities, but because I have rearranged my priorities. William Culbertson, the late president of Moody Bible Institute, once said to me, "We do more by doing less." He was right. I am no longer infatuated with the latest church-growth scheme or intimidated when I fail to attend the latest seminar. Instead of reading the books of the hour, I am concentrating on the books of the ages and learning a lot more.

Above all, I am trying to encourage and help those who are coming along. After all, people encouraged me in those early difficult years, and real Christian encouragement is a rare commodity these days. God changes his workmen, but his work goes right on. I want to be like David and serve my generation in the will of God.

I want to keep growing, even though the older I get, the more difficult it becomes. Why? Because there is no growth without challenge, and no challenge without change. When I was younger, change was a treat; now it tends to become a threat. But I need change—not novelty, but change—the kind of experiences that force me to dig deeper and lay hold of that kingdom which cannot be shaken. There is no time to waste on scaffolding; I must build on essentials, not accidentals.

The same Lord who started me on this path will see me through to the end. I have no desire for a road map of the future; one day at a time is sufficient. I am doing my best to act my age and not trying to imitate a teenager. At the same time, I don't want to drift into what a friend of mine calls "sanctified senility." Balance is the key word, isn't it?

The mind grows by what it takes in; the heart grows by what it gives out. "Age imprints more wrinkles in the mind than it does on the face," wrote Montaigne. I would rather have a wrinkled face than a wrinkled mind. The Indian summer of life has its own glory and beauty because God made it that way, and I hope to enjoy it with him as long as he allows. Ministry thrives on maturity, and time cannot destroy what we do in the will of God. There is no time to wallow in evangelical nostalgia, not as long as there is a world to reach with the gospel.

Middle age? It is just another stage in a grand and glorious life that has been planned for us by a loving Father.

Could we want anything better?

Europe was getting ready for war when Theodore and Matilda Epp, with only sixty-five dollars available, founded Back to the Bible broadcast.* The first program was aired over KFOR in Lincoln on May 1, 1939. Except for the two years the ministry was located in Grand Island, Nebraska, "Back to the Bible" has been produced in Lincoln for over fifty years. From the very

---

*The story is told in Harold Berry's book *I Love to Tell the Story*, published by Back to the Bible. It's unfortunate that none of us—family or staff—could convince Mr. Epp that he should allow somebody to write his biography, because the story would have been exciting and edifying.

beginning, it was a faith ministry; as it grew, it didn't change its basic principles. The Epps were two of the greatest prayer warriors I've ever met. When Mr. Epp preached about prayer or faith, you could tell he wasn't discussing somebody's second-hand abstract theories. Mr. and Mrs. Epp were very familiar with the throne of grace and the promises of God.

If ever a man practiced "this one thing I do" (Phil. 3:13), it was Theodore Epp. He didn't read widely but was a man of one Book, and that Book he knew thoroughly. Even though "Back to the Bible" had helped to found National Religious Broadcasters (NRB) and the Evangelical Council for Financial Accountability (ECFA), Mr. Epp didn't get involved in the wider pursuits of these ministries nor did he try to build a large personal network involving other media leaders. He lived and breathed "Back to the Bible" and left these peripheral matters to Melvin Jones and the departmental directors who were under Mr. Jones.

During its first twenty-five or thirty years, "Back to the Bible" was probably the leading daily Bible-teaching radio ministry in America. During the '40s and '50s, you could listen to M.R. DeHaan and Charles Fuller on Sundays, but there weren't too many daily syndicated Bible study programs. With the expansion of Christian radio and radio agencies, and the advent of religious television, things began to change in the marketplace, and other voices began to be heard by the Christian public. A whole new galaxy of religious media personalities moved on the scene and a new generation with different interests began to turn the dials and push the buttons on their radios and TV sets. It was evident that "Back to the Bible" would have to make changes or face the danger of becoming a media dinosaur.

Theodore Epp was actually one of the most creative leaders in Christian radio. Without abandoning his spiritual principles, he knew how to adapt to a changing world, whether it was in promoting foreign missions, producing attractive literature, or devising new approaches to radio ministry. While most media ministries were seeking to establish a strong home base, "Back to the Bible" was raising money for missionary radio and opening offices overseas. It was as though Mr. Epp realized that the center of gravity of world missions would one day move out of the United States to the Third World. But he and Mr. Jones and their staff knew that "Back to the Bible" was being challenged to minister to a new world. What they needed was a bridge-builder.

# CHAPTER NINETEEN

$$\boxed{1}$$

Once Betty and I were on location in Lincoln, Nebraska, life settled down into a predictable routine that kept both of us very busy.

Unless I was out of the city in conference ministry, or taking a few days' study break, I'd be in the studio each morning, Monday through Friday, producing two programs a day. That meant I had to prepare *ten messages* for each week that I was in the studio taping, and that involved a lot of studying. I was always glad when my Friday morning taping was completed because it meant I had an afternoon and evening without the pressure of getting ready for the next day. Especially happy for us were the weekends when I was able to stay home and not travel somewhere to preach. It was good to attend our own church and listen to our own pastor Curt Lehman preach the Word. He and his wife Claudine became very special friends to us and their encouragement and counsel have helped us.

Many people don't realize that radio speaking is much more difficult than pulpit preaching. Radio listeners can't see your facial expressions or your gestures, so you must communicate everything through your voice. If you're speaking in a studio, there's no congregation present to respond and signal the radio listeners that you've said something witty and they should laugh. (Preachers who broadcast their Sunday sermons have an advantage studio preachers don't have.) Radio time is costly and a speaker can't afford to waste time by beating around the bush. We have thirty expensive minutes in which to raise the dead and we must use it wisely.

I was glad for my years of radio experience at Calvary Baptist Church and Moody Church, learning how to watch the clock and pace the message so that each point receives sufficient treatment. Too many radio preachers go heavy on their first point and then have to rush through the rest of the message or else carry it over to the next program. I made each day's message an independent study, because not all our listeners could tune in to every message in a series. It's not easy to watch the clock, pay attention to the engineer, follow the message outline, and keep your mind on the needs of the listeners, all at the same time. One day, by the grace of God, I produced six radio programs without a mistake or a retake! The two engineers made me a paper "blue ribbon" and pinned it on me after the taping session.

My broadcast responsibilities by themselves would have kept me very busy, but I also brought with me book contracts that I'd signed and that the publishers expected me to fulfill. The *BE* series was doing well and Mark Sweeney, director of Victor Books, kept sending me contracts and urging me to complete the entire New Testament, and I'm glad he did. Mark was a sympathetic listener when I shared my schedule demands with him, and he always encouraged me to do my best. There were some years when I was scheduled to write two *BE* books as well as books for other publishers. How was I to get all this work done?

The solution to my writing and editing needs was very simple: a computer. I confess that for many years I stayed away from computers, telling myself that my trusty typewriters had been good enough to do the job since I'd published my first book in 1945. Certainly they wouldn't fail me now. But the real reason I avoided computers was because I was afraid of them. If you've read my story this far, then you know that I'm not as left-brained as I ought to be; anything electronic or mechanical completely eludes me.

That's where our neighbors came in.

## 2

When Betty and I were searching for a house in Lincoln, we knew it had to meet several specifications. For one thing, because we're "given to hospitality," the house had to have at least three bedrooms and be large enough for entertaining. It also had to provide space for my growing library, which today numbers over ten thousand volumes. (Betty told the real estate people, "I'm looking for a library with a house attached.") The house had to be adequate but modest, because radio listeners visiting Lincoln would look up our address and drive past our house just to see what was happening to their donations. Somebody started the story that the Wiersbes had a big swimming pool and owned a farm! The closest thing we have to a swimming pool is a bird bath in the backyard, and what in the world would a city boy like me do with a farm? Sometimes the saints say crazy things.

The Lord gave us just the house we prayed for, and He added an extra blessing: wonderful neighbors. Among them are Bob and Idonna Florell and (when we moved in) their son Scott, who was about to turn fifteen. Scott sort of adopted us as second parents and dropped in almost daily to chat, eat chocolate chip cookies, and see what Betty was preparing for supper. If he liked the menu, he'd stay and eat with us. Sometimes he came over for a second opinion about a matter. Whenever Scott found me pounding on my manual typewriter, which was often, our conversation would sound like this:

"You ought to get a computer."

"You've said that before," I'd reply. "I don't know how to use one, and I'd probably mess it up and blow every fuse in Lincoln."

**Official Back
to the Bible
photograph.**

**"Preaching"
to the mike.**

"You can't do that with a computer," he'd argue. "All you can do is mess up your file or your program."

"I don't have time to learn how to use one."

"Give me two hours and I can show you everything you need to know," Scott would argue. "After that, you'll learn as you go along. It's not that hard."

I finally capitulated and bought a computer and a printer; sure enough, in two hours one afternoon, Scott showed me the basics and then turned me loose. More than once during those first months I had to phone him for help when I hit a wrong key and goofed up my work, but he'd always come to my rescue — after visiting the cookie jar en route to my library. In time, as I got the hang of it, Scott was able to solve my problems over the phone; then, thanks to his tutelage, I learned to work things out for myself. After Scott went off to medical school, if I had a problem, I could always call our son Bob, and he was able to "read me in"; but, by the grace of God, the problems diminished.

I discovered that Scott had been right: the computer saved me hours of time and helped me do a better job than I could ever have done with my typewriter. I haven't touched the typewriter since.

In time, we computerized the broadcast office, and this made our work much easier, especially when it came to publishing books. A secretary would transcribe my radio messages to a diskette and I'd take the diskette home and do the editing and rewriting on my own computer. Then we'd put the diskette into a special machine that would set the type for the book. Although it was extra work for me, the broadcast saved money and time, both of which are important to a nonprofit faith ministry. When the sacrificial gifts of praying people are helping to pay the bills, you don't waste anything, and no evangelical organization exemplifies that kind of stewardship better than Back to the Bible.

### 3

Nineteen eighty-four was a special year. I was asked to serve on the board of The Evangelical Alliance Mission (TEAM), which Betty and I felt was a real honor. I served with them for almost ten years. When TEAM and Bible Christian Union merged their ministries, I felt it was time for me to step aside and let some of the BCU men serve on the board. Working with Richard Winchell, TEAM's General Director, and the staff and board members was indeed an exciting spiritual experience.

In 1984, Back to the Bible broadcast celebrated its forty-fifth anniversary with a special conference April 30 and May 1 at the new Cornhusker Convention Center across the street from our headquarters office. The guest speaker was Bruce Dunn, for forty years pastor of Grace Presbyterian Church in Peoria, Illinois, and one of Mr. Epp's favorite preachers. Mr. Epp was a faithful listener to "The Grace Worship Hour" and often commented to me about what Dr. Dunn had said. Bruce and I were occasionally in conferences together at Winona Lake and elsewhere, and I had preached many times at Grace church. Bruce went to be with the Lord in 1993. He was a gifted expositor of the Word and a preacher's preacher.

When the broadcast committee was planning the conference, I suggested that we invite soloist Frank Boggs to do the music; the committee, including Mr. Epp, asked, "Who's he?" I was amazed that nobody in the meeting knew Frank Boggs. We'd often had Frank in concert at Moody Church; in my opinion, he's one of the finest vocal interpreters of Christian music anywhere. The committee took my word for it and invited him, and he stole everybody's heart.

Before I say more about the anniversary conference, just a quick story about Frank. In June 1980, Betty and I went to Great Britain for three weeks, along with our younger daughter Judy and our friend Bev Smith from Moody Church, now Bev Johnson. We attended All Soul's Church in London one Sunday evening and discovered that Frank Boggs would be singing, so we waited with bated breath for him to appear on the platform. As he sat there, he surveyed the large congregation, no doubt searching for a face he recognized. When he spied us, he sat up with a jolt. The service hadn't started yet, so Frank left the platform and came down to greet us.

"What in the world are you doing here?" he asked.

"Well," I replied, "we heard you were singing at All Soul's, so we flew over just to hear you. How's that for loyalty?"

Frank and I have often talked about teaming up for an itinerant ministry in Great Britain, where he is greatly loved, but so far, the Lord hasn't given us the go-ahead signal.

Now, back to the forty-fifth anniversary conference. The most exciting thing that happened to me those two days occurred at the board meeting when Mr. Epp resigned and put the mantle on me. I was now General Director.

Some weeks before, he'd called me into his office and asked, "When you become General Director, what will my title be?"

"What title do you want?" I asked. After all, who was I to tell the founder what his title would be?

"Well, I know one thing," he replied; "I don't want to be called *emeritus.* It sounds like an old horse who's been put out to pasture!"

I'm not a believer in prophetic utterances, but I think the Lord gave me a "word of wisdom" at that moment. "How about calling you Founding Director?" I suggested.

Mr. Epp's smile was so broad and spontaneous that it lit up the room.

"Founding Director," he said, more to himself than to me. "Founding Director. I like that. Good! That's what it'll be!"

Of course, the board would have to approve the title, but nobody was worried about that. The board wasn't about to go against his wishes, especially on the day he was taking his first step toward retirement. However, no matter what title I was given, as long as Theodore Epp was alive and well, there would be no question in anybody's mind where the authority rested at Back to the Bible. I was given his former title and his ministry responsibilities, but I did not move into his office until after he'd gone to be with the Lord.

You can understand that it would be difficult for Mr. Epp to turn the leadership of the organization over to a new man, no matter who he was, for "Back to the Bible" had been his very life for forty-five years. He had an agreement with his wife and Mr. Jones that when they detected he was "slipping" in his radio ministry, they should tell him about it, and they did. It was becoming more and more difficult for him to communicate what he wanted to say, and the tapes of his radio messages had to be carefully edited to take out repetitions and other distracting elements. It took a lot of courage for Mr. Epp to set aside his own feelings and step aside for the good of the ministry, but he did it.

For the second time in my life, I was accepting the mantle of a great and godly man who had chosen me to be his successor. I had been through leadership changes before, at Calvary Baptist Church and at Slavic Gospel Association; so I thought I was prepared for what would happen. But I wasn't. Between May 1, 1984, when I was made General Director, and October 13, 1985, when Mr. Epp went to glory, the road that I walked was a difficult one; but the Lord walked with me and taught me many lessons I needed to learn.

Please understand that I'm not trying in any way to tarnish Mr. Epp's reputation. I don't think anybody could do that, because his life was above reproach. He and I may have had our differences during those eighteen months, but never once did I see him as anything other than a man of God who had done an extraordinary work, a man whose wisdom and prayer support were very important to me and the ministry. We often met together and discussed the changes I wanted to make, and, as much as possible, I submitted to his decisions. But there were times when I simply couldn't agree with him and still be true to the vision God had given me for Back to the Bible. At a time when media ministries were experiencing radical changes, I was trying to build a bridge to a new generation of radio listeners, and sometimes I felt like Mr. Epp didn't understand.

It wasn't as though I was new to the staff, because I'd been working alongside Mr. Epp for five years. I was probably more aware of the changes in Christian radio than he was, since he didn't make it a practice to attend NRB or to keep in close touch with others in media ministry. He always depended on Mr. Jones and the staff to do that, and soon Mr. Jones would be retiring too, and Brian Erickson would become executive director.

Mr. Epp was doing what many people do as they get older: he was living in the "good old days." Some anonymous wit has defined "the good old days" as the combination of a bad memory and a good imagination, and sometimes that's true. Mr. Epp enjoyed talking about what he did years ago instead of what God wanted to do now and in the future.

But there was a second problem: Mr. Epp had a difficult time confronting people when he had a disagreement to discuss. I could usually tell when he was disturbed about something because he would walk back and forth past my office door as if he were trying to work up enough courage to come in and talk. I'd been used to the candor of my Youth for Christ associates and of the staff members at Moody Church, and I saw no reason why he and I couldn't discuss our differences forthrightly ("speaking the truth in love"), pray together, and get it over with.

The relatively unimportant "cosmetic changes" that I'd made in the ministry didn't bother him too much. The proposal that disturbed him most was that we change the names of our two magazines, the *Good News Broadcaster* and *Young Ambassador*. I didn't think the names really told people what they'd find in the pages of either periodical. These may have been effective names for reaching people in the '40s and '50s, but the times had changed. We were trying to minister to a nonreading video generation and we needed names for our magazines that would get people's attention.

I wanted to call the adult magazine *Confident Living,* and Roger Morrow and the Youth Department staff came up with *Teen-Quest* for the youth magazine; Mr. Epp didn't like either one. After all, "Back to the Bible" was "broadcasting the Good News," and every Christian teenager was supposed to be a "young ambassador" for the Lord, so why look for better names? He walked back and forth past my office door quite frequently, and then he sent me a handwritten note saying that he was not in agreement with these changes.

"This matter of the change of names for our two magazines [he wrote] has me deeply concerned. (I am being tormented with thoughts day and nights).

"I simply cannot concentrate on my studies, etc. I do not have the authority to stop it, nor to change the names; but as the Founding Director and as a member of the board, I will ask that the matter either be dropped altogether, or if felt important enough to follow thru, then present it to the board at their annual meeting in November.

"I am herewith voicing my conviction, namely that I am 100 percent against any change of name for the *GNB [Good News Broadcaster],* and 99 percent against any change of the name for the *YA [Young Ambassador].*"

All I needed was for the Founding Director to become my adversary at the next board meeting! I knew that one of two things would happen: either the board would side with Mr. Epp and thus start getting involved in administration and possibly oppose other changes; or the board would sidestep the issue somehow and vote it into oblivion. Either way, I was destined to lose. If the board was going to follow Mr. Epp, then they didn't need me, and the best thing I could do for the ministry would be to get out of the way.

Late in September, Mr. Epp became ill; and after a relatively brief time in the hospital, he died of congestive heart failure on Sunday, October 13, 1985. He never got to attend the board meeting. Instead, he had an abundant entrance into the presence of the Lord whom he loved and had served so faithfully.

During his hospital stay, I visited him almost daily and found him confident and trusting the Lord, just as he had always been. He said nothing about the magazines, but he made me promise that I wouldn't replay his messages on the broadcast. I did get him to agree that we could use selected messages during the annual Anniversary Week celebration in May.

The funeral was held at Rosemont Christian and Missionary Alliance Church in Lincoln, where he and Mrs. Epp had attended, and the sanctuary and auxiliary rooms were packed with the people who loved him and appreciated his ministry. The family asked me to give the message; and for the second time in my ministry, I was conducting the funeral of a predecessor. While the service was triumphant, our hearts were heavy because a "prince and a great man in Israel" had been taken from us. In his latter years, Mr. Epp may have been somewhat out of step with the times—just as I may be someday soon—but he was never out of step with the Lord. He was indeed a man of God.

At the November board meeting, I presented my agenda for change, including the new names for the magazines, and I frankly told the men that if Mr. Epp were there, he would oppose them. After a brief silence, one of the Mr. Epp's closest friends spoke up and said, "We wanted to do some of these things years ago, but Mr. Epp wouldn't let us." I breathed a prayer of thanks to the Lord, and then we got down to business.

The week after Thanksgiving, Betty's folks visited us on their way to winter in Prescott, Arizona. On November 29, while driving near Oberlin, Kansas, they were involved in a tragic accident with a truck. The sheriff phoned me that afternoon to give me the sad news, and then I had to tell Betty. We prayed and stayed very close to the phone. Mr. Warren died at 6 o'clock that evening. Mrs. Warren was flown to Denver for surgery but died on the operating table at 9 that evening. Betty lost both of her parents the same day, although, as Vance Havner used to say, "When you know where something is, you haven't lost it."

The funeral service was December 4 at the People's Church

in Beloit, Wisconsin, where they were members; and David and I led the service. I had a hard enough time, but it was especially tough for David. Our children dearly loved their Grandpa and Grandma who had cared for them (and pampered them) so many times when Betty and I were traveling overseas. In spite of their ages, they both had been very much alive and very much involved in the Lord's work, and it seemed a shame that they should be cut off so quickly and so painfully. With Mr. Epp's homegoing in October, and now the Warrens being taken from us, Betty and I were a mournful pair, but, "Precious in the sight of the Lord is the death of His saints" (Ps. 116:15).

One of the hottest issues in Christian radio is music, and that's where "Back to the Bible" had some of its biggest problems. I personally felt that we were keeping a sane balance in our music, but not everybody in Christian radio agreed with me. Some station managers thought our music was too conservative, and they threatened to drop the program or shunt it off to a 3 A.M. spot on their schedule. Others thought our music was too contemporary. They suggested that we go back to using the Hammond organ and the grand piano for accompaniment and abandon the synthesizer and orchestrations. It was even suggested that we drop the music altogether and devote the entire half hour to Bible teaching; but the staff and I were convinced that music was important to the program, just as it is to the local church. Good music helps the listener praise God, and praise is good preparation for Bible study. According to Psalm 119:171 (NIV), praise and study go together: "My lips overflow with praise, for You teach me Your decrees." I don't know that we ever solved the music problem, but we sure tried hard.

I confess that some of today's trends in "Christian" music

disturb me, but there's not much I can do about it. As I turn the radio dial, it's becoming more and more difficult to know when I've located a Christian station. I fear the church may lose the great heritage of hymnody that we have, because too often we're substituting religious entertainment for spiritual enrichment. We're raising a generation of Christians that needs to know the great hymns of the church, but we aren't always giving them the opportunity.

At the same time, let me say that the older generation needs to learn to appreciate what God is saying to the churches through some of the newer music. The best way to do this is for church worship leaders to maintain a creative balance so that the congregation worships God using the best of the old and the best of the new. (Not all the old songs in the hymnal are worth preserving!) This isn't easy to do, but it's the way the Lord told us to minister. "Therefore every teacher of the law who has been instructed about the kingdom of heaven is like the owner of a house who brings out of his storeroom new treasure as well as old" (Matt. 13:52, NIV).

But music isn't the only thing that disturbs the world of Christian media. Money is also a factor. The average listener doesn't realize how many financial cogitations and agitations go on behind the scenes to keep many Christian programs on the air. If you were to eavesdrop on some of the conversations at the annual NRB convention, or at the board meetings of a local Christian station, your eyes might be opened and maybe your faith would be shattered.

Many station managers see Christian radio as a ministry, and they're willing to broadcast programs that may not be "popular" but that have an important message for the Christian public. Other media leaders see Christian radio as a religious business; to them, the bottom line is making money and getting the biggest listening audience possible no matter who the preacher is or what he's saying. Certainly ministry must be businesslike, but with some stations it's difficult to tell where business stops and ministry begins.

But I must be fair and admit that there are also local churches that have this same "corporate merchandising con-

Dr. J. Vernon McGee, me, and Betty at Word of Life, Schroon Lake, New York.

Erwin Lutzer, Alan Redpath, George Sweeting, and me in front of D.L. Moody's pulpit at Moody Church (1985).

cept" of ministry that I think is unbiblical. The pastor is the CEO, the staff is the board of directors, the people are the "customers," and Jesus is the product that the church sells because He has the answers to everybody's problems. "Give the customer what she wants!" and "The customer is always right!" are the two great commandments that govern such ministries, and on these two hang the law and the profits.

The longer I was in Christian radio, the more difficult it became for me to attend the media conventions and conferences.* I enjoyed meeting old friends and making new friends; I profited from the seminars; the missionary radio reports were great; and some of the preachers inspired and instructed me. But the general atmosphere of promotion and religious entertainment made some of these meetings look more like "trade shows" than a gathering of Christ's humble servants who were working together to reach a lost world and revive a sick church. I'm not pointing an accusing finger at anybody, because I served on one national media board and must take as much share of the blame as anybody else.

Many Christians don't realize that broadcasters make regular donations to nonprofit stations that provide them with radio time. These donations aren't classified as "payments," but "Back to the Bible," like many other broadcasters, faithfully sends checks to noncommercial Christian radio stations to help cover their cost of service. As broadcasters, we also participate in the annual "Share-a-thon" to help the station raise additional support. Whenever I hear a local announcer say, "This station is happy to donate this time to 'Back to the Bible' " (or some other broadcaster), I smile to myself, knowing full well that the broadcaster is helping them pay their bills. Certainly there's nothing unbiblical about this arrangement, but sometimes it makes the broadcaster look like a freeloader when he's really helping carry the load.

---

*Mr. Epp once walked out of the plenary session of a Christian media convention when he heard the speaker, a famous television preacher, introduce his address with something like this: "You will notice that I don't have a Bible. I've stopped using a Bible in the pulpit. People don't want sermons; they want to hear what God means to us in our own hearts." I wasn't there to hear what the speaker said; I'm reporting what Mr. Epp remembered and told me.

When it comes to the commercial stations, most broadcasters have to negotiate annually both the cost and the time slot, and sometimes the competition is keen. The time your program is aired determines who will hear it, and every broadcaster wants the widest possible listening audience. Again, if the style of your music or the emphasis of your message doesn't please the station manager, you might not get what you're asking for. When I was General Director of "Back to the Bible," I was glad all these difficult matters were in the capable hands of the staff of our in-house radio agency, Good Life Associates. We had some experiences with the personnel at some stations that almost brought us to tears. These experiences sure brought us to our knees.

Mr. Epp often reminded us that God didn't call "Back to the Bible" to have the biggest network of stations or even the largest listening audience. The Lord called us to teach the Word of God and trust Him to nurture the seed we planted and produce the fruit. During one especially difficult time, when stations were either moving our time slot or canceling the program, God reminded Mr. Epp of the promise He had given him years before in Revelation 3:8, "I know thy works: behold, I have set before thee an open door, and no man can shut it." More than once he shared that promise with me and I appreciated the encouragement.

When the "Pearly Gate" religious media scandals broke in 1987, attracting the attention of the whole world, almost every evangelical media ministry was affected adversely. I wish I had saved some of the hateful letters we received at Back to the Bible, but perhaps it's best that they went into the wastebasket. The activities of a few religious celebrities not only brought reproach to many sincere servants of God, but they also gave some people in the secular media the excuse they needed to announce that fundamentalists were fakes and radio and TV ministers were money-hungry.

There had never been even a suspicion of moral or financial scandal at Back to the Bible during its nearly fifty years of ministry, but that didn't seem to impress the critics. Nor were they impressed that Back to the Bible had helped to found the Evangelical Council for Financial Accountability and had always abided by its standards. The critics lumped all ministries together and declared them wicked.

"Pearly Gate" not only affected organizations, but it also touched the personal lives of those of us who were in positions of leadership. The IRS audited several religious leaders who were involved in media ministries, including my wife and me. We had nothing to hide, but enduring four months of investigation was an additional pressure that we sure didn't need.*

As the public's confidence in ministries eroded, Back to the Bible's income declined; but the Lord saw us through. "Pearly Gate" did a lot of damage, but in the end, some good came out of it. I believe it produced a great deal of heart-searching and housecleaning in many lives and organizations and that Christian broadcasting in general is in better shape today than it was before 1987. That doesn't justify the guilty; but it does remind us that in times of wrath, God still remembers mercy (Hab. 3:2).

---

*For my analysis of the media scandals and what they mean to the church, see *The Integrity Crisis,* published by Oliver-Nelson. It was difficult for me to write that book, but somebody who was in religious media ministry had to say something.

# CHAPTER TWENTY

$$\boxed{1}$$

Whenever I discover that I have more jobs than I can adequately handle, which is frequently, I know I have only myself to blame; I've always been my own worst boss.

I can usually say no to my friends and fellow workers who want me to get involved in some new project, but I have a hard time saying no to myself. During the three years I served as General Director of Back to the Bible Broadcast after Mr. Epp's homegoing, we launched two new radio programs and two new publications.

I don't recall how or when the Lord gave me the idea for the new program "Dyna-Moments." It just seemed to me that Christian radio needed a five minute Bible-teaching program that could be dropped into the broadcast day several times to give the listeners a "blessing break" straight from the Word. Our agency manager Tom Schindler and I worked on the format and "Dyna-Moments" was the result. Each program was based on a brief but complete portion of Scripture from which I would extract one major truth, explain it, and apply it. We added a a crisp musical introduction and conclusion and had ourselves a new program.

During the years that I produced the program, I went

through the entire Book of Psalms,* as well as Proverbs, Matthew, and John, and many of the epistles. It was a helpful exercise for me to have to take one truth from a passage and present it succinctly in a practical way in less than five minutes. A number of the stations that carried "Back to the Bible" also carried "Dyna-Moments" on a sustaining basis. The program is no longer being produced, although some stations are still rerunning the old programs. When people say to me, "I hear you on the radio every day!" I assume they're referring to "Dyna-Moments," because I haven't been on "Back to the Bible" on a daily basis since May 1990.

The second program we started was "Gateway to Joy," featuring Elisabeth Elliot, the well-known missionary, conference speaker, and writer. I thought it was quite a coup that we could get Elisabeth on our Back to the Bible team, but Elisabeth was amazed that we even wanted her! She didn't see herself as a radio personality, but she certainly communicates God's Word in a way that helps both men and women understand God's basic principles for abundant life. One of our broadcast employees who knew her well, Jan Anderson (now Jan Wismer), set the whole thing in motion and was the original producer of "Gateway to Joy." The program succeeded beyond our expectations and at this writing is still being broadcast on several hundred stations.

The two new publications we launched were *Back to the Bible Today*, a giveaway magazine featuring news about broadcast ministries around the world, and *Prokope,*** a four-page bimonthly inspirational piece for pastors. Our editorial department produced *Back to the Bible Today*, but I wrote every word of *Prokope* except for the few times I asked for contributions from our overseas department. It was my one opportunity to minister to the thousands of pastors and other Christian workers whose names were on our mailing list. The emphasis in *Prokope* was on encouragement, which is something most

---

*Back to the Bible and Baker Book House have published the devotionals from the psalms in the book *Prayer, Praise and Promises.*
** Pronounced "PROCK-uh-pay." It's a Greek word from 1 Timothy 4:15 ("profiting" in KJV) and means "pioneer advance." The major articles I wrote for *Prokope* can be found in my book, *In Praise of Plodders,* published by Kregel Publications.

pastors need; and along with my introductory article, I dropped in sermon ideas, quotations relevant to the season, statistics, and book notices, all of which the busy person could read in less than fifteen minutes. Like "Dyna-Moments," the key to *Prokope*'s success was its brevity, and I still get mail from pastors and missionaries telling me they miss this bimonthly chat I used to have with them.

As I look back, I can see that producing "Dyna-Moments" and *Prokope* meant extra work for me, but I enjoyed it; I knew that God's people would be encouraged and helped. I guess no matter what office I fill or title I wear, I'm still a pastor at heart and always will be.

## 2

October 20–23, 1989, Youth for Christ International celebrated its forty-fifth anniversary by hosting a "Celebration of Hope" in Chicago and inviting all the "old guard" and their families back for a reunion. The executive director of the event, Dr. Roy McKeown, asked me to serve on the steering committee, but my schedule at Back to the Bible didn't allow me to attend many of the committee meetings. Roy and his Executive Committee did a splendid job of planning the reunion and making it a happy time of fellowship and ministry for all of us.

I had the privilege of speaking at one of the sessions, and Harold Myra, CEO of Christianity Today, Inc., introduced me. He told how I had nurtured him in his early days as a free-lance writer and then helped bring him on the *YFC Magazine* staff, thus giving him entry into the world of Christian journalism. When he said, "Wiersbe is a legend in his own time," I began to feel very old. I'm not sure what "a legend in his own time" actually is, but the word *legend* is defined as "a nonhistorical or unverifiable story handed down by tradition." YFC is loaded with legends and legendary people, and as the man said, "The legend you are about to hear is true."

The four-day celebration climaxed with an old-fashioned YFC rally at Moody Church with Billy Graham as the main speaker. I think Torrey Johnson and some of the other leaders had hoped that "Celebration of Hope" would spark new interest in YFC and perhaps bring about a "YFC revival," but that didn't seem to happen. Thousands of people like me have reason to thank God for Youth for Christ and its impact on our lives, but now it's a different day. We've got to be careful not to try to duplicate the past, no matter how gloriously successful it may have been. We must remain "geared to the times and anchored to the Rock."

## 3

My YFC experience in helping to plan and promote big events came in handy when "Back to the Bible" celebrated its fiftieth anniversary April 30–May 2, 1989. We started working on the conference early in 1988, and Peter Schroeder and his committee did a great job putting together a program that included all the elements of Back to the Bible's ministry around the world. Along with our many Nebraska friends, hundreds of people attended from all over the United States, Canada, and many foreign countries. All I had to do was speak at a couple of sessions and show up at the rest of them to greet the saints with a smile and a handshake.

Nebraska's governor Kay Orr attended the prayer breakfast and entered into the celebration with enthusiasm. I sat next to her during the meal, and when she opened her purse to get something, I noticed in it a copy of *Our Daily Bread* devotional booklet. It appeared to be well-used, so I don't think it was put there just for my benefit. Some weeks later, I saw Governor Orr at the University of Nebraska commencement, and she called me by name! I was duly impressed.

We chose "The Great American Famine" as our theme for the anniversary year and prepared a video that not only reviewed the history of "Back to the Bible" but pointed out the "famine of the Word of God" in America today. Our theme verse was Amos 8:11 (KJV), "Behold, the days come, saith the Lord God, that I will send a famine in the land, not a famine of bread, nor a thirst for water, but of hearing the words of the Lord."

Theodore Epp had started "Back to the Bible" because American Christians in 1939 needed to do just that — get back to the Bible. Now, fifty years later, the challenge was needed again! A few people criticized us for taking such a negative stance in our anniversary year, but we felt that somebody had to sound the warning. Biblical teaching was slowly disappearing from our land and Christian radio had not escaped. Orthodox Bible teaching was being replaced by a shallow experience-centered kind of ministry that exalted man but almost ignored the Lord.

I don't think the average church member realizes the extent of the theological erosion that's taken place on the American evangelical scene since World War II,* but the changes I've witnessed in Christian broadcasting and publishing make it very real to me. Radio programs that once majored in practical Bible teaching are now given over to man-centered interviews ("talk" radio is a popular thing) and man-centered music that sounds so much like what the world presents, you wonder if your radio is tuned to a Christian station. Some so-called "Christian music" is just plain silly. God's people are getting their "theology" from popular religious music instead of from the Bible and the hymnal. In so much of today's ministry, "feeling good" has replaced being good, and "happiness" has replaced holiness.

When Betty and I visit the exhibits at the conventions that are connected with publishing, sometimes we don't know whether

---

*In his excellent book *No Place for Truth, or Whatever Happened to Evangelical Theology?* (Eerdmans, 1993) Dr. David F. Wells says the same thing and adds careful documentation. I wish his book had been available in 1989. We would have sold hundreds of them.

we should laugh or cry. We rejoice that some of the stalwart publishers are still bringing out books with solid Christian theological content, but the proliferation of superficial "me-centered" books is very disturbing. If anybody's a friend to Christian publishing and to the Christian bookseller, I am; and I've proved it many times. But I become grieved when I see all the "Jesus junk" that's being peddled, the "Christian celebrities" that are being endorsed, and the books without theological substance that are being advertised. As I said before, you wonder where business stops and ministry begins.

The real problem, of course, isn't just that some publishers and broadcasters are wedded to the spirit of the times and want to be "successful." The real problem is that too many Christians have an appetite for this kind of rubbish and don't realize that they're living on substitutes. As long as the church provides a market for that kind of product, somebody will make them available.

I fear that Christian radio can make people "codependent" if they aren't careful. Listeners think that because they've listened to a "great preacher," they've learned something, but that isn't necessarily true. A woman wrote and told me how many Christian broadcasters she listened to in the course of a day, and then she added, "But I'm not a successful Christian and don't know what's wrong." I wrote and told her what was wrong: she was listening to too many voices and not taking time to digest what she heard (if it was worth digesting) and put it into practice.

"Pick out one or two speakers who really get through to you," I wrote, "and listen to them, but be sure to practice what they teach from the Word. Also, spend time alone with the Lord each day, reading the Bible and praying. God doesn't need the radio on to talk to you."

Weeks later, she wrote back and told me how her Christian life had changed for the better because she followed my counsel. She may have stopped listening to "Back to the Bible" for all I know, but that's not important. Now she was listening to the Lord and doing what He was telling her to do.

In spite of the impressive statistics recorded by the evangelical publishing and broadcasting world, and the sensational trade shows that they sponsor, there is in America today a famine of the hearing of the Word of God. Instead of a mirror for revealing Christ and making us like Him (2 Cor. 3:18), the Bible has become a manual for finding "six ways to get along with your wife," "ten steps to successful living" and "seven rules for conquering depression." What the American church needs is obedience to God's four commandments for revival found in 2 Chronicles 7:14.

The fiftieth anniversary celebration actually lasted from January 1989 through May 1990. During that time, the Back to the Bible quartette and I traveled a good deal in radio rallies and church services. The quartette would give a mini-concert, we'd show the "famine" video, and then I'd bring a brief message related to the anniversary theme. It was a tough time for all of us, doing our regular work during the week and then traveling on weekends, but the Lord gave strength to us and blessing to His people. I don't know how many people told us how much they appreciated the Bible-centered ministry of "Back to the Bible Broadcast."

We climaxed the anniversary celebration on May 1, 1990, with a one-day conference in downtown Lincoln that ended with a rally at the Pershing Auditorium in Lincoln where some 5,000 people came to praise the Lord in song and to hear Chuck Swindoll preach the Word. Knowing how busy Chuck is and how many invitations he receives, I will always be grateful to him for speaking at the meeting that launched "Back to the Bible Broadcast's" fifty-first year of ministry. Other speakers that day included Dr. Gary Oliver, Christian counselor and member of the Broadcast board, and Elisabeth Elliot, speaker on "Gateway to Joy."

During that special anniversary year, Betty and I were struggling to understand what the Lord wanted us to do. I'd been working with the broadcast since 1979 and had been General Director since 1984, but I began to sense that my ministry there was about to be completed. It was time for a younger man to take over and make the changes I knew I couldn't make. Brian Erickson and the directors were doing a fine job of managing the machinery of the organization, so a period of transition wouldn't create major problems. The work would go on.

After months of praying, heart-searching, and discussing, Betty and I concluded that I should leave the broadcast at the end of 1989, but stay with the radio ministry until the anniversary celebration on May 1, 1990. On August 30, 1989, I sent a private letter to Brian Erickson, explaining my situation; among other things, I wrote:

> While this is not an official resignation letter, I think I owe you some kind of explanation for what may seem to you a radical decision. I hold you and your directors in the highest esteem and don't want to do anything that would be misunderstood.

> To begin with, I'm not doing much "general directing"; and you and the other directors know it. Ever since the board turned down the scenario of two years ago, I have had no clear "vision" for the ministry, beyond May 1990. Physically and emotionally, I just can't keep up with everything I have to do, especially the daily radio production. Maybe my 1966 accident is finally catching up with me, I don't know; but I have to be honest and confess that the schedule is grinding me down. I don't have the strength for the long haul, and my "creative juices" don't seem to be flowing as they once did.

> The financial picture at the broadcast is not getting better and this baffles me. This is the first time in nearly forty years of ministry that I have been a part of a work that has not seen its needs met. The future of the broadcast de-

pends on the board making some tough decisions and moving the ministry into the future. I tried, but apparently I failed.

Perhaps it was asking too much to expect anybody to follow a man like Theodore Epp. All I know is that I have worked hard and have given the Lord and the ministry my best. I have enjoyed working with you and all the staff and am only too cognizant of my many limitations and failures.

Brian suggested that I send an official letter of resignation to Melvin Jones, chairman of the Broadcast board, so that we could "get the ball rolling" in plenty of time for the November board meeting. Mr. Jones sent a copy of my letter to the members of the board, and then I read a statement in chapel on September 11 that pretty much summarized what I'd written to Brian and the board. Let me quote only two paragraphs:

I want to assure you that this was not an impulsive decision. There are no secrets, no hidden agendas, no organizational conflicts. The main reason for my decision is simply that I no longer seem to have the strength and stamina that it takes to handle the many demands of the broadcast ministry. . . . It is time for someone else to step in who can not only maintain our historic ministry but also relate it to the needs of a new day.

Thank you for your encouragement, your many expressions of love and appreciation, your patience, and your wholehearted devotion to Christ and to the ministry of "Back to the Bible." No leader could have wanted a more cooperative and creative staff, and I thank you for all you have done. Believe me, you are in our hearts and our prayers; and you always will be. God bless you!

The decision was made, the news was announced, and Betty and I had peace in our hearts that we were walking in the will of the Lord. For the most part, the worldwide broadcast family was very supportive, although a few listeners hinted in their letters that I was a quitter and perhaps out of the will of God. After all, Mr. Epp had stayed on the job for forty-five years! But I was just too tired to engage in a ministerial marathon with my predecessor, and I had no desire to stay on the job until I was a hundred years old. As Henry David Thoreau said when he left his cabin at Walden Pond, "I left the woods for as good a reason as I went there. Perhaps it seemed to me that I had several more lives to live, and could not spare any more time for that one."*

God had other things for us to do and we were ready to do them.

---

*Henry David Thoreau, *Walden* (Princeton, N.J.: Princeton University Press, 1971), 323.

# CHAPTER TWENTY-ONE

Nineteen ninety was perhaps the toughest year Betty and I have experienced in all our years of marriage and ministry. Only a few close friends and family members knew what we were going through, and their prayers helped sustain us and eventually bring us out into the "broad place" of victory. I suppose we should have expected some kind of attack because we were stepping out by faith into a different ministry. Also, I was preaching a Sunday evening series on Satan at our church, and every time I do that series, Betty and I end up being assaulted by the enemy in some unusual way. This time we were attacked on several fronts, and at one point, it looked like our ministry might even be destroyed.

I used to criticize Moses and Elijah for wanting God to take them, but by July, I was ready to call it quits. A recurring sinus infection was giving me chronic throat problems, which made preaching difficult, and the oppression of the enemy was starting to smother every desire I had for public ministry. During July, we were scheduled to minister for a week at Word of Life (New York) and then fly to Britain to speak the first week of the annual British Keswick conference. Things looked so bleak, I was tempted to cancel both engagements and just stay home and wallow in my weariness and my wounds.

## Be Myself

I talked to my pastor, Curt Lehman, with whom I regularly confer about ministry matters, and asked what he'd advise me to do, and he encouraged us to keep going. "I'd stick with the schedule," he said. "I think it would do you good to get away and focus on ministering the Word."

We followed his counsel, and I'm glad we did. We had a great week at Word of Life where I preached a series of messages from the Psalms. The conference guests told me they were helped by the studies; they didn't realize that I was preaching to myself as well as to them. More than once during that week, Betty and I awakened in the night, sensing the enemy's attacks; all we could do was pray, weep, and claim God's promises. I spent much time reading the Psalms and asking God to be glorified in all our trials, by life or by death.

After a busy but blessed week at Word of Life, we took the train to New York City, and Sunday morning we attended Trinity Baptist Church and heard Gordon MacDonald preach. After the service, we had good fellowship with him and Gail over a snack at a nearby delicatessen. Betty and I have appreciated their books very much and have benefited from reading them. That evening I preached at the Manhattan Bible Church, founded by Tom and Vicky Mahairas, a remarkable ministry that's being greatly used of God in a most difficult part of the city. It revived my own soul just to be in these two churches and see what God was doing.

Let me interject this story. Some weeks later on a Saturday morning, we were back in Lincoln, and I was in the "slough of despond." The phone rang; it was Gordon MacDonald. The Lord had impressed him to give me a call, and he did so at just the time I most needed a word of encouragement. His call was another evidence that the Lord would bring us through triumphantly, and He did. By the end of the year, the pressures had let up and we felt that the Lord had given the victory.

But back to New York. Monday evening Betty and I flew to Great Britain and were met Tuesday morning at Heathrow by our dear friends Ian and Anne Bull, in whose quiet home in Surrey the Lord has often given us "refuge and strength." If ever we needed their fellowship and support, it was now, and they were lavish in their love. We had an old-fashioned prayer meeting on our knees in their living room, and Betty and I felt it was a turning-point in the battles we were waging.

**In my library at home.**

Before going to Keswick, we visited Roger and Dottie Carswell in Leeds. Roger belongs to an endangered species: he's an itinerant evangelist. He and his older son Benjamin took us to see York Cathedral; and then the Wiersbes and the Bulls headed for the little village of Thwaite where we stayed in a picturesque hotel surrounded by the beautiful Yorkshire Dales. (The Lake District is lovely, but I think the Yorkshire Dales are the most beautiful part of England.) There were thirty people living in Thwaite. When the hotel was filled, it nearly doubled the population! We went out for a walk that evening and met a herd of cows coming up the only street of the tiny village. You can be sure that we walked circumspectly after that.

Betty and I thoroughly enjoyed our week at British Keswick, ministering the Word, seeing old friends, meeting new friends, and being treated royally by chairman Rev. Philip Hacking and the Keswick Committee. The speakers and leaders were housed in a small charming hotel about a mile from the big tent where the meetings were held, and the fellowship at meals and in the prayer times was delightful. The main speaker for the week was Michael Baughen, Bishop of Chester and former vicar of All Soul's in London. Betty and I had met him at All Soul's when Frank Boggs was singing there. It was enlightening to chat with him and his wife during meals and discover that even bishops have their problems. Michael Baughen is a gifted preacher and musician; we enjoying singing some of his songs during the worship times in the big tent.

We enjoyed meeting Billy Strachan, principal of Capernwray Hall in Lancashire, who was one of the speakers. We'd heard him speak over the "Radio Bible Class" and especially appreciated hearing him in person. At Keswick, all the speakers are expected to sit on the platform, even when they're not scheduled to address the meeting. When the program chairman was interviewing me at the pulpit, he talked about my writing and then suddenly asked, "Have you even considered writing a *BE* book on The Song of Solomon?"

A ripple of laughter moved across the crowd, and I replied, "No, I haven't considered that at all, and I don't know what I'd call it."

From behind us came the voice of Billy Strachan: "Call it *Be Careful!*"

The ripple became a tidal wave. I don't know if humor is permitted at Keswick, but it did us all good to laugh, and it made me feel right at home. Anybody who thinks that people in the UK are reserved and restrained has never been around Billy Strachan.

I'm really not sure who was behind my being invited to Keswick; maybe it was Stephen Olford. I certainly didn't feel qualified to stand in a pulpit that had been dignified by such men as Campbell Morgan, Alan Redpath, Stephen Olford, George Duncan (whom we met that week), Donald Grey Barnhouse, Wilbur Smith, and many others. But our being there was one of God's gracious gifts to us, because we desperately needed to hear others minister the Word, and what we heard did our hearts good. Michael Baughen gave a series of Bible readings from Hebrews, and the way he magnified Christ and His finished work nourished our souls and gave us new hope.

I must add that during that year of conflict, I was writing *With the Word,* a devotional commentary on the whole Bible, as well as *Be Patient* on the Book of Job; and the enemy did everything he could to interfere with these projects. *With the Word* is based on material from more than twenty years of notes in my devotional diaries. Day after day, as I worked my way through my Bible and my notebooks, and as I studied Job, the Word of God ministered to my own heart and kept me encouraged when almost everything around me was pressuring me to quit. The sportswriter Red Smith once said, "There's nothing to writing. All you do is sit down at a typewriter and open a vein." When I wrote *With the Word,* I sat down at my computer day after day and opened my heart and a couple of veins! But it was worth it.

Gradually my sinus infection cleared up and I began to feel much better. We finished the summer with a week at Sandy Cove Bible Conference and a week in Bangor, Northern Ireland, where we participated in the annual citywide missions conference sponsored by a number of evangelical churches. Betty and I have enjoyed ministering the Word in Ireland; there's something very special about our Christian brothers and sisters there. I don't know of any city in America that has an annual citywide missions conference, but they've had one in Bangor for many years.

## 2

If you were to read through my date books and devotional diaries, you'd find the notation "sick today" written on many pages. Not many people knew about it, but ever since my auto accident in 1966, I'd been afflicted with recurring headaches, frequent cases of upset stomach, and a tendency to throw up without warning. For years, I told my doctors that I thought I had gallbladder trouble, but all the examinations and tests proved negative. I told Betty to put on my tombstone, "I told you the diagnosis was wrong!"

But for somebody who travels, this kind of problem is a downright nuisance. One Sunday morning in London, I fainted dead away at breakfast and ended up on the floor. The lady of the house thought I was going to die. I didn't die, but I did have to cancel preaching that morning at Duke Street Church, although I was well enough to preach at the evening service. I would get sick in an instant, languish, and then get well in a hurry. My affliction was nothing like what Paul endured (2 Cor. 12), but it was certainly a "thorn in the flesh," and I often had to ask God for much grace to be able to get my work done.

Two weeks before Christmas 1990, I began to experience unbearable pain in my chest, and Betty, thinking it might be a heart attack, took me to the emergency ward of the hospital. The doctor said it was gas, gave me some medicine, and sent me home. The next day, I was still very sick; two days later, the pain was so bad, I wanted to die. This time the doctor said it was my gallbladder and that the only solution was surgery. If I hadn't been so ill, I would have shouted, "I told you so!"

My sick gallbladder had caused my pancreas to get inflamed, and my doctor spent the next four days trying to get my pancreas back to normal. To kill the pain, they put me on Demerol and morphine. For somebody like me who can get high on a decongestant, this combination of painkillers was deadly, and I began to hallucinate. I saw psychedelic drinking straws that became huge spiders which I tried to kill with a rolled-up newspaper. I almost knocked over the IV stand trying to get out of bed one night. (I thought I was at home.) I sat patiently in bed trying to put an imaginary thread through the eye of an equally imaginary needle. One day I woke up with a start and the complete plot of a short story went through my mind in an instant. Betty tells me she wishes she'd recorded some of my conversations. I guess they were pretty wild. But in a few days, my pancreas began to behave and the doctors were able to operate, and my wicked gallbladder fell prey to the skills of the laproscopic surgeon. Two days after the surgery, I was back home and feeling fine, with only three tiny scars to prove I'd had surgery. I was telling the people who phoned that I was now an Israelite in whom there was no bile.

When my fine Christian surgeon, Dr. Lloyd Tenney, came to my room to sign me out, I said, "You know, God gave me a gallbladder and you took it out. Did God make a mistake?"

"Nope," he said, continued to fill out papers.

"If I can do without it," I said, "then why did God give it to me in the first place?"

"So I could send my kids to college," he replied.

Betty and I had planned to visit our family during the Christmas season, but I wasn't able to travel; so we had a quiet holiday at home. Our neighbors the Florells invited us over for Christmas dinner; we talked to our loved ones over the phone; and I got a lot of reading done. (I usually buy myself a stack of books for Christmas!) Unfortunately, I had to cancel a week of ministry at Cedarville College in Cedarville, Ohio, but their president, Paul Dixon, understood the situation and forgave me.

The headaches are gone, the stomach pain is gone, and I don't throw up any more. I told them the diagnosis was wrong!

Some months after I'd fully recovered, I was preaching at the church Dr. Tenney attends; and I saw him coming down the hall. I put my arms around my waist, bent over, got a pained expression on my face, and began to moan. As he walked by, all he said was, "Sorry, warranty's run out."

When I resigned from the broadcast, I urged the board to consider moving the program out of the studio and into a church setting where a live congregation could add a new dimension to the ministry of the Word. The popularity of programs like "Insight for Living," "Turning Point," and "Grace to You" is evidence that people enjoy hearing a taped message given "live" to real people from a real pulpit.

The broadcast board actually interviewed one well-known pastor who, I think, would have merged his embryonic radio ministry with ours. But in order to keep his church and his pulpit, he would have to direct the Lincoln ministry from a distance, and the board didn't think that was advisable. (I didn't tell them how many weeks I had been away from Lincoln during the years I was on staff!) When I heard one or two board members say, "That's not the way Mr. Epp would have done it," I knew the cause was lost.

I gave the search committee a list of the names of men who in my opinion could take the leadership of the ministry. The first name on the list was my pastor friend who wouldn't move to Lincoln and abandon his pulpit. (Since then, his radio ministry has skyrocketed.) The second name was that of a gifted Bible teacher and pastor who didn't feel led to come. The third name was that of Woodrow Kroll, a man I'd met only once at Moody "Founder's Week," but whose ministry I appreciated. For ten years, he'd served as president of Practical Bible Training School in Binghamton, New York, and was well respected as a preacher and Christian leader. I happened to know that one of the Midwest's largest churches was "courting" him to be their pastor, but I hoped the Lord would lead him to "Back to the Bible."

After several months of prayer and discussion, the board invited Dr. Kroll to become General Director and Bible Teacher, and he accepted. He was officially installed at a public convocation in Lincoln on November 16, 1990, so the transition was complete. I felt very relieved. The broadcast was in good hands and the work would go on and expand.

4

On January 12, 1991, Betty and I entertained a few friends at dinner as we celebrated the fortieth anniversary of my ordination. For the occasion, our pastor son David wrote me a letter that I treasure.

January 9, 1991

Dear Dad:

On the 40th anniversary of your Ordination to the Ministry of the Gospel, some reflections are in order. For the past forty years (and more), you have:

Prepared more sermons than you care to figure out;
Wrestled with the Scripture and had it wrestle with you;
Thrown away as many outlines as you've preached;
Dedicated infants, some cooperative, some incorrigible;
Baptized believers; ("Man, that water's cold!")*
Performed weddings that were blessed, and some you'd
    just as soon never done;
Officiated at funerals, triumphant and tragic;
Attended Board, Elder, Building Committee, Trustee,
    Executive Committee, Nominating Committee,
    Sunday School, VBS, Staff, Christmas Program, Budget
    Committee, New Member and Visitor meetings;
Visited people in most of the hospitals and nursing
    homes in northern Indiana, northern Kentucky, and
    northern Illinois;
Candidated at churches at least three times, successfully;
Resigned from five ministries successfully (meaning,
    you're still alive);

---

*This is a "house joke." The thermostat for the Moody Church baptistery went haywire one day and the water was very chilly. The first man I immersed surfaced and said, loud enough for the world to hear, "Man, that water's cold!" The next month the water was so hot, I could have plucked chickens. Count it all joy.

# Be Myself

Been to Winona Lake more times than anyone should
  have to;*
Invested hours in counseling saints and screwballs;**
Endured staff and Sunday School picnics;
Suffered the slings and arrows of outrageous critics;
Enjoyed the enduring friendship of some choice saints
  and their families;
Set high standards for those who model their ministry
  after yours;
Survived a tour of duty as a seminary instructor;
Written over a hundred books (ultra-prolific is the term)
Remained teachable;
Mastered a growing technology (from typewriter to PC);
Endured times of trial with evident grace and faith;
Planned who knows how many orders of worship;
Been wakened by late-night parish emergencies;
Eaten at, and survived, potlucks and banquets;
Heard the best and worst in Christian music;
Stayed married to the same woman and kept her very
  happy;
Learned to disagree with people and not be disagree-
  able;
Come full circle on using "liberal nature songs" in wor-
  ship;***
Publicized some of your children's exploits in sermon
  illustrations;

---

*Another "house matter." David's birthday is July 6, and I always missed the celebra-
tion because I was at the YFC convention at Winona Lake.
**Sometimes they were the same people. Like most pastors, I've met my share of
strange folks: the man who claimed he was the Trinity; the lady who kept phoning me
because "the enemy" was after her legs; the man who sat in the front row at Moody
Church and "played the piano" during the music; the bearded man who wagged his
head like a pendulum as he sang the hymns; the regular attenders who invaded the
visitors' reception at Moody Church every Sunday morning and filled their pockets with
cookies; the man who phoned to argue about the Trinity and then told me he was
divorcing his wife. You had to feel sorry for them because not much could be done to
help them.
***"House matter" number three. When David was pastoring his first church, I criti-
cized him for using songs like "This Is My Father's World" and other "nature hymns,"
arguing that the good old Gospel songs were what people needed. But I matured in my
understanding of the believer's relationship to God's creation; and by the time I wrote
*Real Worship*, I agreed with David.

# Chapter Twenty-one

Never lost your quick wit and sense of humor;

Become a human card catalog for any book having anything to do with life, truth, and human experience;

Demonstrated great strength through not just one, but TWO church building programs;

Faithfully prayed for your flocks, and fed them the very best;

Carried the burdens without losing sight of the blessings;

Served as the church's pastor, the pastor's pastor, and your family's pastor;

Run a great race and fought a good fight;

Not run out of horizons yet.

You've both lived and modeled the Christian faith and ministry for me, Dad. I couldn't have had a better teacher or father. I love you.

[signed] DAVID

I'm not sure I really deserved having all those nice things written about me, but I appreciated them.

Our son's paraphrase of Hamlet ("the slings and arrows of outrageous critics") introduces a subject that I don't enjoy discussing, but there's no way to avoid it if I'm going to tell my story. It's the subject of the critical saints and the things they've written *to* me and *about* me over the years.

When I started my ministry in 1950, there were only two "camps" in the professing church, liberals and fundamentalists. Fundamentalists were people who believed the basics of the Christian faith as expressed in the historic creeds; liberals were people who questioned or denied some or all of these doctrines. While the list varied from time to time, the "fundamentals" usually included: the inspiration and inerrancy of Scripture; the deity of Christ and His virgin birth; the atoning death of Christ; the bodily resurrection of Christ; and the second coming of Christ. These are doctrines I have believed and taught throughout my ministry and that I still believe and teach.

But I've watched the ecclesiastical situation become quite confusing over the years as various "fellowships" have developed within the broader fundamentalist camp. I use the word "fellowships" deliberately because the test of your Christianity depended on the people you fellowshipped with and the leaders who influenced you. Doctrinal fundamentalism was still important, but a "cultic" fundamentalism started to become even more important as various men promoted their causes and sought to exert their influence as widely as possible.

What I call "cultic fundamentalism" was based on fellowshipping with the right people and acknowledging the right leaders. These various "fellowships" were built around strong, high-profile preachers who rallied to themselves pastors and churches looking for direction and protection in a frightening world that was rapidly changing. From my perspective, what church historians call "the fundamentalist movement" may have been more of a temporary cooperative alliance held together by a cadre of men who were independent in their ministries but worked together to promote the cause. If one of these men had a serious disagreement with somebody, he could "pull out" of the fellowship, and his "disciples" would follow him. Then he could start attacking his former friends and branding them as apostates, liberals, compromisers, neo-evangelicals, neo-fundamentalists, or whatever term best seemed to fit.

It was just a short step from *cultic* fundamentalism ("We're following the right leader!") to *cultural* fundamentalism ("We live as he lives!"). When that happened, the tests of fellowship became the personal convictions (or prejudices) of the leaders, such things as length of hair, length of skirts, translations of the Bible, styles of music, separation from worldliness (which was not always clearly defined), and being friendly with the wrong people. "The wrong people" included believers who were too friendly with people who didn't belong to your particular fellowship.

**Our whole family at Betty's and my fortieth anniversary, June 1993.**

There developed from this new approach to biblical separation a concept called "secondary separation." To get in trouble with your fellowship, you didn't have to deny the fundamentals or break the cultural standards. All you had to do was have fellowship with somebody who did break the rules, and you were in trouble. If I preached to a congregation whose pastor had been on the steering committee of a Billy Graham crusade, or if I shared a conference with a speaker associated with an unapproved organization, I was no longer a separated saint or a bona fide fundamentalist. Separation ended up separating the saints and bringing anger, accusation, and fragmentation among people who claimed to believe the same Bible and love the same Savior.

Even Bible translations became a test of orthodoxy and fellowship. A "King James Only" movement penetrated churches

in the United States and Canada, and some churches and conferences let their guest speakers know that no other translation
would be permitted. When I was on the board of Slavic Gospel
Association, pastors of fundamentalist churches supporting our
missionaries would send us questionnaires to determine if our
ministry was acceptable by their standards. One questionnaire
asked, "What translation of the Bible do your missionaries
use?" The answer, of course, was *Russian*. However, the answer wasn't satisfactory, because the pastor wrote back and
asked, "Is it the Russian King James?" We replied that there was
no such translation as "The Russian King James," and the
church then dropped its support.

Sometimes the survey would have a page devoted to the
question, "Does your organization endorse or cooperate with
any of the following groups?" and there would follow a list of
ministries such as Campus Crusade for Christ, the National
Council of Churches, Dallas Theological Seminary, World Vision, the Billy Graham Evangelistic Association, and so on. It
also asked, "Do you object to the term 'Fundamentalism' in
describing your doctrinal position or association?" Now we'd
come to the point where the very word "fundamentalism" (or
"Fundamentalism") was a test of fellowship!

I have in my file a thick folder of literature written to warn
people about me and my ministry. If I mentioned a "disap-
proved" writer or preacher in one of my *Moody Monthly* columns, I received mail from readers who accused me of being a
liberal, and editorials would appear in some of the fundamentalist publications attacking me, Moody Bible Institute, and
Moody Church. Billy Graham's associate evangelist John Wesley
White spoke at Moody "Founder's Week" in 1976, and so did I;
and the meeting was held at Moody Church. I got blamed for
causing both the church and the Institute to apostatize!

The strange thing is that the position these people took toward me was quite inconsistent. During the ten years I pastored Calvary Baptist Church in Covington, Kentucky, these
separatist groups approved of my ministry and invited me to
speak at their meetings; *and yet Calvary Baptist Church belonged to the Southern Baptist Convention, a denomination*

*branded as liberal by many fundamentalists.* When I went to Moody Church, widely known as "the citadel of fundamentalism," I became suspect. Within a few years, my attackers were calling me a compromiser and a neo-evangelical. However, their accusations didn't seem to hinder my ministry. I still received many invitations to speak at leading fundamentalist schools and conferences, and those invitations came back year after year. In fact, two schools in the fundamentalist camp gave me honorary doctorates!

Church historians say that "neo-evangelical" was first coined by Harold John Ockenga, but I question if that's correct. In his fascinating book *A History of the Evangelical Party in the Church of England\**, G.R. Balleine informs us that the term "neo-evangelical" was coined by writers in an "ultra-militant" publication called the *Rock,* which began publication in 1868. Its purpose was to "expose the compromise" of ministers in the Church of England, men who didn't identify with the militant wing of the church. The *Rock* first applied the term "neo-evangelical" to John Charles Ryle, author of so many excellent books, especially *Expository Thoughts on the Gospels.*

A recent fundamentalist newsletter called me "the king of the neo-evangelicals." I don't think I qualify; but if I do, I'm certainly in good company with a godly man like J.C. Ryle! Without apology, I affirm that I'm a doctrinal fundamentalist; I believe and preach the historic Christian faith. To the best of my knowledge, I have never knowingly cooperated in ministry with anybody who denied any of the fundamentals of the faith.

When this barrage of unfounded criticism first started, it hurt me deeply. I would write lovingly to those who attacked me and refute their accusations, but usually I received either no reply or a reply so bland that it said nothing. Then I realized that Satan was using these articles to upset me and hinder my spiritual life, so I stopped reading them altogether. When they arrived in the mail, I either dropped them in the wastebasket or put them in the file and went on with my work.

"A disputatious spirit is a sure sign of an unsanctified spirit,"

---

*G.R. Balleine, *A History of the Evangelical Party in the Church of England* (London: Church Book Room Press, 1908), 215.

wrote Alexander Whyte. "They are usually men least acquainted with the heavenly life who are the most violent disputers
about the circumstantiality of religion. Yea, though you were
sure that your opinions were true yet when the chiefest of your
zeal is turned to these things, the life of grace soon decays
within."*

# 6

I thank God that He has given me a ministry of the Word that
leaps over denominational walls and manmade barriers, and
that I belong to a wide and loving fellowship of people who
seek to honor Jesus Christ and bring sinners to faith in Him. I
guess it's the broadness of my ministry that has upset the people who have a more narrow outlook on the Christian life than
I do. Like Joseph, I've been privileged to see my branches "run
over the wall" (Gen. 49:22); and like Joseph, I've felt the attacks of "the archers" who have shot at me (v. 23). But if that's
what it takes to be a "fruitful bough," it's worth it.

I'm grateful that God has opened the doors of opportunity
for me and that I've never tried to force my way into any ministry. The Lord has given me far more opportunities than I ever
deserved, and I trust this will continue until He calls me home
or comes to receive all of His people.

However, as I get older, there are times when I feel like a
dinosaur. So many of my friends with whom I ministered in
Bible conferences are now in glory, people like Fred Brown,
Howard Sugden, Vance Havner, J. Vernon McGee, Bruce Dunn,
and Jacob Gartenhaus. They were all a great encouragement to
me.

But I don't want to be the kind of preacher who spends all

*Alexander Whyte, *Bible Characters from the Old and New Testaments* (Grand Rapids:
Kregel Publications, 1990), 832.

his time remembering the good old days and criticizing what's going on today. I think that some of today's younger leaders would do well to get acquainted with some of us dinosaurs because we might have something worth sharing. And I wish more of my fellow dinosaurs would make friends with younger preachers and find out that God is doing some exciting things today. My younger friends have done me a world of good and I thank God for them.

A few years ago, on a drizzly day when my arthritis was reminding me of the creeping consequences of getting old, I asked the Lord in my morning devotional time to give me a promise that would sustain me for the "declining" years to come. (No sense fooling myself!) In the course of my regular Bible reading, I came to Isaiah 58:11 (NKJV); and I said, "That's it! Thank You, Lord!" Here's the verse He gave me:

> The Lord will guide you continually, and satisfy your soul
> in drought, and strengthen your bones; you shall be like a
> watered garden, and like a spring of water, whose waters
> do not fail.

Then I remembered the godly British preacher F.B. Meyer who, in the latter years of his busy life, said to a friend, "I do hope my Father will let the river of my life go flowing fully till the finish. I don't want it to end in a swamp."*

Gilbert K. Chesterton's definition of old age was "to be left alone at a banquet, the lights dead and the flowers faded." As much as I admire Chesterton, I don't agree with him here. For one thing, we Christians are never alone and the banquet never ends, because Christ has promised to be with us "even to the end of the age." If I should have to walk through the valley of the shadow of death, Jesus Christ will be right there with me (Ps. 23:4), so there's no need to be afraid.

And the lights never go dead, because "The path of the just is as the shining light, that shineth more and more unto the perfect day" (Prov. 4:18). God's people are going to a land where

---

*W.Y. Fullerton, *F.B. Meyer: A Biography* (London: Marshall, Morgan and Scott, n.d.), 169.

the flowers never fade and God's glory is the light forever. The flowers around us on earth may fade, and the tent we live in may gradually decay, but we don't lose heart. "Even though our outward man is perishing, yet the inward man is being renewed day by day" (2 Cor. 4:16, NKJV).

Sometimes in the early evening, I go to my library and sit in the rocking chair and meditate on things eternal. I think of what it will be like to meet Jesus Christ face to face. Then the words of Thomas à Kempis come to my mind: "Of a surety, at the Day of Judgment, it will be demanded of us, not what we have read, but what we have done; not how well we have spoken, but how holily we have lived."*

I have one desire.

After I've attended my last meeting and preached my last sermon, written my last book and answered my last letter, told my last joke and said my last good-bye, and I wake up in the presence of my Lord, I want to be able to say to Him what Jesus said when He came to the end of His earthly ministry: "I have glorified You on the earth. I have finished the work which You have given me to do" (John 17:4, NKJV).

I don't want my life to end in a swamp.

A swamp is no place for a bridge-builder.

---

*The Imitation of Christ, III.5.

# APPENDIX
## An Informal Bibliography

This is a nonacademic ramble through an annotated bibliography of my books. I won't name every tract, booklet, or magazine article I've written because I can't remember them all, and I didn't save copies of everything I published. Robert Benchley said it took him fifteen years to discover he wasn't a writer; but his books were so popular, he had to keep writing.

**Wiersbe, the Magician**
*Action with Cards* (1944), *Mental Cases with Cards* (1946), and *Tantalizing Thimbles* (1948), all published by the L.L. Ireland Magic Company, Chicago.

It was sort of imbecilic for a fifteen-year-old amateur magician to have the audacity to write a book and send it to one of the nation's leading magic houses, but I didn't know any better. Nothing ventured, nothing gained. Francis Ireland and their resident card expert Ed Marlo were very kind to me. Having three books published before I was twenty gave me a lot of confidence when I started writing for the religious press.

**The Youth for Christ Years (1958–1961)**
I wrote *A Guidebook to Ephesians* (1957) and *A Guidebook to Galatians* (1958) for the YFC quizzers who wanted some kind

of brief introduction and commentary to these epistles. I got an upfront royalty of $300 for each one, which was a lot of money in those days and probably helped us pay some doctor bills. I also wrote *A Guidebook to Proverbs,* but it was never published. Bob Pierce convinced the YFCI board that Proverbs wasn't a good book for quizzing, so it was dropped. *A Guidebook to Proverbs* is one of two manuscripts I wrote that never were published. The other one is *The Life I Now Live,* a terrible book on how to live the Christian life, based on Galatians 2:20. Whenever I want to aggravate my wife, all I have to say is, "I think I'll get out that Galatians 2:20 manuscript and work on it." Back in 1955, Dr. J. Sidlow Baxter was kind enough to read the manuscript, but he didn't give me much encouragement.

In 1958, I assembled ten articles we'd published by Billy Graham, and we called the book *Billy Graham Talks to Teenagers.* I think the Billy Graham Evangelistic Association is still distributing the book.

I edited a book on rock music called *Teenage Rock* (1959), which was to be sold at the showings of the Gospel Films movie of the same name. The chapters were originally published in *YFC Magazine.*

I did a series of articles for *YFC Magazine* on "teenage spiritual diseases," and they were compiled into a book we called *Quaran-Teen* (1960). *Teenagers Anonymous* (1961) was a compilation I edited of *YFC Magazine* "as-told-to" articles describing the lives and problems of young people who were better off remaining anonymous. I think Ken Anderson and I wrote most of the original articles; fortunately, we were also anonymous. The chapter titles were pretty daring for a youth publication in that era, like "I Went Too Far!" and "I Wish I Had Never Met Him" and "I'm Glad We Broke Up."

Ted Engstrom had published a rather successful book with Zondervan called *52 Workable Youth Programs,* and they asked for a sequel, so we collaborated on *52 Workable Junior High Programs* (1960). Ted had a file of ideas, to which I added my own brain children; and I took a week off from work to write the book. I think the up-front royalty helped to pay the bills for our Judy to come into this world.

# *Appendix*

*How to Study Successfully* and *Successful Christian Living for 20th Century Teens* both came out in 1962 and were forgotten by 1963. By then, our family was in Covington, Kentucky, and I was completely involved in pastoral ministry.

One day Pete Gunther phoned me from Moody Press and asked if I could come to the Institute to chat with him and Harold Shaw about a couple of books for teenagers. Ken Taylor was then director of Moody Press and was working on what we now know as *The Living Bible.* Ken and Pete and Hal were a great encouragement to me in those days when I was trying to get a foothold in Christian publishing, and I'll always be grateful to the Lord for their friendship. I ended up writing three books for Moody Press: *Byways of Blessing* (1961), an adult devotional book; *A Guidebook for Teens* (1962) and *Teens Triumphant* (1962). The latter two titles were later combined into *The Wonderful World of Teens* (1968), and material from *Byways of Blessing* went into *Thoughts for Men on the Move* (1970).

## The Calvary Baptist Church Years (1961–1971)

Frank Randolph was the Fleming H. Revell representative who serviced our Calvary Book Room and I always looked forward to his visits. He knew the Christian publishing world intimately and kept me informed. Frequently, he urged me to write for Revell; the result was *Be a Real Teen-Ager* (1965) and *Creative Christian Living* (1967). Later, Moody Press picked up *Be a Real Teen-Ager* and reissued it in 1982 as *Be Challenged.* I'm not sure Victor Books liked the way they hitchhiked on the *BE* titles which were then becoming widely known. Material from *Creative Christian Living* was reworked and used in *The Strategy of Satan,* which was published in 1979 by Tyndale House.

I think that the most important writing I did during my Calvary Baptist Church years was the weekly material for "The Whole Bible Study Course." These outlines were published by Calvary Book Room in offset form as *Expository Outlines on the New Testament* (1965) and *Expository Outlines on the Old Testament* (1968) and later became the foundation for my *BE* books. These outlines are now published by Victor Books as *Wiersbe's*

327

*Expository Outlines on The New Testament* (1992) and *Wiersbe's Expository Outlines on the Old Testament* (1993). Mark Sweeney had to twist my arm to get me to agree to have my name in the title.

Scripture Press asked me to write a little book on the subject of "change" to supplement the youth curriculum lessons for one quarter, and I wrote *So What's New?* (1971) I had a good time researching what philosophers and theologians had to say about change and the so-called "generation gap."

## The Moody Church Years (1971–1978)

I've already told about the beginning of the *BE* series. *Be Real* on 1 John was published by Victor Books in 1972. Baker Book House published a collection of my "Songs in the Night" radio messages in 1973; we called it *Songs in the Night.* A few years later, we changed the title to *Turning Mountains into Molehills,* and the book started to do better. You'd be surprised what a difference the title can make!

My beloved friend Howard Sugden and I collaborated on *When Pastors Wonder How* which was published by Moody Press in 1973. In 1980, it was reissued as *Confident Pastoral Leadership.* Howard and I worked on a revision a year before he was called home, and Lucile Sugden and Betty provided material for a chapter for the pastor's wife. The book has especially helped younger pastors and has elicited many phone calls from bewildered and burdened ministers seeking counsel.

*Be Joyful* (Philippians) was published by Victor Books in 1974 and turned out to be the *BE* book that's sold the most copies. I don't think it's the best exposition I ever wrote, but the approach to the epistle seems to meet people's needs. At least I've had more positive response to *Be Joyful* than to any other *BE* book.

During 1972–73, I devoted almost every Thursday (my day off) to gathering information on Dr. William Culbertson and writing a biography of the late president of Moody Bible Institute. Pete Gunther at Moody Press had asked me to write the book, and I felt honored to be given the assignment. I read hundreds of letters and magazine articles, interviewed the family members and dozens of people who knew him well, and the result was *William Culbertson, a Man of God* (1974).

With the thousands of MBI alumni who knew and loved Dr. Culbertson, I thought the book would have a wide ministry, but it turned out to be one of the best-kept secrets in evangelical publishing. People whose opinions I trust tell me they enjoyed the book and felt I did a good job writing it, but the Christian public in general and the MBI constituency in particular chose to ignore it. Maybe someday I'll find out why.

*Be Free* (Galatians) came out in 1975 and it had the garish subtitle: "CAUTION: This book may be hazardous to your ideas of Christian living!" But the subtitle turned out to be true. I know of two missionaries working under a very legalistic mission board who read *Be Free* and resigned from the board to join another mission. I've had phone calls from pastors and Sunday School teachers asking for help in counseling believers who didn't want to accept their freedom in Christ because they were afraid to apply the lessons of Galatians and trust the Holy Spirit for the wisdom and strength they needed.

*Be Rich* (Ephesians) was published in 1976 and really should have been called *Be United*. I think my exposition missed the main theme of the epistle, which is the unity of God's people. I dedicated the book to my immediate predecessors at Moody Church: Frank Logsdon, Alan Redpath, Howard Hermansen (who served frequently as interim pastor), and George Sweeting. As of this writing, only George is still with us.

At Moody Church, I did a series of sermons on The Beatitudes, and Les Stobbe at Moody Press asked me to put them into a book. The result was *Live Like a King*, published in 1976 and reissued several times through 1993, when they dropped it. Some of my close friends have told me they thought *Live Like a King* was the best book I ever wrote.

Herman Baker, founder of Baker Book House, loved books and knew books as few people know them. We had many good times together and I learned a lot from him. He suggested that I compile some of the *Moody Monthly* "Insight for Pastors" columns, and the result was *Walking with the Giants*, published in 1976. This was followed by *Listening to the Giants*

(1980), and *Giant Steps* (1981). The latter volume is a devotional book comprised of seven selections from fifty-two of the "giants" so that the reader can spend a whole year with them. The biographical chapters of *Walking* and *Listening* were compiled into *Living with the Giants* (1993), and I added a long chapter on D.L. Moody that I'd written for Back to the Bible's magazine *Confident Living*.

The *Giant* books have been used as textbooks in a number of Bible schools and seminaries, and many pastors have told me that the bibliographical material in the books has helped them build their own libraries. I've devoted a good part of my life to researching the lives and ministries of the "giants" and introducing them and their writings to a new generation. Like Isaac, we must dig the old wells (Genesis 26) or we may find ourselves spiritually dehydrated.

After a long and fruitful life and ministry, Herman Baker went to be with Christ February 10, 1991. Everybody in the evangelical publishing world felt the loss of a dear friend and a dedicated bibliophile.

One of my delightful friends in the publishing world is Wendell Hawley, vice president of Tyndale House, which was founded by Ken Taylor to publish *The Living Bible*. We met shortly after I went to Moody Church, and Wendell suggested that I do a series of devotional books styled after the small Hallmark gift books that were then very popular. I took my Advent series on Isaiah 9:6 and wrote *His Name Is Wonderful*, which Tyndale House published in 1976. I later enlarged the book to include chapters on Isaiah 61:1-2, and this was published in 1984.

The fifth *BE* book, *Be Right*, on Romans, came out in 1977; it was joined by *Five Secrets of Living*, on John 15, the second in the "devotional series" for Tyndale House. This little book has had a wide ministry, and a number of pastors have told me they've preached it in their own churches. When Betty and I visited Bill and Stella Taylor in Madrid in 1978, Bill told me that he knew an itinerant Spanish preacher has given that series all over Spain. Praise the Lord!

Our good friend Bob Kregel, a great bibliophile in his own

right, was president of Kregel Publications when I was at Moody Church; he suggested to me that I go through the ten-volume set compiled by Grenville Kleiser, *The World's Great Sermons,* and put together a one-volume edition. I've tried to avoid using the word "great" when referring to sermons, because I'm not really sure I know what a "great" sermon is. (My own series of volumes of "great" sermons with Kregel Publications is called *Classic Sermons.*) Not every sermon in the Kleiser set was worth preserving, and some of the preachers, though perhaps effective in their day, are now forgotten. The result of my reading ten volumes of sermons and selecting 122 of them was *A Treasury of the World's Great Sermons,* published by Kregel in 1977. The 1993 edition in paperback erroneously gives the impression that I wrote the brief biographical sketches of the preachers, when actually we used the original sketches written by Kleiser, with very little editing.

*Be Mature* (James) was published in 1978 and is second only to *Be Joyful* in sales. I guess people want joy before they want maturity. That year Baker Book House published *The Best of A.W. Tozer* which I had compiled from his many books. It wasn't an easy task because just about everything Tozer has written has done my heart good and enriched my ministry. The book met a ready audience and was later reissued in paperback. Then the editors at Baker Book House compiled a sequel, *A Treasury of A.W. Tozer.* (It would be difficult to have a second *Best* book.) I didn't make the choices but the editors did use my original preface from *The Best of A.W. Tozer.*

### The "Itinerant" Years (1978–82)
I left Moody Church because my work was done and because I felt the Lord wanted me to devote more time to writing and a wider conference ministry. If my count is correct, between the time I resigned from the church and we moved to Lincoln, Nebraska, at least twenty books were published. This has to be a miracle of God's grace when you consider that during those years I was teaching one day a week at Trinity Evangelical Divinity School, continuing to produce "Songs in the Night" programs for Moody Church, chairing the Slavic Gospel Association

board, doing a quarterly teaching cassette for the youth division of Scripture Press, speaking at conferences and churches week after week, and flying regularly to Lincoln to produce programs for "Back to the Bible." Betty and I also made our share of overseas trips.

The Victor Books titles included: *Be Ready* (Thessalonians, 1979); *Windows on the Parables* (1979); *Meet Your King* (Matthew, 1980), later retitled *Be Loyal; Be Complete* (Colossians, 1981); *Be Faithful* (Timothy, Titus, Philemon, 1981); *Be Confident* (Hebrews, 1982); and *Be Hopeful* (1 Peter, 1982).

In 1979, Tyndale House published *The Strategy of Satan,* and in 1982 *Listen! Jesus Is Praying!* an exposition of John 17, which was later reissued as *Prayer: Basic Training* (1988). Baker Book House published a second series of "Songs in the Night" messages, *The Bumps Are What You Climb On,* as well as an edition of William Quayle's *The Pastor-Preacher,* which I edited and introduced with a biographical preface. Baker also issued *Listening to the Giants* (1980) and *Giant Steps* (1981). I don't know of any book I've written that's given people more help and encouragement than *The Bumps Are What You Climb On.* Without a doubt, the title helps to promote the book.

In 1980, Moody Press published my *Annotated Pilgrim's Progress.* I so enjoyed doing the research for *The Annotated Pilgrim's Progress* that when the book was completed, I felt like I'd lost a friend. But the book didn't sell\*; Moody Press dropped it; and Discovery House reissued it in 1989. I'm a purist when it comes to great literature and hate to see condensations and "modernized" texts published, but I yielded to the suggestion of Bob DeVries that we update the text for the contemporary reader.

By 1980, Back to the Bible was publishing booklets containing edited transcriptions of some of my radio messages. *Come Share the Glory* contained six messages on Christ's transfiguration; *The Most Expensive Thing in the World* dealt with David's

---

\*Mark Twain was right when he defined a "classic" as a book everybody talks about but nobody reads. Occasionally I've polled congregations to see how many present had read *The Pilgrim's Progress,* and the statistics are deplorable. Charles Spurgeon read the book over a hundred times and got a great deal of his theology from Bunyan and the Puritans.

sin with Bathsheba and his confession in Psalm 51; and *The Wonderful Names of Jesus* was a Christmas series on nine of the names of our Lord in the New Testament. Two titles were published in 1981: *Jesus' Seven Last Words,* a Lenten series, and *How to Be a Caring Christian,* a study of twelve of the "one another" statements in the New Testament. These books were for sale, but they were used primarily as "giveaways" to encourage our radio listeners to write the broadcast. Receiving letters and building a strong mailing list are very important to the ongoing of a media ministry.

Bob Kregel asked me to revise Sir James Marchant's *Anthology of Jesus,* which had been published in 1926; the new edition was published in 1981.

My 1982 Back to the Bible titles were *Be God's Guest,* a study of the feasts described in Leviticus 23, and *Key Words of the Christian Life,* a series on Bible doctrine, including justification, sanctification, adoption, regeneration, etc. I got the idea for the series from H.A. Ironside's book *Great Words of the Gospel. God Isn't in a Hurry* was published in 1982, a collection of nine editorials I'd written for *The Good News Broadcaster.*

**The "Back to the Bible" Years (1982–1990)**
When Betty and I moved to Lincoln in September 1982, it meant serving full time on the broadcast staff, and this meant having less time for writing. I would be answering radio mail, attending staff meetings of one kind or another, preparing Bible messages, producing programs, and representing the broadcast in a wider conference ministry in the States and overseas. I would also be writing editorials and articles for the magazine, and eventually would begin producing *Prokope,* our bimonthly mailing to pastors and Christian workers. However, from 1982 to 1989, when I resigned from Back to the Bible, Victor Books published eleven *BE* books plus *Meet Yourself in the Psalms* (1983), and other publishers, including Back to the Bible, brought out twenty-six titles, a total of thirty-seven books published during the eight years from 1983 to 1990.

The *BE* titles included: *Be Wise* (1 Corinthians, 1983); *Be*

*Encouraged* (2 Corinthians, 1984); *Be Alert* (2 Peter, 2 and 3 John, Jude, 1984); *Be Victorious* (Revelation, 1985); *Be Alive* (John 1–12, 1986); *Be Transformed* (John 13–21, 1986); *Be Diligent* (Mark, 1987); *Be Dynamic* (Acts 1–12, 1987); *Be Daring* (Acts 13–18, 1988); *Be Compassionate* (Luke 1–13, 1988); and *Be Courageous* (Luke 14–24, 1989). With the writing of *Be Courageous*, the New Testament *BE* series was completed. In 1989, Victor Books combined all twenty-three books into the two-volume *Bible Exposition Commentary*.

In 1983, Back to the Bible published *Lonely People: From Worry to Worship*, a study of Habakkuk; *Enjoy Your Freedom*, a series of studies on the freedoms we have in Christ; and *Meet Your Conscience*. *Something Happens When Churches Pray* came out in 1984, a series of messages on The Lord's Prayer and prayer in the Book of Acts. I confess that the title was a direct steal from my friend Evelyn Christenson whose *What Happens When Women Pray* is now a classic.

While Betty and I were still living in Chicago, our son David and I wrote *Making Sense of the Ministry*, which was published by Moody Press in 1983. It's a handbook for the new pastor to help him put to work in the church what he studied on the campus. Baker Book House published a new edition in 1989 to which David added a new chapter. The "ten principles of ministry" found in chapters 3 and 4 have been quoted by Chuck Swindoll on his "Insight for Living" program.

Moody Press published *The Wycliffe Handbook of Preaching and Preachers* in 1984, a book that my beloved professor Lloyd M. Perry and I wrote together. Dr. Perry covered the historical and technical aspects of preaching, while I contributed biographical and anecdotal material. We thought it could become a standard resource book for professors of homiletics and serious students of preaching, but the book never "took off."

Another loser that year was *Steps of Faith*, an edition of the NIV New Testament and Psalms "for growing Christians." I prepared what I thought was a unique series of cross references, plus footnotes, to help the new believer get started right in Bible study and the Christian life, but the book died aborning. The first edition ended up being given away by Ben Hayden and other TV preachers and there never was a second edition.

But there was at least one "winner" in 1984, thanks to my good friend Dr. Victor Oliver, now president of Oliver-Nelson Publishers. He was then associated with Fleming H. Revell. Rabbi Kushner's book *When Bad Things Happen to Good People* had been very popular, and Victor urged me to write an answer from a Christian perspective. I wrote *Why Us? When Bad Things Happen to God's People*, and it's had a good ministry.

In 1984, Baker Book House published a collection of my *Good News Broadcaster* biographical articles and called it *Victorious Christians You Should Know*.

But 1984 introduced a new series of books that I edited for Kregel Publications called "The Classic Sermon Series." (As I mentioned before, I hesitate to use the word "great" when referring to sermons. Sermons that appear dull in cold print may have been "great" when they were actually preached, but I wasn't there to hear them.) Each book contained a dozen or so sermons by well-known preachers dealing with a specific theme. I was careful to choose preachers who were evangelical, who were deceased, and who preached sermons that expounded biblical texts.

At this writing, the series includes: *Classic Sermons on Suffering* (1984); *Classic Sermons on Faith and Doubt* (1985); *Classic Sermons on Prayer* (1987); *Classic Sermons on Worship* (1988); *Classic Sermons on the Attributes of God* (1989); *Classic Sermons on the Prodigal Son* (1990); *Classic Sermons on Christian Service* (1990); *Classic Sermons on the Cross of Christ* (1990); *Classic Sermons on the Birth of Christ* (1991); *Classic Sermons on the Resurrection of Christ* (1991); *Classic Sermons on Overcoming Fear* (1991); *Classic Sermons on the Second Coming and Other Prophetic Themes* (1992); *Classic Sermons on Spiritual Warfare* (1992); *Classic Sermons on the Names of God* (1993); and *Classic Sermons on Family and Home* (1993).

In 1985, Back to the Bible published *Don't Lose Your Crown*, a series of studies on the life of King Saul, and *Put Your Life Together*, an exposition of the Book of Ruth. Tyndale House published an exposition of Hebrews 11, *Run with the Winners,* and Moody Press brought out *Comforting the Bereaved,* a book David and I wrote to help pastors with their ministry to grieving people.

Back to the Bible published three of my radio series in 1986: *Scriptures that Sing,* messages from the texts that form the basis for our well-known hymns and Gospel songs; *Famous Unanswered Prayers,* a study of eight Bible prayers that God refused to answer; and *What to Wear to the War,* an exposition of our Lord's temptation and of the spiritual armor in Ephesians 6. Oliver-Nelson published *Real Worship: It Will Transform Your Life,* a book that was so difficult to write that I almost gave up. I had a terrible time getting started and threw away four or five drafts of the first chapter. Then I realized that the book had to be personal and describe my own spiritual pilgrimage in worship; once I'd turned that corner, the going was easier. Baker Book House published *Devotional Talks for People Who Do God's Business,* which David and I wrote together, forty devotional talks that church leaders can use to open their business or committee meetings on a spiritual level. Please don't ask me which chapters I wrote and which chapters David wrote, because I can't tell! Tyndale House brought out *The Elements of Preaching,* which I co-authored with David, a small book patterned after Strunk and White's famous *Elements of Style.* In about 100 pages, we give twenty-six "preaching principles" and fourteen "preaching prohibitions" to help all of us preach better sermons.

Also included in 1986 is *A Time to Be Renewed,* published by Victor Books and edited by my good friend Jim Adair, at that time Executive Editor of Victor Books. It's a compilation of "meaty" excerpts from the New Testament *BE* books, arranged as daily devotional readings for the year. Jim was good enough to go through the books, make the selections, and then add the "action assignments" for each day. Jim retired from Scripture Press in 1988, after many years of faithful service.

Accent Books published *My Favorite Verse* in 1987, an attractive book that I wrote on my life verse, Psalm 16:11. In 1988, I did a series of studies over "Back to the Bible" on John 11, and they were published as a thirty-day daily devotional with the title *Jesus and Your Sorrows.* The broadcast also published my magazine series on D.L. Moody, *Meet Mr. Moody; Angry People;* and *What Shall We Name the Baby?* Tyndale House released my study of twelve pictures of God's people in Scripture, entitled *Be What You Are.* (Everybody was getting in on the *BE* titles!)

On Sunday morning, July 12, 1987, I was privileged to give the message at the worship service of the Christian Bookseller's Convention in Anaheim, California; I felt led to speak on Nehemiah and "Living in a Day of Reproach." All of us were feeling the impact of the "Pearly Gate" scandals and I felt that we needed to get some positive direction from the Word. After the message, both Victor Oliver and Sam Moore, president of Thomas Nelson Publishers, urged me to expand the message into a book on "the integrity crisis." Since I was then deeply involved in Christian radio, they felt that what I had to say would carry more weight. It was a tough book to write, but if the letters in my file are any indication, the Lord used *The Integrity Crisis* in a wonderful way.

Since 1989 was the fiftieth anniversary year of "Back to the Bible," the broadcast published four booklets containing radio messages based on John 17 and dealing with what I called the four priorities of "Priority Christian Living": glorifying God, living a holy life, reaching a lost world, and building Christian unity. They also published ten booklets of "Dyna-Moments," messages covering the entire Book of Psalms. These devotionals were later reworked and expanded, and the result was *Prayer, Praise, and Promises: A Daily Walk through the Psalms* (1992).

### The Recent "Itinerant" Years (1990– )
I don't like it when people ask me how I'm enjoying my "retirement," because I'm still a very busy person who is not yet living on Social Security or a pension. Since my leaving Back to the Bible, at least a dozen books have been published, and the Lord willing, more are on the way.

The first in the Old Testament *BE* series was published by Victor Books in 1990, *Be Satisfied* (Ecclesiastes); and *Be Pa-*

*tient* (Job) and *Be Obedient* (Abraham) followed in 1992. *In Praise of Plodders,* a collection of my *Prokope* articles, was published by Kregel in 1991, but *With the Word,* a devotional commentary on the whole Bible, was the major work for 1991. With over a thousand pages in the manuscript, it's the biggest book I've ever written. Like *The Integrity Crisis,* the book was suggested to me by Victor Oliver and Sam Moore, and at first, I turned them down. But I had over twenty years of material in my devotional diaries and often yearned to get some of it into print, so I finally yielded, and I'm glad I did. The material is also included with the complete text of *The New King James Bible* in *The Essential Everyday Bible Commentary* published in 1993 by Thomas Nelson.

My two *BE* books for 1992 were *Be Comforted* (Isaiah) and *Be Determined* (Nehemiah), and Victor Books also published *Wiersbe's Expository Outlines on the New Testament.* Their computer people had scanned my original outlines, published by Calvary Baptist Church in Covington, Kentucky, and put them on computer disks. All I had to do was put the disks in my computer and revise and expand the material, except that it wasn't that easy because I had all sorts of problems with the disks. Then I realized that I needed a more powerful computer to handle what Victor Books had sent me. So I bought a new computer; after that, editing the material was quite easy.

As I studied this material that I'd written as a busy pastor a quarter of a century ago, I must confess that I was sometimes embarrassed and occasionally had to stop and ask the Lord to forgive me for what I'd written. I realize that I prepared those outlines for a specific local church, and that the religious climate has changed since the '60s, but that's no excuse for the sexist writing I did, the unkind things I wrote about groups whose theology I disagreed with, and the immature interpretations I gave of too many passages. Needless to say, as I edited both the Old and New Testament outlines, I deleted objectionable material, rewrote sections, added a good deal of new material, and did my best to make the books useful to God's people today. I'm not aware of any drastic theological shifts. I threw out some furniture, but I didn't change the foundation.

# *Appendix*

Along with *Wiersbe's Expository Outlines on the Old Testament,* two *BE* books were published by Victor Books in 1993: *Be Committed* (Ruth and Esther) and *Be Strong* (Joshua). Oliver-Nelson published *On Being a Servant of God,* thirty informal "chats" about what it means to serve God. Again, it was Victor Oliver who suggested this book.

I rejoice that many of these titles have been translated into other languages and are being read in many nations of the world by people whose tongues I don't understand. A believer in Poland sent me a copy of *Why Us? When Bad Things Happen to God's People* which he had translated without permission of the publishers. I doubt that he'll have any trouble because of it! I've received letters from believers in many nations telling me that the books have helped them, and this always warms my heart.

**Soli Deo gloria!**

# Index

342